TRADITION AND DESIGN
IN
THE ILIAD

TRADITION AND DESIGN
IN
THE ILIAD

BY

C. M. BOWRA
FELLOW OF WADHAM COLLEGE

GREENWOOD PRESS, PUBLISHERS
WESTPORT, CONNECTICUT

Library of Congress Cataloging in Publication Data

Bowra, Cecil Maurice, Sir, 1898-1971.
   Tradition and design in the Iliad.

   Reprint of the 1930 ed. published by Clarendon Press,
Oxford.
   Includes index.
   1. Homerus. Ilias. I. Title.
PA4037.B63 1977   883'.01   77-3065
ISBN 0-8371-9561-6

Originally published in 1930 at the Clarendon Press, Oxford

This reprint has been authorized by the Oxford University Press.

Reprinted in 1977 by Greenwood Press, Inc.

Library of Congress catalog card number 77-3065

ISBN 0-8371-9561-6

Printed in the United States of America

TO

KENNETH AND JANE CLARK

PREFACE

THIS book makes no claim to add any new facts to our knowledge of Homer, and indeed it is doubtful whether any new facts are likely to be discovered. But so much industry and acumen have been spent on the study of the *Iliad* that it seems worth while to see if any satisfactory conclusions on its character and authorship can be drawn in the present state of our information. In this book I have tried to use the work of scholars in an effort to reconstruct the conditions under which the *Iliad* was formed and to explain some of its more peculiar characteristics by reference to those conditions. For some years I have felt that the *Iliad* has suffered from two opposed methods of treatment. On the one side it has been treated exclusively as an historical document and subjected to an analysis which disregards it as poetry. On the other side it has been treated as a poem produced like great modern poems with all the resources of literature behind it. Both these views have led to serious errors. The first has resulted in incompatible theories of multiple authorship, which assume the existence of many great poets of remarkably similar gifts. The second has refused to reply to questions that must be answered and contented itself with highly dubious dogma. Under such circumstances my aim has been to steer between these two courses. I have tried to show that the *Iliad* is a poem and must be treated as such, but I have also tried to show that it is far nearer to the beginnings of poetry than most epics and must therefore be judged by different standards from those applied to them.

Fortunately we possess enough early epics to know what this type of poetry is like, and we are able to note the appearance of common characteristics and in some measure to account for them. In many ways the *Iliad* shows these characteristics, and may because of them be classed as an early epic. But its standard of construction and its poetical quality are far higher than those of works even so good as the *Song of Roland*. The conclusion then follows that the *Iliad* was composed at a stage when the traditional or primitive epic was passing into real art, and to this peculiar state of affairs it owes its peculiar character.

I have read as much of the vast literature on the *Iliad* as time has allowed. Among Unitarians I have found much in the work of J. W. Scott and C. Rothe, and I owe special thanks to the titanic industry of E. Drerup. To scholars of the opposite school my debt is no less great, and I must acknowledge my deep gratitude to E. Bethe, W. Leaf, P. Cauer, and U. von Wilamowitz-Moellendorf. Nor can I pass by the name of my old teacher, Professor Gilbert Murray. There is much here with which he will disagree. But I know that he is the most generous of opponents and the first to see what justice there is in views opposed to his own. To him I owe more than I can well express, and I hope he will take gratitude as an adequate substitute for agreement.

Any treatment of Homer must be largely hypothetical, and there is much here which is far from certain or proved. Analogy is an inspiring but treacherous servant, and I am well aware that I may have been misled by her. Nor do I feel any full confidence in the treatment of historical matters before Homer. The evidence is scanty and hard to interpret, and for much of it I have to rely on other men's opinions. But the question seemed too important to be lightly dismissed, and I have done my best with it. I can only hope that the critics of my historical chapter will regard it as an attempt to state the evidence and to form an opinion, not as a dogmatic solution of problems beyond my capacity.

Finally I must put on record my gratitude to three friends from whose conversation I have learned much, to my colleague Mr. H. T. Wade-Gery, to Mr. J. D. Denniston, Fellow of Hertford College, and to Mr. J. H. A. Sparrow, Fellow of All Souls' College.

C. M. B.

IGHTHAM,
14 *August* 1930.

CONTENTS

I

TRADITION AND DESIGN

FOR more than a hundred years Homeric scholarship concentrated on a single, vital, and fascinating problem —Who wrote the *Iliad* and the *Odyssey*? The struggle between Unitarians and Analysts created such an atmosphere of controversy that hardly any conclusion met with common acceptance. But in recent years both sides have begun to agree on the opinion that, whatever the authorship of the *Iliad* may be, it is still in some sense a work of art and has undergone some formative influence from a single poet.[1] This poet may have composed the whole poem or he may have transformed independent poems into a unity, but in either case the poem may, and indeed must, be considered as a single work of art. This conclusion alters the conditions of Homeric criticism, and shifts the burden of scholarship from the special question of authorship to other general questions which the *Iliad* raises. It is now possible to take the *Iliad* as we have it and to consider it as poetry, and particularly we may try to distinguish in it those elements which belong to the traditional epic art and those which seem to betray the hand of the creative poet. Such an inquiry does not assume that the *Iliad* is the unaided work of one man, but it does assume that its present form is the product of a single mind transforming traditional material into an artistic whole. On the one hand it excludes the view that the completed poem is largely the result of chance and caprice, and on the other hand the view that the poet was completely his own master and the *Iliad* is what it is simply because Homer chose so to compose it. It seems probable that there was a single poet called Homer, who gave the *Iliad* its final shape and artistic unity, but who worked in a traditional style on traditional matter. If this assumption can be accepted, we may try to differentiate between the traditional heritage and the uses

---

[1] Cf. E. Bethe, *Homer*, i, pp. 57–68; C. Rothe, *Die Ilias als Dichtung*; J. T. Sheppard, *The Pattern of the Iliad*; H. van Leeuwen, *Commentationes Homericae*, pp. 1–45; K. Goepel, *Von homerischer Kunst*.

to which the poet puts it. It must, however, be freely admitted that any such inquiry can only achieve general results. It may never be possible in the present state of evidence to decide whether Homer was entirely responsible for this or that element in the poem or whether he took it over from some anonymous predecessor.

But it may well be possible to consider some general features of the poem, and to distinguish in them the traditional and the later elements. The presence of the different elements may often be detected by the uneasiness they cause us or by some awkwardnesses they create in the poem. Such difficulties exist, and the Higher Criticism has done well to detect them. But it has failed to find any satisfactory scheme of authorship based on their consideration. For this it is not to be blamed. The tradition is so strong that individual authors obey it closely, and stylistic tests are foiled by a remarkable unity of style. But, if we assume that any ultimate analysis of the *Iliad* into the work of different authors is impossible, we may still use the evidence which the critics have found for quite a different purpose—the explanation of certain remarkable characteristics, on the hypothesis that they are due to a single poet working on given material in a manner dictated by a tradition of which he was the inheritor.

The traditional character of Homeric art must be clear to all but those who will not see. Some points will be considered in detail later, but here it is essential to see that the *Iliad* in its method of narration presumes an audience acquainted with the main outlines of its story. The poet composed for listeners who knew of his characters and their histories. His art assumes this acquaintance and makes use of it. On this depends his allusiveness and seeming disregard for much that is common in story telling. A good example may be found in the opening lines. After the few words which set forth the scope of the poem we are at once introduced to the protagonists of the quarrel, Achilles and Agamemnon. Of their previous history nothing is said. We are told simply that they quarrelled and that Apollo was the cause. The details of the quarrel, being less well known, are given in full. The priest Chryses, evidently an unfamiliar figure, is given the definite article—τὸν Χρύσην (*A* 11)—as an introduction among familiar figures.[1] It is soon made clear that the quarrel is at Troy (*A* 19), and the audience of course knows that there was a quarrel at Troy. The story is unravelled, and mentions in an off-hand way characters who are to be important later. A casual reference tells us that Agamemnon has a wife who is called Clytaemnestra (*A* 113), and another mentions two heroes, Aias and Odysseus, who seem to be nearly as important as Achilles or Agamemnon (*A* 138), but for the present we are told no more of them. Achilles implies that his home is in Phthia, though his remarks would be obscure if we did not know it already (*A* 155), and we hear in passing that he rules over the Myrmidons (*A* 180). When he goes back to his tent, he goes with the son of Menoetius, of whom no further mention is now made, but the audience know that he is Patroclus who is to play an important part in the story and is the bosom friend of Achilles (*A* 307). When Achilles in his grief calls on his mother and she answers him, we are not at first told her name nor her divine origin (*A* 352 ff.). The audience know it, and there is no need to be verbose about it. In all this the poet assumes that his hearers know the general outline of the story, the names and antecedents of his main characters. His concern is to tell the old story again in a new way, and therefore he concentrates on the details of the quarrel and on the new characters, like Chryses, whom he makes important in it. But he does not expect too much from his hearers. When the characters are less familiar, he adds a short note on their history. He tells us that Calchas was a seer and brought the Achaeans to Troy by his art (*A* 69), that Talthybius and Eurybates were Agamemnon's heralds and servants (*A* 321). Even Nestor is introduced with a short note on his age, kingdom, and power of speech (*A* 248 ff.). These characters may well have existed in earlier poems, but they were not entirely familiar and needed words of explanation.

The assumption that the audience know the main outlines of the story persists through the poem. Characters, who are

---

[1] Cf. U. von Wilamowitz-Moellendorf, *Die Ilias und Homer*, p. 246.

later to play an integral part and whose previous action is
assumed to have been important, are mentioned casually as
if we knew all about them. Hector is never formally introduced. We first hear of him from Achilles, who says that
his own abstention from battle will lead to many Achaeans
being killed by Hector (*A* 242), and when he does appear on
the scene it is assumed without more ado that he commands
the Trojans (*B* 802). So too with Priam and his city of Troy.
The words Πριάμοιο πόλιν (*A* 19) show that the audience knew
of Troy and its king Priam. Helen, who began all the
trouble, is first named by Hera as the cause of many deaths,
but her early history is taken for granted (*B* 161). Her lover,
Paris, gets even less introduction. He appears on the battle-
field and his armour is described (*Γ* 16 ff.), but his abduction
of Helen is only mentioned later when Hector wishes to
cause him shame (*Γ* 53). So too the audience must have
known that Hector's mother was called Hecuba. When he
meets her on the wall, her name is not given, and then a
little later it slips out when she makes an offering to Athene,
and we should be puzzled if we did not know it already
(*Z* 293). This practice indeed is so obvious that no multipli-
cation of examples is necessary. It implies a knowledge of the
main events and characters, and such a knowledge can only
have been based on earlier stories which told the same tale.
Such a characteristic is common in literature based on tradition. In the *Song of Roland* we are plunged in the same way
among characters and events which the poet assumes to
be familiar. He takes it for granted that we know the
characters and antecedents of Charles and Oliver and
Roland, even of Ganelon and Turpin and King Marsilies.
Charles's conquests are dismissed rapidly, for every one knew
of them. And, as by Homer, the result of the story is foreshadowed, as if the audience had some idea of it. The simple
announcement

Des ore cumencet le cunseill que mal prist,[1]

tells them what to expect—it is the old story of the betrayal
and the fight at Roncesvalles. In poetry which is more
sophisticated and breaks new ground, such an assumption

[1] l. 179. 'The council then began which ended ill.'

of knowledge is impossible. Chaucer used much traditional art, but some of his stories were new in England and their characters unfamiliar. So he introduced them with full details, giving the early history of Palamon and Arcite, the appearance and ways of Alison and Absolon. It is only when literature becomes more sophisticated still that it can afford to assume that its readers will recognize a casual name or reference. Dante or Milton, writing for well-educated men, can throw out casual references to Caesar or Averroes, to Thammuz or Galileo. Superficially their method is like Homer's. But fundamentally it is quite different. They assume a knowledge ranging over many fields and gathered from heterogeneous sources. Homer assumes only a knowledge of poetry similar to his own, dealing with a tradition of great things done in a heroic age. He has a background and he demands a knowledge of it, but it is a background of saga, not of learning.

The contents of this saga, though limited in time and character, are much wider than the scope of the *Iliad*, and of this Homer gives many hints. He assumes that his hearers know not merely of the siege of Troy but also of many other events in the heroic history of Greece. He makes passing mention of the famous heroes of an older generation, of Perseus ($\mathit{Ξ}$ 320), Daedalus ($\mathit{Σ}$ 592), Theseus and Peirithous (A 263, 265), and, though he sometimes adds a picturesque detail, it is clear that his hearers know who they are. So too with the great events of heroic story. The war of the Seven against Thebes is assumed in the boasts of Sthenelus and Agamemnon's account of Tydeus ($\mathit{Δ}$ 372 ff.), the first siege of Troy by Heracles in a speech of Zeus to Hera (O 25), the fall of Cronus and the Titans in a passing reference to their existence below the earth ($\mathit{Ξ}$ 274). Even more recondite episodes are rapidly recorded, such as Priam's wars against the Amazons on the Sangarius ($\mathit{Γ}$ 187) or the wars of Pylians and Arcadians by the river Celadon (H 133). These casual mentions show that a great body of saga was known popularly and taken for granted. The widespread existence of this saga can be seen in its diffusion through Greek literature. The fall of the Titans was fully dealt with by Hesiod and the

poet, whoever he was, of the Τιτανομαχία. Heracles was the
subject of many poems by the followers of Hesiod, and the
Shield of Heracles survives to show what these short epics were
like. The war of the Seven was the subject of epics attributed
to Homer, the Θηβαΐς and the Ἐπίγονοι. Chiron, the wise
centaur, is a favourite hero of Pindar's, who employed all
manner of traditional literature. There is no reason to believe that Homer knew any of these poems, but he used the
same sort of sources that they used, and in all probability
these sources were epic poems, whether short or long. The
song or poem is the usual method for spreading stories
among an unlettered people, and no doubt Homer's contemporaries heard such tales from their earliest childhood
and knew their outline. But as the old story was always being
retold, they expected new turns and details, and with these
the poet presented them.

Another traditional trait in the epic is its anonymity. The
poet nowhere mentions his own name, and hardly passes an
explicit judgement or gives a personal opinion.[1] He uses the
first person singular only to say that he is not a god to give a
list of all the deaths caused at the Achaean trench (*M* 176).
In this the *Iliad* differs from Hesiod and from some of the
Homeric Hymns. Hesiod sets out to deliver a lecture to Perses
and makes no attempt to hide his personality or his views. So
too his imitator, the author of the *Theogony*, describes how
the Muses appeared to him and told him to sing. The
author of the *Hymn to Apollo* speaks of himself as a blind old
man living in Chios (l. 172). But Homer gives us no such
personal touches about his life or appearance. His anonymity
indeed recalls Shakespeare's. Shakespeare has the same gift
for disappearing behind his characters and baffling us when
we try to trace his spiritual history through his plays. With
him there is always the suspicion that, when we think we
have at last found his own opinion, we have only been de-
ceived by a dramatic utterance of one of his creations. But

---

[1] Possible exceptions are when he praises good advice in *Z* 62, *H* 121 (αἴσιμα
παρειπών) or condemns foolishness in *B* 38, *M* 113, 127, *Π* 46, 686, *P* 236, 497,
Σ 311. On the question generally cf. J. Schmidt, *Das subjektive Element bei
Homer*, Vienna, 1889.

in spite of the dramatic convention some of his personal predilections eventually come clear. He liked aristocrats and hated puritans, he had an extraordinary interest in the law, he made mistakes in geography. This may not be much, but it is more than the *Iliad* gives us of its author. Above all, Shakespeare's style is his own, but Homer's style is largely the style of a school and cannot easily be distinguished from that of any of the *Homeric Hymns*. His language is as composite as Shakespeare's, but its creation must have been done for him largely by his predecessors. His stories, as we have seen, he must have taken from a common pool. Even some of the traits of his characters, the anger of Achilles, the strength of Aias, the guile of Odysseus, have the marks of ancient tradition. Of his own life we have not even such information as we have of Shakespeare's. The *Lives* are late, and derived entirely from the poems.[1] His birth-place was claimed by many cities. No wonder that his name has been denied and he himself divided into a school of bards. Yet the *Iliad* postulates a final author, and, if he existed, his anonymity needs explaining. It might well be the case that the bard was not a man of sufficient importance to obtrude his own views or personality on his royal patrons. His business was to tell a story, and to go farther were bad manners. But such a view contradicts the high regard in which the poets whom the *Odyssey* describes were held. Demodocus and Phemius were men of some standing, and their views might well be listened to. The blind singer of Chios was not afraid of mentioning his circumstances, and Hesiod is full of advice and moral judgements. The explanation would seem rather to be in the traditional view that the poet was merely the mouthpiece of the Muse. He was an inspired agent of the gods, and it was they, not he, who spoke or sang. Such a view would be the more readily held when poets were a hereditary guild with secrets belonging to their craft. In their anxiety not to betray these secrets or to reveal their art, they naturally ascribed them to divine agency. But for this mystification the poet paid a price, and if he invoked the

---

[1] G. Wiemer, *Ilias und Odyssee als Quelle der Biographen Homers*, Programm Ostern 1905 u. 1908. But cf. Wilamowitz, *I. und H.*, pp. 413–39.

Muse he could not claim that the poem was his own. In this the *Iliad* differs even from the *Song of Roland*. Turoldus, whoever he was, has his name in the last line, and the author of the poem as we have it says that he found the story written in the cathedral at Loum by St. Giles who was present at the fight. The Norman poet was a Christian and could claim saintly authority, and all was well. But Homer could claim only the authority of the Muse and had to be careful not to betray his secrets. This anonymity is most obvious in the Homeric style, and though we have nothing older than the *Iliad*, it is probable that Homer's immediate predecessors wrote much the same language that he did. His successors, the authors of the *Hymns*, wrote a language that is almost identical. A certain love of accumulated decoration in the *Hymn to Hermes* or the *Hymn to Pan* is the chief point of divergence. The fragments of the Cyclic poems are in good Homeric Greek. Even Hesiod, who wrote for a mainland audience and was no great master of his technique, used a Homeric vocabulary. The poems of Corinna show how different his poetry might have been. This standardized style has few parallels in poetry. The French epic shows some resemblance to it, but there is far more difference between the *Song of Roland* and the later epics than there is between the *Iliad* and the *Hymn to Apollo*. The *Iliad* implies a long history before itself, and a long series of poems written in much the same style. Only a guild with strict rules and jealously held secrets could have maintained a style so homogeneous through so many years. The nearest parallel may perhaps be found in the history of the Church of England Prayer Book, where a homogeneous style has persisted through some four centuries and where great masterpieces, whose authors are known to be different, are written in the same manner.

So far, then, the *Iliad* is the work of a tradition, and so far the tradition is so strong that the personality of the poet disappears and we are left with what is practically impersonal art, that is, art standardized by a succession of poets, and learned and mastered by its exponents. This tradition reaches far into the workmanship of the *Iliad*, and its influence in other directions will be considered in its place. But no living tradition is mere tradition. Each poet worthy of the name makes something new of it, even if he is bound by the closest rules and conventions. No matter how strict the form may be or how overmastering the rules, a poet of genius may still impose his personality and create a new thing without contravening the inherited laws of artistry. Just as Villon created masterpieces in the time-worn forms of the *rondeau* and *ballade* when they seemed dead in the hands of Deschamps, so too Homer preserved the proprieties and created a work of art on which he laid the impression of his own great, if elusive, personality. As a man he may elude us, but as a poet we know him and catch his individual utterance. Behind the style there is still the poet. So for the Greeks he was ὁ ποιητής *par excellence*; so even for Wolf there was *unus color* in the poems. Out of the traditional material a whole was made, and it can only have been the work of a single creating poet.

His creative work can be seen most simply in the construction of the whole poem. Despite its many characters, despite its plot and counter-plot, it remains a whole. To call it a 'Flickwerk', as Wilamowitz does, is to miss this essential feature. In Aristotelian language the *Iliad* has a beginning, a middle, and an end, and it achieves its emotional effect as well as any great poem ever written. It presents us with a world full of events and characters, but this medley is so shaped that it all leads to a great emotional climax in the results of the wrath of Achilles.

It is easy to see why the *Iliad* has been thought chaotic and inartistic. It deals with a great mass of themes and it does not trouble to subordinate them to a common end. Threads are taken up only to be broken and thrown aside. Episodes are told which seem to have no real relation to the central theme. It is not surprising that critics have tried to disinter a fundamental *Achilleid* and to claim that all else is later addition. No doubt there was once an *Achilleid* and Homer made use of it, but what we have to consider is the present *Iliad* and its artistic unity. This unity is of a particular kind dictated by the necessities of recitation and the desire of

the poet to treat a wide subject. In this the *Iliad* differs from
the *Aeneid*, which is concerned with a single man who holds
the poem together, or from the *Song of Roland*, which deals
with a single event, the treachery of Ganelon. It differs too
from the *Odyssey*, where different strands of story are united
into the single event of the return of Odysseus. Its subject
is announced by the poet himself in the opening lines,
and it is frankly the wrath of Achilles and its results. This
is eminently a composite theme, such as few poets have
since attempted. If we must find parallels, we must look to
such works as the history of Herodotus, which deals with the
quarrels of Greeks and Barbarians, and has in its course to
relate of many men and events which are connected only by
the central theme. Or we might find a parallel in such a
book as *Wuthering Heights*, whose concern is not with a person
but with a family set in certain surroundings which affect
their lives, or in Hardy's *The Return of the Native*, where
the chief character is no man or woman but the vast tract
of Egdon Heath. The theme of the *Iliad* is set out so
emphatically by the poet that it needs some consideration.

The poet opens with a prayer to the Muse to tell the story
of the wrath of Achilles, and the first seven lines of the poem
are devoted to a rough summary of what is to be told.
The summary is, as might be expected, both incomplete and
rather superfluous. As soon as it is finished, Homer plunges
into the middle of his story and begins to unravel the
plot. But the superfluity is only apparent. A poem must
begin somehow, and a short summary is as good a way as
any other. So at least thought Virgil and Milton, so, to a far
less excusable extent, thought Euripides, and, at times,
Shakespeare. The reason for this slight sketch of coming
events was that the audience had to be told which of many
stories was going to be recited. The poet took his story and
characters from a traditional stock and gave them a new
interpretation, but his hearers knew the main outlines of
most stories and were entitled to know which they were going
to hear. So the poet announces the story of the Wrath of
Achilles. The company then knew what was coming and
could prepare itself to appreciate a new version of an old

tale. Such being its object, the prologue cannot justly be accused of being incomplete. No summary is ever complete, and there is certainly no obligation which binds a poet to tell us in advance all that he means to say later. In the prologue of *Paradise Lost* Milton says nothing of the books to be devoted to the science and theology of the Archangel Raphael which fill so large a portion of the poem, and in the opening lines of the *Aeneid* there is no mention of the name of Dido. So here there is no mention of Hector or Patroclus, no hint of the events described in the last seven books. Yet in essence these seven lines give a fair account of the plot. The story is to be of the wrath of Achilles and of its terrible results for the Achaeans, and that is just what the story is. The prologue anticipates not only those portions of the poem which tell of Achilles, but also those which tell of the misfortunes of the Achaeans while he is absent from the battlefield. In other words, it implies a poem telling a great deal more than the mere story of Achilles which so many have tried to postulate as the original and authentic *Iliad*.

The poet announces not merely the wrath of Achilles, to which he at once proceeds and to which he recurs throughout the poem, but also its dire consequences. These are sketched at great length in those books which describe the fighting when Achilles is away. In the words

> πολλὰς δ᾽ ἰφθίμους ψυχὰς Ἄϊδι προΐαψεν
> ἡρώων, αὐτοὺς δὲ ἑλώρια τεῦχε κύνεσσιν
> οἰωνοῖσί τε πᾶσι [1]

is forecasted in general terms the great slaughter which takes place in the various ἀνδροκτασίαι and ἀριστεῖαι. All this is due to the wrath of Achilles, which emboldened the Trojans to attack the Achaean camp and allowed Hector to make such havoc. It is absurd to take these lines as referring to some quite different conclusion, in which Hector plays a far deadlier role than he does in the *Iliad*.[2] The results of Achilles' abstention are deadly enough, as any reader can

---

[1] 'and many strong souls of men he sent on their way to Hades, and their bodies he made a prey for dogs and all birds'.

[2] Maintained by D. Mülder, *Homer und die altionische Elegie*, p. 46. Criticized by C. Rothe, *Die Ilias als Dichtung*, p. 146.

see, and, in particular, they produced one death which is of cardinal importance to the plot. The main consequence of this anger was the death of Patroclus, and when the poet speaks of strong souls sent to Hades, he hints at this. Of its details he says nothing, and the whole of the part played by Patroclus may be his own invention, which he wishes to keep as a surprise for his patrons. It is true that neither the body of Patroclus nor the body of any of the greater Achaeans is thrown to the birds or the dogs, and at first sight the poet might seem to be exaggerating. But he often recurs to this idea, and if the fate was too horrible for the greater heroes, it often fell to the less. Such is the fate foretold to the fallen by Glaucus (*P* 153), Aias (*P* 241), and others.[1] Such must have been the fate of many killed in battle, whose funeral is never described. To be eaten by dogs or birds was the normal fate of the unburied dead, and it needed no elaboration. Its mention in the prologue helps to give a hint of the horrors which follow Achilles' refusal to fight.

So far then the prologue gives a correct account of the plot, even if it leaves many important episodes unannounced. No doubt the poet had surprises, which he wished to keep concealed and only vaguely foreshadowed, suggesting horror and disaster but giving no indication of what precise form they would take. He finishes his summary with the words Διὸς δ' ἐτελείετο βουλή. The scholars of Alexandria explained this by an account given in the *Cypria*, in which Zeus, wishing to reduce the number of human beings on the earth, caused the Trojan war.[2] Such an explanation implies that both the poet and his audience knew this story well enough for it to be mentioned and dismissed in three words. This is certainly

---

[1] Δ 237, Λ 452, 455, Χ 42.

[2] *Cypria*, fr. i, ed. T. W. Allen:

ἦν ὅτε μυρία φῦλα κατὰ χθόνα πλαζόμεν' ἀνδρῶν
. . . . βαθυστέρνου πλάτος αἴης.
Ζεὺς δὲ ἰδὼν ἐλέησε καὶ ἐν πυκιναῖς πραπίδεσσι
σύνθετο κουφίσαι ἀνθρώπων παμβώτορα γαῖαν,
ῥιπίσσας πολέμου μεγάλην ἔριν Ἰλιακοῖο,
ὄφρα κενώσειεν θανάτου βάρος· οἱ δ' ἐνὶ Τροίῃ
ἥρωες κτείνοντο· Διὸς δ' ἐτελείετο βουλή.

wrong. There is not the slightest trace of any such divine plan anywhere else in the *Iliad* or the *Odyssey*, and a reference so obscure would be intolerable in a poem where the main motives are superbly clear. The author of the *Cypria* certainly described such a plan of Zeus, but it is far more likely that he chose to misinterpret these words than that Homer thought the story so well known that the merest hint of it was enough. The words must mean something else, and coming as they do at the end of this summary they must be important. They mean simply that the will of Zeus was fulfilled, that, as Wilamowitz says, events happened κατὰ βουλὴν Διός.[1] Here, too, the poet anticipates in a general phrase much of what is to happen. He foretells those passages in which Zeus determines the course of the action by giving the advantage to the one side or the other. And more than this. The poet announces that in all these events the will of Zeus was accomplished, and prepares his audience for the large part to be taken in the poem by Zeus and his subordinate gods. This view recurs in the poem, and the poet more than once puts on the lips of his heroes his own feeling of the responsibility of Zeus for the war. When Agamemnon tries to test his followers he says:

" οὖτω που Διὶ μέλλει ὑπερμενέϊ φίλον εἶναι,
ὃς δὴ πολλάων πολίων κατέλυσε κάρηνα
ἠδ' ἔτι καὶ λύσει ".   (B 116–18)[2]

The same idea in other words is expressed by Idomeneus:

" μέλλει δὴ φίλον εἶναι ὑπερμενέϊ Κρονίωνι
νωνύμνους ἀπολέσθαι ἀπ' "Αργεος ἐνθάδ' 'Αχαιούς,"
(N 226–7)[3]

and recurs again elsewhere.[4]

So in these first five lines we get a just account of what is going to happen. The audience know that the story is to be the old story of the wrath of Achilles and that they are going to hear of the dire results which Zeus wills. More than this

[1] *I. und H.*, p. 245.
[2] 'Such must, it seems, be dear to mighty Zeus, who has destroyed the crowns of many cities and will yet destroy others.'
[3] 'It must be dear to the mighty son of Cronus that the Achaeans should perish here unknown away from Argos.'   [4] e.g. *T* 270.

the poet does not say, partly because there is no sense in telling a story twice over, and partly because, though the main features of the story may be known, he is a poet and has new creations of his own with which he wants to surprise his patrons.

The poem then has strictly speaking two themes, a special theme, the wrath of Achilles, and a general theme, the results of the wrath. The second depends on the first and is derived from it, but in the development of it we are sometimes led far from Achilles. So composite a plot is rare in literature, but a similar form of construction was employed by one of the most careful and conscientious writers who ever lived, Gustave Flaubert. The plot of *Salammbô* resembles that of the *Iliad* in having both a special and a general theme. The centre of the story is Salammbo and her personal history, but this at times disappears in the general story of the fate of Carthage and the war conducted by Hamilcar against the revolting mercenaries. So too in the *Iliad* there is the special theme of the wrath of Achilles and the general theme of the siege of Troy, or, more accurately, of the siege of Troy in the tenth year. Hence the poem is not an *Achilleid* but an *Iliad*. Though we hear only of a small part of the siege, we are deeply concerned with the fate of Troy, and when Hector dies there is no need to describe its capture. With him its hopes are gone, and though the first antagonist is always Achilles, the second is not so much Hector as Troy, of which he is the defender and heroic embodiment. One by one Troy's defenders perish or desert her. Sarpedon is killed (Π 502), the river-god Scamander is defeated (Φ 382), Ares and Aphrodite are driven off the field (Φ 416 ff.), Artemis retires before Hera (Φ 479 ff.), and Apollo leaves Hector to fight his battle alone (X 213). Through the poem a note of impending doom is reiterated. The warlike goddess, Athene, refuses to hear the supplication of Hecuba and her women (Z 311), and Hector knows that there is no real hope of victory when he tells Andromache :

> ἔσσεται ἦμαρ ὅτ' ἄν ποτ' ὀλώλῃ Ἴλιος ἰρὴ
> καὶ Πρίαμος καὶ λαὸς ἐϋμμελίω Πριάμοιο.   (Z 448–9) [1]

[1] 'There shall be a day when holy Ilium shall perish, and Priam, and the people of Priam of the good ashen spear.'

When he dies the city bewails him as if it had already fallen and were weeping for its own doom (*X* 411).

Because the poem is an *Iliad*, Homer is able to surround the central character of Achilles with a great galaxy of portraits, both Achaean and Trojan. These diverse men and women are of great importance, for they are all affected by Achilles' anger and refusal to fight. His absence gives the other Achaean heroes a chance to prove their mettle, and in turn we get to know Diomedes, Menelaus, and Odysseus. His absence brings out the kingly qualities of Agamemnon, which have been overlaid by his masterful temper. Above all we get to know Patroclus, who is overshadowed by his friend when he is near and needs independence to show his heroic character. For the Trojans Achilles' abstention means the rise to prominence of Hector and, to a lesser degree, of Glaucus and Sarpedon. Achilles is too great a fighter for them to play such a role when he is near, but in his absence we learn to see them at their best and to know the stuff of which Trojans are made. In these books, when Achilles is off the scene, the poem is truly an *Iliad*. The two sides are sharply contrasted, and we see the battle fluctuating between them. When at last he returns, the plot is at once simplified and the contest between Achaeans and Trojans is reduced to a contest between Achilles and Hector, the champions and symbols of their races. The plot leads up to this simplification, but even when it comes, we are fully conscious of the camp life behind Achilles and the family life behind Hector. And when Hector is killed, Troy is doomed and the Achaeans have won the day.

Such then is the theme, the wrath of Achilles and its consequences. But such a theme is not in itself enough to make a work of art. It must be put into shape and organized into a whole. And this Homer has done. The poem is built on a plan at once simple and majestic. The *crescendo* of the opening is paralleled by the *diminuendo* of the closing books. In *A* we hear of the outburst of Achilles' anger and the prayer of Thetis to Zeus that her son may win glory through the defeat of the Achaeans. In *Ω* we hear how Thetis at the request of Zeus persuades her son to forgo his anger and to give back the body of Hector for burial. The poem begins with an uncontrolled scene of wrath and it ends with the appeasing of wrath in reconciliation. In the second book, *B*, one by one the Achaean heroes are shown us as they hold council of war: we see them in their martial temper, each with his own individuality and idiosyncrasies. In the penultimate book, *Ψ*, we see them clear of war during a truce, when their more peaceful characteristics are revealed in the sports held at Patroclus' funeral. In the third book, *Γ*, we have the duel between Paris and Menelaus and the home-life of Troy with Priam and the old men, with Helen and Aphrodite. In the last book but two, *X*, we have the duel between Achilles and Hector which ends not in the bridal chamber as the first duel ended, but in death and the broken-hearted lamentations of Andromache.[1]

Inside this frame the story falls into three main sections, separated by the books in which Achilles first refuses, and later decides, to change his mind and fight. *I* and *T*, in which the discussions are described, not only provide interludes in the narrative of violent action, but also mark vital changes in the course of affairs. In the first section the terrible results of the quarrel are told. The Achaeans, deserted by Achilles, are driven back in the field and penned in their camp by the victorious Hector. Their defeat gives a great chance to the heroes to distinguish themselves, and they take it. But one by one they are vanquished, and Hector lights his fires near the Achaean ships. In despair they appeal to Achilles, and the section ends. The embassy fails, and, after an interlude of night operations in *K*, the Achaeans start their efforts afresh. This second section begins with some short-lived triumphs. Agamemnon at first carries all before him, but then the trouble begins. The leading heroes are wounded, and the Trojans assail the Achaean wall. Idomeneus gives a temporary relief, but the Trojans are soon back. And then Patroclus persuades Achilles to let him go. He does well, but his victories are quite counterbalanced by his death, and, even if his body is saved, the section ends in disaster. The second turning point comes in *T* when Achilles, stung to

---

[1] E. Bethe, *Homer*, i, p. 61.

remorse by grief at Patroclus' death, makes up his quarrel
with Agamemnon and prepares to go to battle. Then comes
the swift series of battles which end in the death of Hector.
The last two books are an epilogue to what has gone before,
just as the first two were a prelude to what is to come after.

Such is the shape and outline of the poem, and it is truly
an *Iliad*. But inside this frame, causing the different events
and holding them together, is the story of Achilles' wrath,
and this has an essentially tragic character. On this the poet
rightly laid special emphasis in his opening words, and it is
the kernel of the story. The other events derive from it and
are full of poetry, but this makes the *Iliad* a great poem.
Here too, moreover, the poet's own hand is most manifest.
For the tragedy of Achilles is essentially a moral tragedy, and
implies a series of values which must be largely the poet's
own. Certainly, only one great poet could have created a
poem so profound in its moral sensibility and so skilful in
adapting moral judgements to an artistic end. The theme
is how Achilles' temper leads him both to disaster and to
moral degradation. The disaster is clear enough. If he had
not preferred his injured pride to his duty as a soldier, he
would not have sent his only friend to his doom. This he
admits himself when he first hears of Patroclus' death. In
the shock of the terrible news he makes no attempt to conceal
that he is to blame—τὸν ἀπώλεσα he tells his mother (Σ 82),
and he knows that his own quarrelsomeness and anger are the
cause. He found pleasure in them before, but now he wishes
that they had never existed (Σ 107–10). But the loss of his
friend is not his only tragedy. He has fallen from heroic
standards of virtue, and there is another tragedy, in his soul.
It is hard to recapture the morality of the heroic age, but
this particular tragedy is vital to the plot of the *Iliad*, and we
must try to judge Achilles by the same standards as those by
which Homer's audience judged him. Only so can we see
that the *Iliad*, in spite of its many strands and patterns, is
essentially a unity.

The first lapse of Achilles is in his quarrel with Agamemnon. The poet prepares us for something terrible when he
announces that he will tell of the μῆνιν οὐλομένην. The

adjective gives a hint of what will come. It is used by Homer of anything disastrous, but particularly of anything wrong. It leads us to expect that Achilles' wrath is wicked as well as unfortunate, and this expectation is fulfilled. In the quarrel, Achilles is by no means so much in the wrong as his leader, but he is still in the wrong. When Agamemnon tells him that he loves quarrelling—αἰεὶ γάρ τοι ἔρις τε φίλη πόλεμοί τε μάχαι τε (A 177)[1]—he makes a legitimate point. What is wrong is Achilles' determination to dispute his commander's decision, and it is simply to stop the dispute that Athene intervenes. The moral is pointed clearly by Nestor, who knows the rules of chivalry. Both are in the wrong, Agamemnon for taking Briseis and Achilles for quarrelling with his liege lord. Agamemnon's power comes from Zeus, and he is a superior being with whom Achilles may not dispute (A 277). So far the wrath of Achilles is regarded as unfortunate because of its results, but not highly reprehensible. Nestor's advice to both is to control their tempers and make up the quarrel; he does not add any word of reproach. In this scene Achilles is guilty of a lack of αἰδώς to his superior lord. In heroic morality a king was owed αἰδώς by his vassals and subjects, and so Homer makes it plain. It is a feeling of respect for superiors.[2] When Agamemnon chides Diomedes for shirking the fight, Diomedes makes no answer because of his αἰδώς for the king (Δ 402), and reproves his comrade Sthenelus when he tries to reply in his stead. This case is precisely the antithesis of the quarrel between Achilles and Agamemnon. In both Agamemnon is in the wrong, but in the second case Diomedes is enough of a perfect knight to know that he must make no answer— αἰδώς forbids it. In the quarrel the poet wins our sympathy for Achilles by making Agamemnon far more in the wrong than he. Agamemnon also violates αἰδώς, but in another aspect—the respect that should be shown to subordinates,[3] but he violates it more brutally and with less justification than

---

[1] 'For ever is strife dear to you and wars and battles.'
[2] e.g. K 238, O 129, υ 171. Hesiod, *Theog.* 91; Aesch. *Pers.* 699; Soph. *Ajax*, 1076. Cf. R. Schultz, *ΑΙΔΩΣ*, 1910; M. Hoffmann, *Die ethische Terminologie bei Homer*, Tübingen, 1914.
[3] Hence Achilles' taunt, " ὦ μοι, ἀναιδείην ἐπιειμένε, κερδαλεόφρον ". (A 149)

Achilles. His sin is ὕβρις (*A* 203), and he merits most of the
abuse which Achilles throws at him. Even after Nestor's
intervention he refuses to reconsider his decision and remains
unrepentant. So the poem begins with two good men in the
wrong, though Achilles is less in the wrong than Agamemnon
and therefore gets more of our sympathy.

When Achilles next appears, the situation changes and his
moral tragedy deepens. Because of his defection the Achaeans
have been defeated in the field, and to secure his support
Agamemnon offers handsome amends, proclaims his own
guilt, and is prepared to end the quarrel. Achilles makes an
unequivocal refusal. The heroic view of this refusal is given
by his old friend, Phoenix. Achilles has now become the
victim of Ἄτη, the infatuation that leads to disaster. By
refusing the entreaties of the embassy he neglects the Λιταί
—the Prayers who follow after Ἄτη and undo the harm she
does. Achilles scorns them and perseveres in his wrath.
Once again he lacks αἰδώς, but this time it is the gods and
not man he neglects (*I* 508 ff.). This is a grave fault, the
same fault as that of the suitors in the *Odyssey*, who are
punished for it (*v* 169). And it is all the worse because the
divine ordinance which Achilles now violates is one of the most
sacred, the law that mercy must be shown to suppliants.[1] The
embassy comes with all the appearance of suppliants making
a sacred request in the name of the gods. To such, mercy
and consideration were due. When the request has failed,
Aias makes a last attempt to move Achilles by pointing this
out; he shows that the envoys are friends under his roof who
demand and deserve respect (*I* 640 ff.), but the only answer
to this is Achilles' determination to continue in his wrath.
The embassy leaves him and reports its failure. The best comment is that of Diomedes: they should never have attempted
to move him (*I* 698). In this scene Achilles definitely moves
a step in the wrong direction. The recovery and repentance
of Agamemnon removes what excuse he had before, and now
he alone is to blame for the dire position of the Achaeans.

---

[1] Φ 74, ρ 577, χ 312. Cf. J. Engel, *Zum Rechte der Schützflehenden bei Homer*,
Progr. Passau, 1899; T. Sorgenfrey, *De vestigiis iuris gentium Homerici*, Diss.
Leipzig, 1871, p. 12 ff.

For Achilles himself the results of this action are as terrible as they are for the other Achaeans. As Phoenix has shown, he has set himself up against the divine law, and he must expect the consequences. They come soon enough. The Achaeans are again defeated, and their defeat makes the generous Patroclus want to help them. Achilles cannot restrain him; he goes and is killed. When the news comes, Achilles realizes that he himself is to blame. He allowed his comrade to fight, and never thought of being at his side to protect him (Σ 98 ff.). His wrath is to blame, and now he knows it when it is too late. The ἄτη, against which Phoenix warned him, has indeed played its part and hurt him, when he might have listened to the prayers of the embassy and prevented disaster.

By the death of Patroclus, Achilles is punished for his lack of αἰδώς, for the ὕβρις which made him flout the laws of God and the prayers of men. But his tragedy does not end here. The saddest chapter is yet to come, and in it the poet shows his finest sensibility and sense of construction. Achilles has anger in his soul, and, though the death of Patroclus gives him a deep sense of guilt, it does not cure him of his anger. It turns from the Achaeans to the Trojans, and especially to Hector. Now his main idea is revenge. Revenge was quite legitimate in heroic morality. When Odysseus kills the suitors, he would be thought entirely justified by the poet and his hearers. But when Achilles seeks revenge on Hector, his mood is different and its results are less laudable. In the first place, his fury extends to others who are quite innocent. He slays Lycaon and refuses him the rites of burial, though Lycaon has addressed him with all the language of a suppliant.

"γουνοῦμαί σ', 'Αχιλεῦ· σὺ δέ μ' αἴδεο καί μ' ἐλέησον·
ἀντὶ τοί εἰμ' ἱκέταο, διοτρεφές, αἰδοίοιο." (Φ 74–5)[1]

And in the second place, he is not content with killing Hector. He has to maltreat his body after death. He drags it after his chariot and intends to throw it to the dogs. Out of his

---

[1] 'On my knees I beg you, Achilles. Do you show ruth and pity me: for, goddess-born, I am as a suppliant who deserves ruth.'

own mouth the poet condemns him (X 395, Ψ 24). These actions are ἀεικέα ἔργα—shameless deeds—and not to be pardoned. The phrase is one of severe condemnation. Elsewhere it is used only of the unjust burdens laid by Eurystheus on Heracles (T 133) and of the fate which awaits the fatherless Astyanax (Ω 733). The poet's condemnation of Achilles in these acts accords well with the treatment given by his heroes to their dead. Both sides are ready for a truce that the dead may be buried. The true heroic note is sounded by Odysseus when he forbids any rejoicing over the dead suitors:

οὐχ ὁσίη κταμένοισιν ἐπ' ἀνδράσιν εὐχετάασθαι. (χ 412)[1]

Achilles' behaviour is the opposite. He has had his revenge, and he is not content with it. There is still a burning wrath in him, and it continues, although the gods prevent him from doing all that he wants to Hector's body. When the burial is over and the ghost of Patroclus has disappeared, this anger begins to die. There is nothing for it to feed on, and Achilles is busy with the funeral games. But Homer is not content to leave Achilles and his story thus. His hero has sunk to degradation through a fault in his own character, and he can only be restored to honour and sympathy when this fault is healed.

The healing comes in the last book, with the visit of Priam to ransom the body of Hector. Achilles, who has lost his αἰδώς, regains it before the old man, and so conforms to the will of the gods who expect the old to be honoured and pitied:

ἀθάνατοι τιμῶσι παλαιοτέρους ἀνθρώπους. (Ψ 788)[2]

The recovery is worked out in detail. At the beginning of the book Achilles drags the body of Hector three times round the tomb of Patroclus. The gods see it, and Apollo expresses the general feeling on Olympus, when he says that Achilles has lost his wits and raves like a lion, and finally:

" ἔλεον μὲν ἀπώλεσεν, οὐδέ οἱ αἰδὼς γίγνεται " (Ω 44–5)[3]

[1] 'It is unholiness to boast over slaughtered men.'
[2] 'The immortals honour old men.'
[3] 'He has lost pity, and he has no ruth.'

The judgement is severe, but only Hera disputes it. Even
Thetis knows that Achilles is not quite in his right mind and
keeps Hector's body φρεσὶ μαινομένῃσιν (Ω 135). The solution
is that he must give the body back to Priam, and for this the
gods combine with Thetis. It is the only hope for the recovery of Achilles. But the general impression is still that he
has no reverence nor pity. So, at least, Hecuba thinks when
she tries to dissuade Priam from going:

" ὠμηστὴς καὶ ἄπιστος ἀνὴρ ὅ γε, οὔ σ' ἐλεήσει,
οὐδε τί σ' αἰδέσεται ". (Ω 207–8)[1]

And Priam himself is none too sure that his visit will not end
in his death. But when he reaches Achilles, he makes an
appeal to his αἰδώς, asking him for pity in the name of his
old father. The key of the appeal lies in the words:

" ἀλλ' αἰδεῖο θεούς, Ἀχιλεῦ, αὐτόν τ' ἐλέησον
μνησάμενος σοῦ πατρός ". (Ω 503–4)[2]

Achilles does not respond to the appeal at once, but he is
touched to tears and weeps for Patroclus. This makes him
pity Priam:

οἰκτίρων πολιόν τε κάρη πολιόν τε γένειον, (Ω 516)[3]

and in his pity he cannot withstand the request which comes
from the gods that he should release the body of Hector. In
this act he recovers his true nature. His anger has passed
away, and he is himself again.

The story of the wrath of Achilles, as the poet announces it,
is thus the kernel of the *Iliad*. It is a tragic story in so far
as it involves waste and loss or excites pity and fear. And
the tragedy is essentially moral. It turns on the failure of
Achilles to keep his αἰδώς for gods and men, and it does not
end till he has regained it. This failure is due to his imperious temper, and is thus derived from the same source
as his heroic qualities in war and council. His great gifts
have their tragic side and lead to the death of Patroclus and
his own humiliation. His tragedy bears some likeness to that

[1] 'Ravening and faithless man that he is, he will show no pity nor ruth to
you.'
[2] 'But reverence the gods, Achilles, and pity me, remembering your father.'
[3] 'Pitying his white head and white beard.'

of Coriolanus. Both are the victims of their imperious
tempers, and both are splendid in their darkest hours. But
the tragedy of Achilles is perhaps more intimate and more
moving, because it lies even deeper in his soul.

Such is the kernel of the plot, so far as Achilles is concerned.
But the main story too has its tragedy, and it is the tragedy
of Troy. We have seen how the poem is truly an *Iliad* and
deals with the fall of Troy. But like the disasters which
befall Achilles, this disaster too has a moral significance
which makes it the more painful. It is not Homer's way to
underline his moral judgements or expressly to state his
axioms, but here also, as with Achilles, he makes his meaning
plain enough. The Trojans are guilty because of their
support of Paris, and it is he who not only causes their
sorrows but refuses to end them. That Paris is the cause of
the war is clear enough to the Trojans. Hector makes it
plain at his brother's first appearance on the battlefield,
when he chides him with being mad after women, and says
that it would have been better if he had never been born.
His guilt is that he has carried off another man's wife and
brought shame on himself because of it (Γ 39 ff.). A little
later Hector is not afraid to tell both Achaeans and Trojans
that Paris is the cause of the struggle (Γ 87). His view is
clearly accepted by the other Trojans. In the nocturnal
debate Antenor suggests that they should end the war by
restoring Helen and her possessions to the Atreidae, and
Priam, though he yields to Paris, still admits his responsibility (H 353 ff.). To the Achaeans, and especially to Menelaus, his guilt is even plainer. He has broken the ties of
hospitality, and it is right that he should be punished (Γ 350),
if only as a warning to others not to abuse their hosts' kindness. Paris cares little for their censure and enjoys himself
while he can. But Helen, the partner in his guilt, though the
old men excuse her and Hector is always kind, knows that
she is to blame. Her guilt weighs heavily on her, and she
wishes that Paris had been killed in the duel with Menelaus
(Γ 428), and that the storms had carried her off or the sea
swallowed her before she could have committed her sin (Z 34
ff.). Yet, though both are thought guilty, it is plain that the

poet does not condemn them overmuch. He has his excuse
for them. It is not they who are to blame, but the gods,
and especially Aphrodite. When Hector chides him, Paris
answers that even if we do not want them, the gods' glorious
gifts must not be thrown away (Γ 65). And the same excuse
holds for Helen in the great scene where she tries to maintain
her will against Aphrodite, and then has to yield and sleep
with the man whom she despises. In her struggle with the
goddess Helen pours scorn upon her, telling her to stay
with Paris and avoid the path of the gods. She herself will
not go to him—her words are clear and unequivocal—
" νεμεσσητὸν δέ κεν εἴη " (Γ 410)—there will be righteous
indignation against her if she does. But Aphrodite overrules
her and threatens her with hatred. Then Helen goes with her
to Paris, and though she blames his cowardice, she yields to
him. He dismisses her taunts and tells her how he loves her,
and then the poet ends the scene in a few poignant words:

ἦ ῥα, καὶ ἄρχε λέχοσδέ κιών· ἅμα δ' εἵπετ' ἄκοιτις. (Γ 447)[1]

This touching scene shows, more clearly than does Paris'
careless denial, that Helen is not her own mistress. She is the
victim of Aphrodite, who is relentless in breaking her to her
will. No wonder that Paris was thought the victim of powers
beyond his control. The poet lays the blame on Aphrodite,
and this is important for the story. She has laid an ἄτη on
Paris, and the Trojans suffer for it. Paris begins the war, and
his obstinacy makes it continue. He offers to fight Menelaus,
but his curse prevents a conclusion being reached. In the
moment of victory Menelaus finds him snatched away by
Aphrodite. This makes it easier for the solemn oaths of
truce to be broken, and for the fighting to begin again with
the Achaeans firmly convinced of the justice of their cause.
Later, when the Trojan council meets at night, Antenor
suggests that Paris should restore Helen and her property.
Paris refuses, and the fight has to go on. Even at the very
last when Hector's dead body is being maltreated by Achilles
and most of the gods pity it, Hera and Poseidon are opposed
to any attempt to save it—because of Paris, ᾿Αλεξάνδρου ἕνεκ'

[1] 'So spake he and led the way to the bed, and his wife followed with him.'

ἄτης (Ω 28). A curse is on him, and Troy pays for it. The curse comes from Aphrodite, and is none the better for that. Her character is suspected, and she is the least honoured of the Olympian goddesses. The heroic world seems to have regarded her with a mixture of amusement and horror, and Homer, who at times makes her ridiculous, makes her terrible when she forces Helen to obedience. We may laugh at her when she gets wounded in battle and cries to her mother for comfort, or when she helps Hera to trick Zeus with her magic girdle (Ξ 214 ff.). But her gift is μαχλοσύνη ἀλεγεινή (Ω 30), hateful wantonness, and the hard words are intended to be hard. In her treatment of Helen there is no tenderness. If her will is thwarted, she sticks at nothing. Because of her, Achilles finds Helen ῥιγεδανή, something that makes him shudder (Τ 325). As an ally in battle she is of little use, and she leaves the Trojans in their danger (Φ 416). Hera, when she no longer needs her for her own purposes (ib. 421), calls her 'dogfly', κυνάμυια. Yet it is she who, working through Paris and Helen, brings the destruction of Troy, she who prevents the solution afforded by the duel between Paris and Menelaus. Troy falls because the Trojans condone the guilt of Paris. This is clear from the emphasis which Homer gives to that guilt. His crime passed all the limits allowed the heroic age; it violated not only wedlock but hospitality. His friends stood by him, and they were punished. The Trojans also, like Achilles, fall because of their high qualities. The loyalty of Hector to Troy makes him forgive Paris while he condemns him. Troy is under the protection of Aphrodite, or rather in her thrall, and for this it falls.[1]

It may seem fanciful to attribute the fall of Troy to the power of Aphrodite, but to the Greek mind sin was sooner or later followed by punishment, and by hinting at a cause for the fall Homer would appeal to deeply ingrained opinion. But he writes not as a moralist but as a poet. His scheme of sin and punishment is transformed into poetry by the

---

[1] That Homer was so understood in antiquity may be seen from Ibycus, *Ox. Pap.* 1790, ll. 8–9.

⟨Πέρ⟩γαμον δ' ἀνέ⟨β⟩α ταλαπείριο⟨ν ἄ⟩τα
⟨χρυ⟩σοέθειραν δ⟨ι⟩ὰ Κυπρίδα.

pathos with which he invests its victims. There is no condemnation of Helen's action in his wonderful picture of her. She is the plaything of fate, and calls only for pity. Nor is there much is the picture of Paris. He is not indeed a man of heroic stature, but he still loves Helen and refuses to give her up. The fall of Troy comes from the fate which has sent her Paris and delivered her to Aphrodite. From this follow the other disasters, the perjury of the broken oath and the hostility of powerful gods.

The *Iliad*, then, both in its particular and general aspects, is a profoundly moral story. This scheme of sin and punishment runs through it and holds its parts together. Homer is not a teacher like Aeschylus, and he does not preach his views. He takes them largely for granted, and is content to let them be merged in his story. They are important because they make the *Iliad* tragic in character. In this it differs from the *Odyssey*, which is, as Longinus said, largely a comedy of manners.[1] The suitors, like Achilles or Helen, are the victims of ἄτη, but they lack heroic or even lovable qualities, and their death stirs not our pity but our sense of justice. We do not feel that there is waste in it. In the *Iliad* these great souls are caught in the grip of circumstances and made to suffer from the defects of their own high qualities. And that is the essence of tragedy.

[1] Περὶ Ὕψους ix. 15 οἱονεὶ κωμῳδία τίς ἐστιν ἠθολογουμένη.

THE ORIGINS OF THE EPIC

THE *Iliad* implies a long history. It must have grown from something, but from what? The poet tells us nothing of himself, and we are left to draw our conclusions from analogies and casual references. The best evidence should be in the *Iliad* itself, but the *Iliad* says little about poets or poetry. Fortunately the *Odyssey* is more explicit, and its evidence may be taken as the best that can be found. The *Iliad* assumes that great doings are subjects fit for song, and Helen says that Zeus has given an evil doom to her and Paris, that in days to come they may be the theme of songs for men (Z 357–8), but the *Odyssey* tells how such doings came to be made part of poetry. Demodocus sings at the court of Alcinous, and in Ithaca Phemius sings to the suitors. These singers are not amateurs but professionals. They rely on their craft for a living. Their social position, if we may believe Eumaeus, is similar to that of seers, doctors, and craftsmen (ρ 383–4). Demodocus indeed is called a hero (θ 483), and Agamemnon's minstrel was sufficiently important to be put in charge of Clytaemnestra when her husband went to Troy (γ 267–8). But these social claims do not hide the fact that a minstrel's rank was well below that of a chieftain. He belonged to a class dependent on princes for patronage and livelihood. When Odysseus kills the suitors, he lends a merciful ear to Phemius, who claims that he has sung for the suitors under compulsion: they were more numerous and stronger than he, and they took him to Ithaca by force (χ 351–3). But in spite of such humiliations the bard is honoured in his own way. Odysseus tell Alcinous that nothing is better than to listen at a feast to a bard whose voice is like that of the gods (ι 3), and when Alcinous in his turn wants to congratulate Odysseus on the excellence of his narrative, he can find no better praise than by comparing him to an ἀοιδός—with such craft has he told his story (λ 368). Such distribution of compliments may of course be due to the poet's desire to emphasize the dignity of his own profession, but there must be a germ of truth in them. Otherwise his patrons would not have tolerated them, and his livelihood would have been ruined.

The themes of which Demodocus and Phemius make their song are like the themes of the *Iliad* and *Odyssey*. They are, as Penelope says, ἔργ' ἀνδρῶν τε θεῶν τε (α 338),[1] and the details confirm the description. Demodocus' song on the loves of Ares and Aphrodite differs little in temper from the *Διὸς ἀπάτη*. The songs of men are mostly from the Trojan Cycle. Demodocus sings of the Wooden Horse (θ 499–501) and the Quarrel of Odysseus and Achilles (θ 73–8), while Phemius sings of the Return of the Achaeans (α 325–7). The bard's business is to tell of the latest news, and the newest song (as Telemachus tells his mother) is the best and most honoured (α 351–2). The stories are regarded as strictly historical, and Odysseus compliments Demodocus on telling his tale λίην κατὰ κόσμον (θ 489)—as it should be told. These songs are separate entities and sung separately. Demodocus and Phemius sing what they are asked to sing, and they can start at any point. But their songs nearly all concern Troy and deal with a coherent set of stories. That some sort of continuity existed is shown by the poet's words when Demodocus, after being pressed by Odysseus, sings of the Wooden Horse:

ὁ δ' ὁρμηθεὶς θεοῦ ἄρχετο, φαῖνε δ' ἀοιδὴν
ἔνθεν ἑλὼν ὡς οἱ μὲν ἐϋσσέλμων ἐπὶ νηῶν κ.τ.λ.   (θ 499–500)[2]

This seems to mean that there was a set order for the story and that the bard took it up at a definite point.

In the *Odyssey* then we have a clear and consistent picture of how the poet imagines bards to have lived and sung in the heroic age, and the picture is so vivid that it must be based on his own experience. The songs of Demodocus and Phemius recall certain aspects of the *Iliad* and *Odyssey*. They deal with similar themes, they are addressed to leisured, aristocratic audiences, they imply the existence of a large body of

---

[1] 'the deeds of men and gods'.

[2] 'He, stirred by the god, began, and made his song, starting at that point how they on their well-benched ships, &c.'

poetry from which the particular piece demanded could be drawn. All these are essential features of the Homeric poems as we have them. Moreover, the bards of the *Odyssey* make the same claim to divine inspiration as the poet of the *Iliad*. Homer says:

" ἀργαλέον δέ με ταῦτα θεὸν ὣς πάντ' ἀγορεῦσαι " (M 176)[1]

and such is the claim of Phemius:

" αὐτοδίδακτος δ' εἰμί, θεὸς δέ μοι ἐν φρεσὶν οἴμας
παντοίας ἐνέφυσεν " (χ 347–8)[2]

Homer calls his bards ἀοιδοί, and so he must have called himself, if we may judge by the first words of the *Iliad* μῆνιν ἄειδε, θεά. The conclusion follows that, however much the poet may create an imaginary past elsewhere, he reproduces historical conditions when he writes of poets and poetry. This conclusion, natural in itself, is fortified when we compare the conditions he describes with those which we know to have existed elsewhere.

The existence of a professional bardic class is a commonplace of history. When soldiers thought it below their dignity to read or write, the bard recorded their great deeds for them and was an indispensable servant in court and camp. In Finland and Serbia there still exist professional bards whose only business is the recitation of traditional poetry,[3] and in the Middle Ages every court or army had its poet. But the parallel goes closer than this. The lays of Demodocus seem to cluster round a single subject, the siege of Troy, and this recalls other early literatures. The Icelandic *Edda Poems* largely cluster round the story of Sigurd and Gudrun, and the medieval French epics centre on Charlemagne. The body of the saga, from which the single lays were drawn, was not a single great poem. It was a collection of complete poems. The *Edda Poems* are perfect in themselves, but they tell a consecutive and fairly consistent story. And they are short, like the lays of Demodocus. In its youth narrative poetry

---

[1] 'It is hard for me to tell of all these things like a god.'

[2] 'I taught myself, but a god made all manner of lays to grow in my mind.'

[3] D. Comparetti, *The Traditional Poetry of the Finns.* M. Murko in *N. Jahrbücher f.d. kl. Alt.*, 1919, pp. 273 ff.

prefers short lays: length seems the result of age and development. The lays of Demodocus were short enough for several to be heard in one evening, and resemble the separate poems which were artificially built into the Finnish *Kalevala*.

The picture, then, which Homer gives us, has its parallels in other cultures and may well be true, but it does not reveal conditions under which the *Iliad* can have reached its present form. The differences between it and these lays are greater than the similarities, and reveal a vast gulf between the two types of poetry. The lays of Phemius and Demodocus are of their own heroic times. The Trojan War is as real history to them as the battles of Maldon and Brunanburh were to the Anglo-Saxon poets who celebrated them or the European War is to bards now living in Herzegovina or Cyprus. But Homer sings of a past beyond recall, when gods walked on the earth and men were stronger and better than in his day. His picture is of bards in the hey-day of the heroic age when daily deeds were done worthy of song, but he himself belongs to a later generation which looks for inspiration not to the present but to the past. Other Greek poets, like Aeschylus, could write of the high events of their own time and invest them with the glamour of heroism, but Homer is not of this company. He writes of an irrecoverable past, and he knows it. He can only have found his matter in lays like those which he ascribes to Demodocus. Other early poets may use prose chronicles. Such at least seem to have been known to the author of the *Song of Roland* who attributed them to St. Giles, and we possess in the Welsh *Mabinogion* and the Icelandic *Prose Edda* collections of stories intended for translation into verse. But Homer makes no mention of a prose chronicle, and it is improbable that such a thing existed in his day. Such writing came with the days of Ionian enlightenment long after the *Iliad* was composed. The only hint he gives of his sources is in his invocations of the Muse, and these seem to imply not only his own inspiration but the secrets of the singers' guild to which he belonged.

Another difference is that of length. The songs of the Odyssean ἀοιδοί are short. Demodocus can fit three into a single evening, but the *Iliad*, if recited from beginning to end without a break, would take nearly two days. It is true that just as Demodocus draws from a collection of lays, so any bard might select a portion of the *Iliad* and recite it separately, and such a selection might well be a unity by Aristotelian canons. But in spite of this the *Iliad* is still a whole such as Demodocus' collection can hardly be thought to have been. Yet this difference gives us the clearest evidence of what pre-Homeric poetry was like. Many portions of the *Iliad* may be detached from the whole and made into separate songs, and pieces like these must have been the forerunners of the poem as it now exists. Several books, such as the *Embassy to Achilles*, the *Story of Dolon*, the *Ransoming of Hector*, are complete unities, each with its own story and atmosphere, and might well be recited separately for their own merits. It is true that they imply a general knowledge of the plot and are only fully intelligible if we know what has come before or what is to come after. But such a knowledge is expected in most audiences of saga. The story of Gudrun was indispensable to the men who listened to the *Edda*, and the outline of the Siege of Troy was probably part of the education of every Ionian child. Or again other detachable unities might be found embedded in the text of the *Iliad*, which posterity did not honour by making into separate books. The episode of Glaucus and Diomedes in *Z* is a self-contained poem. It begins in the right narrative manner by plunging *in medias res*:

Γλαῦκος δ' Ἱππολόχοιο πάϊς καὶ Τυδέος υἱὸς
ἐς μέσον ἀμφοτέρων συνίτην μεμαῶτε μάχεσθαι (Z 119–20)[1]

and ends brilliantly with the interchange of armour:

χρύσεα χαλκείων, ἑκατόμβοι' ἐννεαβοίων. (Z 236)[2]

Here we have the rapidity and completeness of the separate lay. It is excellently placed in the *Iliad*, but none the less detachable and complete in itself. The same may be said of other episodes, such as the single combats between Paris and Menelaus or between Aeneas and Achilles. Both belong to a

---

[1] 'Glaucus, the son of Hippolytus, and the son of Tydeus came together in the midst of the two armies desiring to fight.'

[2] 'bronze for gold, what was worth a hundred oxen for what was worth nine.' Cf. Bethe, *Homer*, i, p. 28.

type of narrative which is known to have existed separately. An example survives in the combat between Heracles and Cycnus in the Hesiodic *Shield of Heracles*. Such episodes are short, complete, and look as if they were drawn from a large repertoire. They are written without the elaboration of some other parts of the *Iliad*. Similes are few in them, and they have none of the delays and postponements which bulk so large in other sections of Homeric narrative. They have often a genealogical interest, which shows their ancient character. In them the *Iliad* retains an earlier phase of epic art. Episodes like the *Ransoming of Hector* are less primitive than they, and, so far as their art is concerned, lie half-way between these simple lays and the highly complex books which lead up to the making of Achilles' armour. They are complete in themselves, but their movement is more leisurely, they have more irrelevances, they are stories told for stories' sake.

From short poems like these the *Iliad* must have developed. Can we trace its history still farther back? Homer indeed gives a hint, and we may follow it. When Odysseus and Aias find Achilles in his tent, he is singing to his lyre, and he sings of κλέα ἀνδρῶν. By him sits Patroclus, waiting for Achilles to stop that he may pick up the song and continue it (*I* 156–91). This method of singing is quite different from that of Demodocus. Achilles is not a professional bard, and his singing is *impromptu*. He has, moreover, a partner who can continue when he himself is tired. This type of minstrelsy has its historical parallels, both in literature and in history. Good examples come from the age of migrations at the beginning of the dark ages of Europe. In *Beowulf* such improvised songs were the occupation of nobles in King Hrothgar's court,[1] and Procopius records that the Vandal king, Gelimer, comforted himself in his troubles by composing songs about them.[2] The amoebaeic song, practised by Achilles and Patroclus, is recorded to have existed recently in Finland, where pairs of bards improvised in turn with rapid alternation.[3] Such royal improvisation, as the *Iliad* depicts, can exist by the side of professional poetry. As a pendant to Gelimer's songs we have the picture, given by Priscus, of the two German bards who sang

[1] *Beowulf*, ll. 866–74.   [2] Procopius, iv. 6. 33.   [3] Cf. Comparetti, l.c.

songs at Attila's banquets of his prowess and victories,[1] and by Jordanes of the Goths who 'cantu maiorum facta modulationibus citharisque canebant'.[2] But though the two types existed side by side, the inspired amateur is really the predecessor of the professional, whose livelihood depends on a whole society appreciating his art and being prepared to support him for it. The change from the one to the other is ultimately a change from improvised to remembered poetry. Such a change is never absolute, and the bard who retold old poems was often called upon to recite one of his own compositions. But he could not follow his fancy freely, and had to be prepared to sing of some popular theme. The natural result of this was that lays were circulated from one bard to another, learned by heart, and recited at demand. The rise of such a professional class meant at first a great growth of poetry, even if in its decline it meant the growth of conventions and the standardization of poetical forms. In Germanic countries we find a similar development from improvised poetry to poetry learned and repeated. The earliest Icelandic poetry must have been improvised, but later the class of skalds largely repeated earlier compositions, improving on them as they thought fit but keeping in essentials to the traditional material. Demodocus, of course, keeps up the air of an improviser, and such no doubt Homer meant him to be. But his historical prototype must have reached a high level of conscious art and composed his songs before he was asked for them. Otherwise the Greek epic would never have attained its great strength in style and construction.

So far our evidence takes us without much difficulty. The question is whether the sung lay can be taken still farther back. E. Bethe has made a brilliant attempt to derive the epic ultimately from the song and dance from which most Greek poetry can be derived.[3] This type of song survived on the mainland in the work of Corinna, Pindar, and Bacchylides. It is derived, he claims, from the same original as Homer, but preserves its features in a purer form. In his own words, 'as the recited heroic epos is developed from the sung heroic

---

[1] Priscus, *F.H.G.* iv, 92 b. Cf. Sidon. Apollin. *Ep.* I. 2. 9.
[2] *Chron.* 5.   [3] *Homer*, i, pp. 14 ff.

song, so is the single song of the bards, originally divided into strophes, derived from the heroic song of the dancing chorus'. Prima facie this theory has one great merit. Most poetry is derived from some combined ritual of song and dance, and if the heroic lay can be traced to such an origin, it would be in good company. The evidence adduced by Bethe is complicated and needs stating at some length. The basis of it is a distinction which he makes between sung and recited poetry. The characteristics of sung poetry, he says, are two. It is divided into strophes, and it has a particular style of narrative, which consists of giving only the important moments, in moving abruptly from one scene to another, and in being concise where the epic is full. This is a perfectly fair account of lyric narrative as we possess it, and Bethe ably exemplifies his views with examples drawn from the *Fourth Pythian Ode* of Pindar and the *Sixteenth Ode* of Bacchylides. Both these poems have the characteristics he describes. In both we are plunged *in medias res* and moved by abrupt transitions from one brilliant scene to another. The manner of both narrations is the same and may well be called 'the song style'. This manner, he continues, can be found in the *Iliad*. The first book is a good example of it. We plunge straight into the story, and the scenes succeed each other rapidly. Bethe asks: 'Has the opening of the *Iliad* a truly epic style? Has it not rather the conciseness, the breathless impetus, the concentrated dramatic art of the song?'[1] He contrasts it with the leisurely movement of the *Odyssey*, and with other parts of the *Iliad* such as the fighting round the Achaean trench in *M*.

Having found traces of the song style in the epic, and thereby derived the epic from the song, Bethe is able to provide a literary parallel to such a development. In Dalmatia, Herzegovina, and old Serbia there are still heroic songs which celebrate long-perished deeds. These are sung to a simple recurring melody played on the *guslé*, a kind of fiddle. All verses have ten syllables and a caesura after the fourth syllable. The verses are grouped into units of from five to ten verses each. From a verse form similar to this

[1] *Homer*, i, p. 24.

Bethe thinks the Homeric epic was derived, and he finds a survival of such in the poetry of Corinna, who tells stories in the lyric manner composed in strophes for musical accompaniment. Corinna, despite her date, preserves an early form, but in essentials her art is the same as that of Pindar and Bacchylides. The independence of this lyric narrative is seen by its popularity in southern Italy and Sicily, where it dealt at some length with stories not known to Homer, and was presumably free of his influence. The best example of this is to be seen in the long lyrical narratives of Stesichorus, which have names like Ἰλίου πέρσις, Νόστοι, Γηρυονηΐς, Εὐρώπεια, Ἄθλα ἐπὶ Πελίᾳ. These poems were sung by a choir. The change from such an art to the heroic lay was not rapid. The chief crisis came when the leader of the choir gave up his choir and sang by himself, still keeping the rhythm and strophe of the song form. The next change came when song gave place to recitation and the strophe disappeared.

This ingenious and complicated theory is in many ways attractive. It accounts for actual features in the epic and it has analogies in other literatures, but it is open to grave objections. It is quite true that the *Iliad* shows traces of the song style in its narrative, but it may well be doubted if the similarity is due to its being derived from a song form. The epic is concerned chiefly with telling a story, and this is its paramount object, but the stories told by the lyric poets are only incidental to the whole poem, and they imply a far greater knowledge of the story than is implied in the epic. Pindar's method of narration is hardly narrative at all. He illuminates a few beautiful details of a well-known story, and leaves it at that. Corinna indeed seems more concerned with her story than Pindar is, but she too writes with an ulterior purpose. Her aim is really religious. Like Hesiod, she wishes to tell a story of the gods or heroes, but it is to explain some local usage or cult. She writes to instruct and not to please. Her art is plainly in a close relation with some religious rite, but in the epic there is no trace of any such relation. Nor can the literary parallels adduced by Bethe be treated as final evidence. His theory depends on his view that the epic lay cannot ultimately be a separate form, but must be derived from a song form. But in some of the most primitive literature known we find the two forms existing side by side. Thus in Turkish literature we find on the one side a lyric form with a four-lined strophe, alliteration, assonance, and end rhymes, and on the other side improvised narrative poetry whose unit is not the stanza but the line, and which lacks the graces of the lyric.[1] The use of the line instead of the strophe is a common practice in narrative poetry, and can been seen in early German and Anglo-Saxon verse. So it is not surprising that there is no trace whatsoever of the strophe in the Greek epic. And indeed, if analogies may be pressed, the lyric narrative as used by Stesichorus seems to be less an ancient type than a later combination of the two original forms of song and narrative verse. At least, among the Kirghiz Tartars we find by the side of purely lyrical songs, historical songs composed in strophes of four, six, or eight lines.[2] So, too, among the Serbs to-day the old improvised epic has been replaced in many districts by lyric-epic songs composed in strophes and accompanied by music. In Germanic literature there appeared early not only the long alliterative lines of the epic, but also a four-lined strophe which produced the *Edda Poems*, and, under Viking influence, the strophic ballads of the Irish. It seems then that in early literatures we may roughly distinguish two forms of poetry, the epic or narrative poetry written in lines, and the sung poetry written in strophes, and sometimes accompanied by dancing. The two seem to be independent of each other from the start, and only to be combined in a more sophisticated stage of culture.

When we look into Homer we find that he indicates just such a distinction. On the one side he presents us with the narrative poetry, perhaps improvised, as it is by Achilles when he sings κλέα ἀνδρῶν, perhaps learned from the Muse, as it is by Phemius and Demodocus, and on the other side he indicates quite a different form of song, accompanied with dancing and sung by more than one person. This second class falls naturally into different divisions, which correspond

---

[1] E. Drerup, *Das Homerproblem in der Gegenwart*, p. 72.
[2] E. Drerup, *Homer*, p. 146.

with the oldest known types of sung poetry. The first type is the Hymn. When his daughter is returned to Chryses, the whole company first feast, and then sing to Apollo:

οἱ δὲ πανημέριοι μολπῇ θεὸν ἱλάσκοντο
καλὸν ἀείδοντες παιήονα κοῦροι Ἀχαιῶν,
μέλποντες ἑκάεργον· ὁ δὲ φρένα τέρπετ᾽ ἀκούων. (A 472–4)[1]

Here it is clear from the words μολπῇ and μέλποντες that it is a case of song and dance, and it is equally clear that the singing is done not by one man but by the whole company. Such hymns must always have existed, and we have ancient examples of them in the Athenian *Hymn to Zeus* for rain, quoted by Marcus Aurelius (5, 7), or the hymn to Aphrodite, quoted by Plutarch (*Q. Conv.* iii. 6. 4), asking that old age may be postponed. These hymns are quite different from the *Homeric Hymns* or προοίμια. It was in their essence that they were sung by a company with dancing or rhythmic gestures. To this class too belongs the *Linus Song* of the *Shield of Achilles*.

τοῖσιν δ᾽ ἐν μέσσοισι πάϊς φόρμιγγι λιγείῃ
ἱμερόεν κιθάριζε, λίνον δ᾽ ὑπὸ καλὸν ἄειδε
λεπταλέῃ φωνῇ· τοὶ δὲ ῥήσσοντες ἁμαρτῇ
μολπῇ τ᾽ ἰυγμῷ τε ποσὶ σκαίροντες ἕποντο. (Σ 569–72)[2]

What the *Linus Song* is, is made clear by the context. It is vintage-time, and the song is a song of vintage. Such songs long survived in Greece, like the *Eiresione* sung at Athens when the first-fruits were sent as a thank-offering.

The second class concerns games, and it also comes from the *Shield of Achilles*. On it young men and women are dancing, and a crowd watches.

πολλὸς δ᾽ ἱμερόεντα χορὸν περιίσταθ᾽ ὅμιλος
τερπόμενοι· δοιὼ δὲ κυβιστητῆρε κατ᾽ αὐτοὺς
μολπῆς ἐξάρχοντες ἐδίνευον κατὰ μέσσους. (Σ 603–6)[3]

[1] 'They, the young men of the Achaeans, besought the god with song all day long, singing a fair hymn, chanting of the Far Shooter, and he rejoiced in his heart when he heard.'

[2] 'And in the midst of them a boy with a shrill lyre played a lovely tune on the strings, and he sang to it the fair Linus Song in a delicate voice. And they broke into song with it and accompanied it with dancing and shouting, beating time with their feet.'

[3] 'A large company set up a delightful dance round it, rejoicing. And among them two tumblers leading the dance wheeled in the midst.'

While the tumblers do their turn, they lead the audience in song. Here ἐξάρχοντες is the clue. The ἐξάρχων leads both the song and the dance. The tumblers show the way, and the crowd follows with song and gesture. So, too, songs survive which were sung at the beginning or the end of a race.[1]

The third class is that of the θρῆνος or lament, like that sung at Troy when the body of Hector is brought home:

> παρὰ δ' εἶσαν ἀοιδοὺς
> θρήνων ἐξάρχους, οἵ τε στονόεσσαν ἀοιδὴν
> οἱ μὲν ἄρ' ἐθρήνεον, ἐπὶ δὲ στενάχοντο γυναῖκες,   (Ω 720-2)[2]

or when Thetis hears of the death of Patroclus and appears with her Nereids:

> τῶν δὲ καὶ ἀργύφεον πλῆτο σπέος, αἱ δ' ἅμα πᾶσαι
> στήθεα πεπλήγοντο, Θέτις δ' ἐξῆρχε γόοιο,   (Σ 50-51)[3]

or when Achilles laments his dead comrade with his Myrmidons:

> αὐτὰρ Ἀχαιοὶ
> παννύχιοι Πάτροκλον ἀνεστενάχοντο γοῶντες,
> τοῖσι δὲ Πηλεΐδης ἀδινοῦ ἐξῆρχε γόοιο.   (Σ 314-16)[4]

Here the ritual is much the same as in the other songs. In each case there is an ἔξαρχος, who sets the lead and provides the words, while the remainder beat their breasts and join in the lament.

These songs are different from the lays of κλέα ἀνδρῶν sung by Achilles or professional bards. They are sung not by one man but by many, or if not by many, at least many accompany them or take some part in them. And they are combined with some sort of action. They are examples of the μολπή, the song accompanied by dance, and associated with definite occasions, harvest, rejoicing, and death. They are quite different from the lays of Demodocus, which are accompanied by no action, are sung only by the bard himself, have no connexion

---

[1] Julian, Caes. 318. Lucian, Demon. Vita 65.
[2] 'And by the bier they set singers, leaders of the dirge, who led the dolorous song, and the women wailed in concert.'
[3] 'The silver-shining cave was filled with them, and they all beat the breast while Thetis led the dirge.'
[4] 'And the Achaeans all night wept and lamented for Patroclus, while for them the son of Peleus led the vehement lamentation.'

with any special occasion, and are intended only to beguile the leisure of princes and nobles at the feasts held in their halls.

In one case, however, a song of Demodocus seems to be of the pure song type. When he sings of the loves of Ares and Aphrodite, he appears to be accompanied by the dancing of young men.[1] This is plainly of the ritual type, and the dance is explained by the song being addressed to the gods and not being purely narrative. Yet at first sight this lay looks like the other lays of Demodocus, and seems to contradict the distinction we have made between the narrative lay and the lay accompanied by dancing. It is true that here the story is given in detail and has all the technique of Homeric narrative, and yet it is accompanied by young men dancing. But really this song belongs to the pure type of song. It is sung to the gods, and therefore the young men dance to it, as they would to any other hymn. It is simply put into the narrative style and metre because that was demanded by the conventions of the epic.

The distinction between the two types of poetry seems, then, ancient and fundamental. The short heroic lay existed by the side of the μολπή but was radically different from it. At a later period the two types may well have influenced one another. Perhaps Homer learned something from the neatness and rapidity of lyric narrative, perhaps Stesichorus, and certainly Pindar, learned something from the full vocabulary and style of the epic.

In the last analysis the distinction between the two types may be considered as a distinction between court poetry and popular poetry. Such a distinction exists in early French literature. Charlemagne's noble, William of Aquitaine, was the subject of many songs because of a defeat he inflicted on the Saracens in 793. These songs were short and essentially popular. They had no influence on the epic which described his doings. A great achievement like his had many literary results, but the songs which told of it on the lips of ordinary men were quite different from the longer and more formal *Chansons de Geste* which beguiled princes and their courts. So too *Beowulf*, though it presents some similarities to the

[1] θ 256–65.

early ballads, is radically different from them. Its complications and sophistications show that it was meant for a different type of society. Only professional singers could produce and perform an epic like this. Its character is aristocratic, not popular, its art highly elaborate, its ancestry lies not in songs or ballads but in short epic lays like the *Fight at Finnsburh*.

Such seems to have been the origin of the heroic lay, but the *Iliad*, as we have seen, is not a heroic lay, but something far more complicated and literary. How did the lay develop into the full epic?

The *Odyssey* describes poetry sung in courts, but when the Homeric poems first appear in recorded history they are performed at large popular gatherings. The προοίμια or 'hymns' which preceded their recitation give a good idea of these gatherings. In the Delian *Hymn to Apollo* the scene is set before our eyes:

ἔνθα τοι ἑλκεχίτωνες Ἰάονες ἠγερέθονται
αὐτοῖς σὺν παίδεσσι καὶ αἰδοίης ἀλόχοισιν.
οἱ δέ σε πυγμαχίῃ τε καὶ ὀρχηθμῷ καὶ ἀοιδῇ
μνησάμενοι τέρπουσιν ὅταν στήσωνται ἀγῶνα.   (147–50)[1]

The Ionians come with their families to Delos, and amongst the other attractions is an ἀγών in which poems are recited. The ἀγών is competitive, and in his hymn the bard asks his patron god or goddess that he may win the prize. These competitive recitations took place in different parts of Greece.[2] They existed in the sixth century at Sicyon, where they were stopped by the nationalist Cleisthenes, because the poems had too many mentions of Argos and the Argives.[3] At an early date there were such ἀγῶνες at Sparta, and, like other Spartan institutions, the introduction of Homer was ascribed to Lycurgus.[4] The rhapsode Cynaethus, the reputed author of the Delian *Hymn to Apollo*, was credited by Hippostratus with performing them at Syracuse in 504 B.C.[5] They seem even to have been performed so far away as Cyprus. For one

---

[1] 'There in your honour gather the long-robed Ionians with their children and shy wives. Remembering you, they delight you with boxing and dancing and song, so often as they hold the gathering.'

[2] Cf. J. Frei, *de Certaminibus thymelicis*, Basle, 1900.   [3] Herodotus v. 67.

[4] Heraclides, *F.H.G.* ii. 210; Plutarch, *Lycurgus*, 4; Aelian, *V.H.* xiii. 14; Dio Chrys. ii. 45.   [5] Schol. Pind. *Nem.* ii. 1.

of the prologues invokes the Cyprian Aphrodite in whose honour the ἀγών was held.

χαῖρε θεὰ Σαλαμῖνος ἐϋκτιμένης μεδέουσα
εἰναλίης τε Κύπρου· δὸς δ' ἱμερόεσσαν ἀοιδήν.

(*Hom. Hymn* x. 4–5)[1]

But the best and fullest evidence comes, as might be expected, from Athens. Here there was an ordinance by which the *Iliad* and *Odyssey* were recited every fifth year at the Panathenaic festival. Who made the ordinance is not known. In antiquity it was attributed variously to Solon, to Peisistratus, and to his son Hipparchus.[2] The more reputable authorities do not say who was responsible. The fourth-century writers, Lycurgus and Isocrates, speak vaguely of οἱ πατέρες and τοὺς προγόνους.[3] Probably the fourth century did not know who started the custom, but merely knew that it had existed in the fifth century. Fortunately the manner of the recitation is better known than its origin. The poems were recited by ῥαψῳδοί, the professional reciting class. They were recited ἐφεξῆς, i.e., the whole poems were recited complete, and not in excerpts.[4] It is recorded that the regulations demanded that they should be recited intact, and popular favourites were not allowed to be performed separately.[5] The task of reciting the whole of the *Iliad* and *Odyssey* was too much for one man, and it was done in relays, ἐξ ὑπολήψεως or ἐξ ὑποβολῆς as the authorities say. When one rhapsode stopped, the recitation was taken up by another at that point. The Athenian method of recitation was no doubt employed elsewhere, as Pindar in a *Nemean Ode* describes how the Sons of Homer—another name for the rhapsodes—begin their recitation with a Hymn to Zeus, and he calls them ῥαπτῶν ἐπέων ἀοιδοί (*Nem.* ii. 2). The natural meaning to attach to these 'stitched lays' is that they were performed in relays by different bards.

---

[1] 'Hail, goddess, queen of well-built Salamis and sea-girt Cyprus, and grant me a lovely song.'

[2] For Solon, cf. Dieuchidas ap. Diog. Laert. i. 2. 9. For Peisistratus, cf. Paus. vii. 26. 13. Aelian, *V.H.* xiii. 14. For Hipparchus, cf. Pseudo-Plato *Hipparchus* 228 b.   [3] Lycurgus, *in Leocratem*, 102. Isocrates, *Panegyricus*, 159.

[4] Ps.-Plat. *Hipparchus* 228 b.

[5] Diog. Laert. l.c. ὅπου ὁ πρῶτος ἔληξεν, ἐκεῖθεν ἄρχεσθαι τὸν ἐχόμενον.

The conditions revealed by this evidence are different from those described in the *Odyssey*. The ἀγῶνες are not private entertainments but great public gatherings. Not one but several bards are necessary for the performance. And the bards are no longer attached to a single court. They are men like Cynaethus, who comes from Chios and is found following his profession in Delos and Syracuse.[1] Finally the poems are so long that a single man cannot recite them, and their character is so well known that selections from them are not allowed, no matter how popular. Between Demodocus and this lies a great division, and somewhere in it we must place Homer and the composition of the *Iliad*. What we have to consider is not when or where it was composed, but how. By what process did the full-fledged epic grow from the small lay?

On this question the epic itself is silent, and other authorities also are silent. We are again reduced to the precarious and difficult use of analogy. In other countries we find full-grown epics developed from shorter poems, and we might expect that the *Iliad* was developed in a similar way. But the question is not easily settled, as the growth of the epic poem seems to have followed different paths in different countries. Critics of the nineteenth century thought they had found an exact parallel in the growth of the Finnish *Kalevala* from separate lays. The poem existed as a whole, and in country places the separate lays were still sung. Here seemed to be a parallel to the growth of the *Iliad*. The belief was not severely shaken when it was known that the composition of the whole poem was the work of a nineteenth-century savant, Lönnrot. It was thought that he had merely restored to its pristine unity an epic which had been broken into fragments by the habit of piecemeal recitation. But now it is clear that the *Kalevala* is an artificial composition. It lacks any coherent unity, and is simply a series of separate lays strung together. The contradictions involved in the composition are far greater than in the *Iliad*, and it is clear that the lays were always separate, even though they deal, like the *Edda Poems*, with one group of stories. A consecutive poem can and has been made out of them, but it is not a

[1] Schol. Pind. *Nem.* ii. 1.

unity like the *Iliad*. So, too, the *Mahabharata* has grown from humble origins into an enormous epic. In its earliest form it has 8,800 verses, in a later form 24,000, and in its final version 107,000. But in the process of expansion the original story, which crystallized round the internecine war between Kuru and Pandava, has been quite lost in a mass of religious and political themes superimposed on it. It is now a compendium of information on subjects human and divine, but it has ceased to be a literary unity. A more exact parallel can, however, be found in the Middle High German *Nibelungenlied*. This epic is essentially a unity. It adapts for the age of chivalry the ancient saga of the Ring of the Nibelungs, and in adapting it, achieves a unity of tone and a consistency of character such as we find in the *Iliad*. But its origins are of great antiquity. Much of its story can be found in the *Edda Poems*, and it has a short epic forerunner in the ninth-century *Song of Hildebrand*. It resembles the *Iliad*, then, in having achieved a development from the short lay to the full epic. In the process it has changed much of its character and been adapted to fresh social conditions. The change must be due to a long bardic tradition which continually adapted and remade old stories to suit new audiences. The history of the *Iliad* must be similar to this.

But though the *Nibelungenlied* grew out of the short lay, the growth of the *Iliad* cannot be compared to it at all points. In the first place, as Matthew Arnold pointed out,[1] the German poem is essentially an enlarged ballad, whereas the *Iliad* is not. This difference is not merely the difference between great and indifferent poetry, it is the difference between simple and highly developed poetry. The *Nibelungenlied* is the legitimate descendant of its ancestors in its metre and manner as well as in its stories. But it is hard to believe that the Homeric manner and outlook were possessed by many generations of poets before Homer. The *Iliad* owes much to tradition, but it has qualities such as no tradition can impart, qualities which are lacking in the *Nibelungenlied*. The presence of these qualities separates it sharply from its German counterpart, and provides a special problem in

[1] *Last Words on Translating Homer.*

elucidating its origins. The untraditional elements in the *Iliad* are the elements which it shares with other great poetry, and the only explanation of their existence is that they are the work of a great poet. Like the *Nibelungenlied*, it is based on earlier stories, but unlike the *Nibelungenlied* its existing form is the work of genius. If we allow for this distinction, the parallel between the two can be properly estimated. Both tell stories which have often been told before, not incorporating earlier poems verbatim, but remodelling them to suit the changed taste of their age. To assume that Homer incorporated earlier work without reshaping it, is not only to ignore his remarkable unity of style and temper, it is to misunderstand the method by which short lays grow into a great poem. Stories persist, but what suits one age in the way of narration will not suit another, and the poet who deals with traditional material has to remodel his stuff entirely.

But the question still remains whether this reshaping was fundamental or merely superficial. Literary history provides us with two main types of such reshaping, and we must decide to which of these the *Iliad* belongs. On the one hand, we have the *Nibelungenlied*, where the old story is entirely retold. The language and the morality belong to the twelfth century instead of to the ninth as in the *Song of Hildebrand*, and this alone makes a great difference. But there is also a difference of scale. The long epic, like the *Nibelungenlied*, can give far fuller accounts of events and speeches than the short lay, and the later poet may spread himself where the earlier had to be extremely economical. The result is not so much a new and up-to-date edition of an old poem as an entirely new poem on an old theme. On the other hand French literature shows quite a different process at work. The *Song of Roland* is the earliest example of a long series of poems on the same subject. In the twelfth and thirteenth centuries the poem we possess in the Oxford manuscript was often retold, but the retelling was not the creation of a new poem but a very simple adaptation of the old poem to new manners. The taste of the age of chivalry succeeds that of the crusades. Love interests are introduced, and the stature of Charlemagne is lowered. But the poem remains essentially the same in story and structure. The chief difference is in language, as the old practice of assonance gives way to the new practice of rhyme. The result is a group of modernized versions of an old poem, not a new poem on an old theme. The relation of the *remaniements* to the original *chanson* is more like that of Dryden's *Tales from Chaucer* to the original, than like that of Tennyson's *Idylls* to such poems as *Gawain and the Green Knight*. Here then are two sharply contrasted processes of literary development. The one is real development, the other is little more than adaptation. We must decide to which of these two classes the *Iliad* belongs. Is it a completely new version of an old story, like the *Nibelungenlied*, or is it a mere *remaniement* of an old poem, like the later versions of the *Song of Roland*?

This question is highly important, as Homer's reputation as a poet largely hangs on its result. Is he a great creative poet or is he a mere adapter of an earlier poem? The answer can best be found in a consideration of the scale on which Homer treats his themes. Most early poetry is highly economical and achieves its effect in a very few lines. At its highest this economy gives us the concentrated power and passion of the *Edda Poems*. But Homer, like the *Nibelungenlied* and the Icelandic prose sagas, treats his themes on a generous scale. The single episode of the *Embassy to Achilles* takes over seven hundred lines, and no important action in the poem is treated on a less generous scale. This fullness is in strong contrast to the conciseness of the English ballads or the *Song of Hildebrand*. Though Homer is never diffuse, he enjoys details and he gives us full measure. But his fullness is the very opposite of the garrulity of the French *remaniements*. Though some of the later versions of the *Song of Roland* are twice the length of the early poem, they add nothing significant or fundamental. They merely say more elaborately what has already been said simply. And this is the point where the *Iliad* differs from them. The *Iliad* is indeed rich, full, and exuberant, but it is not diffuse. The narrative has, to quote Matthew Arnold, 'a flowing, a rapid movement', not the sluggish garrulity of the *remaniements*. If the *Iliad* were really the result of a series of such *remaniements*, as Professor

Murray seems to think it,[1] it would not possess this amazing rapidity and liveliness which distinguish it from all other epic poems. It would be slow and diffuse, full of irrelevant detail and verbiage; it would have none of that fire, which in Pope's words 'burns everywhere clearly and everywhere irresistibly'. It follows then that the *Iliad* must resemble the other type of epic poem, the new poem on an old theme. Just as the *Nibelungenlied* tells again in quite a new way the most ancient stories, so Homer must have taken the old stories of Greek saga and told them again in the *Iliad*, not quoting his predecessors word for word, nor adapting their verses to suit new fashions, but telling the stories fresh from the beginning, altering them to please his own taste and suiting them to the great style of which he was a master. And this conclusion, though based on the precarious evidence of analogy, is after all what we should expect. The *Iliad* is great poetry, and the *remaniements* of the *Song of Roland* are bad poetry. Any one can write bad poems, and in the twelfth century there were not lacking men in France to degrade a noble poem in the interests of fashion and profit. But only a great poet can produce a great poem, and he can only produce it if he creates something new, not if he is chained to an original and has no task but to inflate it with verbosity and unnecessary appendages.

The *Iliad*, then, is a new version of older stories. These stories must have been told in poems far shorter than the *Iliad*, but in it they are told on a generous scale, which makes the most of their possibilities and is far removed from the dramatic concentration of early lays. In this it resembles the *Nibelungenlied* and hardly any other early epic. It remains to decide how conditions can have made such a scale of treatment possible. What causes contributed to the growth of songs like those of Demodocus into the great panorama of the *Iliad*? The fundamental cause of such a development must be a change in the conditions under which poetry was performed. The songs which Achilles sung in his tent were suited to the camp or to the march and were necessarily short. They must have resembled that version of the *Song of*

---

[1] *C.R.* xliii. 1929, p. 170. 'Lang once came so far as to agree with me that there must have been many *remaniements* of the epic tale of Troy.'

Roland which Taillefer sang at Hastings. But as the Ionian colonists settled down to a life of comparative peace and ease after the tumult of the migrations, court life must have developed and social conditions changed. Longer songs were demanded to break the monotony of feasting, and this demand increased the prestige and opportunities of professional bards. The *Odyssey* knows of the existence of such a professional class. It speaks of a φῦλον ἀοιδῶν whom the Muse teaches and men honour (θ 479–81). This class of course claimed that their inspiration came from Heaven, and demanded all the respect shown to real improvisers. But the poet gives his case away and shows that his trade needed training and learning. Telemachus may tell his mother that the poet must follow his fancy—τέρπειν ὅππῃ οἱ νόος ὄρνυται (α 347)[1]—but casual phrases teach a different lesson, as when Odysseus tells Demodocus that the Muse has *taught* him (θ 488), or Alcinous congratulates Odysseus on telling his story like a bard—ἐπισταμένως (λ 368). The professional class was known to Homer, even if he was not going to betray its secrets. Its existence meant the preservation of old stories. The old tale was handed on and the inspired poet retold it in his own way. By this means extremely ancient tales were preserved from generation to generation, and Homer was able to tell of the Siege of Troy. So, too, the author of *Beowulf* was able to tell his Anglo-Saxon audience of events which took place in Scandinavia in the first quarter of the sixth century.[2] The continual telling of the same theme could in an age of lively poetry only result in an extension of scale and a growth of long poetry. So the Icelandic *Lay of Atli* is much shorter than the Greenland version of the same story. In England the scale of *Beowulf* yields gradually to the great expanse of Layamon's *Brut*. This process of growth is largely due to the stabilization of political conditions. The earliest lays were sung in the camp or on the march, when the confusion of the migrations forbade the composition or the performance of the epic on any large scale. But as conditions became more settled in Ionia, and the camp gave place to the court, poets could

---

[1] 'to give delight as his mind is stirred'.
[2] Cf. R. W. Chambers, *Beowulf, An Introduction*, 1921.

compose with more confidence that the lay of to-day could be continued to-morrow. Under such circumstances poetry could really develop and achieve an ampler manner and scale.

In such a question there can only be too many doubts and uncertainties. The *Iliad* grew, and possibly it grew on the lines here indicated. In unskilful hands such a process might have ended in a chaos like the *Mahabharata*, but in Ionia the epic was luckier. It found in Homer a poet of such gifts that he took the traditional material and made it his own, enlarging and elaborating it, giving it a singleness of style and outlook which transformed the diverse materials into a single poem. His work was so successful that the life of the Greek epic really ended with him. Long after him other poets wrote epics, but they modelled themselves on him, and he fixed their style. His work was far from being a compilation. He employed the traditional methods and stories, but he subordinated them to his artistic purpose and impressed his own personality upon them. The result was the *Iliad*.

So far the development of the *Iliad* may be paralleled by the development of other epics. But over one aspect of its growth so much controversy has raged that it needs separate consideration—the question whether Homer was in any way indebted to the use of writing. The writers of medieval epics unquestionably employed writing. To its use they were indebted for their knowledge of earlier versions of the stories which they used, and to it they confided their own works. But in Homer's case the problem is obscure and the evidence scanty. Writing existed early in Greece. If we exclude the Mycenean Age, we can still be certain of its use in the seventh century and probably in the eighth. The inscriptions on Thera are of a very early date, and by the seventh century writing is common on vases. The Spartan lists of Ephors go back to the end of the ninth century, and the laws of men like Zaleucus and Charondas imply written codes in the later part of the eighth. But of course, though writing may have existed in Homer's time, it may not have been common or used on a large scale for long works like the *Iliad*. Homer himself does not enlighten us, and on the only occasion where he mentions writing he wraps it up in mystery. We might indeed feel that an epic poem so long as the *Iliad* must have been written, being beyond the power of any man to remember. This consideration appealed strongly to Wolf and plays an important part in his *Prolegomena*. But modern research has disproved his contentions. Men whose memories have not learned to rely on books can remember enormous quantities of verse. Among the contemporaries of Xenophon were those who knew the *Iliad* and the *Odyssey* by heart.[1] And in modern times such feats have been equalled if not excelled. At Zagreb, between 2nd January and 15th February, 1887, a Croatian bard, Salko Vojniković, sang ninety lays with a total of some 80,000 ten-syllabled lines, i.e., approximately double the number of words in the combined *Iliad* and *Odyssey*.[2] And there is to-day in Birmingham a forge-worker who knows by heart the whole of Byron's poetical works.[3]

At first sight the *Iliad* might easily belong to either written or recited poetry. Neither view is fundamentally untenable, and it may be impossible to decide between them. At the outset, however, it is important to distinguish between poetry which is written merely for the poet's convenience and poetry which is written that it may be read. Much poetry meant to be recited was written down that the bard's memory might be saved from an unendurable strain. The Oxford manuscript of the *Song of Roland* is simply the text carried by a minstrel and used by him to refresh his memory. On the other hand the only surviving manuscript of *Beowulf* seems to be intended for the reading of the learned. The epic lies between two prose works, an account of *The Wonders of the East* and a version of the *Letter of Alexander the Great to Aristotle*, and was clearly put there for the instruction of those who liked to read of monsters and strange places. That the *Iliad* belongs to the second class seems out of the question. Homer says nothing of the reading of books, and

---

[1] *Symp*. 3. 5.   [2] Murko, l.c., p. 294.
[3] Private information. My friend Mr. H. V. Yorke tells me that all efforts to find him wrong have so far proved futile.

his whole art is governed by the necessities of recitation. But it may well belong to the first class, and indeed it seems for good reasons to belong to it. The poem has its architecture and shape, as the poet meant it to have, and it is improbable that if he had composed only in his head, he would have given it its balance and unity. The correlation of different scenes, the echoes which a later passage has of an earlier, the interdependence of seemingly separate anecdotes, seem unaccountable if the poet did not have his manuscript before him, and was not able to refer back when he wanted or to consult what he had written. It is true that Milton, who was used to writing, was able to compose *Paradise Lost* in his head and still to make it a masterpiece. But though he could not read, the words were written for him by his daughters, and he could always consult them when he wanted. Yet it is still possible that a highly-trained memory could dispense with a manuscript, and such a memory may well have been Homer's. So by itself the argument, though persuasive, is not conclusive. The *Iliad* has not the closely knitted texture of a poem like the *Divine Comedy*, and, it might be argued, it has not because it was not composed on paper. But the case for its being written becomes stronger when we compare it with epics which are known not to have been written but composed in the head and transmitted orally. The epics of the South Slavs were not written down until the last century, and even now they are learned and recited by professional bards without recourse to books. The result is a real *Volksepik*, known to every villager, and continually altered and renewed. But the character of this epic is different from that of the *Iliad*. Though its central theme remains constant to the Prince Marko, the result of continued recitation is an enormous divergence between different specimens. Each district has its local version, and these versions differ greatly from each other. It is impossible to find a standard epic among them, as each is suited to its own *milieu*. Now it is unlikely that the *Iliad* ever took so many varied forms. The editions κατὰ πόλεις, which the Alexandrians collected, seem to have varied from the accepted text only in the smallest points of language, and in any case they were not of great antiquity.[1] The themes which vase-painters took from the *Iliad* may not be numerous, but on the whole they agree with the *Iliad* as we have it. The early quotations and reminiscences show no very notable divergence. This remarkable homogeneity would be impossible if the *Iliad* had come into existence like the Slav epics. Then there would have been a large number of competing Iliads, each with its own allegiance and special family connexions. It is no argument against the *Iliad* having been written that in antiquity the text was full of variant readings. The methods of Homeric narrative make misquotation easy, and in any case an ancient text was liable to corruption and interpolation, if not to expansion. The present design of the *Iliad* forbids the notion of expansion as it is found, for instance, in the Byzantine epic of Digenes Acritas. But interpolations there certainly were. The lines in the catalogue referring to Athens (*B* 558, 573) were regarded in antiquity as having been inserted by Solon or Peisistratus to justify the Athenian claim on Megara,[2] and there was a tradition that among his other activities the rhapsode Cynaethus tampered with the text and made insertions of his own.[3] But the mere fact that such interpolations were noted shows that the text was known and could be consulted. If it was not written, it would have been almost impossible to identify any addition or interpolation. The so-called fluidity of the text is certainly a real fact, but it does not prove that in its early days the *Iliad* was a memorized poem existing in highly variant versions. It proves that as with other early poems its manuscript tradition was inaccurate and corruptible.

The root of the difficulty lies in Homer's own attitude to writing. His heroes cannot and do not write. When they cast lots to decide who is fight Hector, each makes his mark on his own lot and throws it into the helmet, but no one can decipher any mark but his own.[4] So it follows that they have no common system of writing. But Homer recognizes the existence of writing in the story of Bellerophon. Proetus sends him to the King of Lycia:

---

[1] Cf. G. M. Bolling, *The External Evidence for Interpolation in Homer*, pp. 37–41.
[2] Strabo 394; Plutarch, *Solon* 10; Quintilian v. 11. 40; Diog. Laert. i. 2. 57.
[3] Schol. Pind. *Nem.* ii. 2.   [4] *H* 185–9.

πόρεν δ' ὅ γε σήματα λυγρά,
γράψας ἐν πίνακι πτυκτῷ θυμοφθόρα πολλά,[1]

and he is to show the message to the king ὄφρ' ἀπόλοιτο (Z 168–70). The king receives the message—it is called σῆμα and σῆμα κακόν—and sends Bellerophon on a series of deadly errands. Here is a case of writing, but Homer wraps it in words of mystery. The πίναξ πτυκτός is not the ordinary Greek way of recording a message: it recalls the folded wooden tablets of the Babylonians and Assyrians. The vague θυμοφθόρα πολλά and the repeated σῆμα are not the natural words for writing. Homer is out to mystify. The message is strange, sinister, and outside ordinary experience; and the language is suited to its character. Elsewhere in the *Iliad* there is no mention of writing. The conclusion to be drawn is that writing existed, but that Homer's audience did not care about it and regarded it as something abnormal. For the poet things may have been different. He may have learned writing as a secret of his craft and have been careful not to disclose the mystery to his audience. Such a hypothesis would explain why in the one place where he mentions it his language is vague and mysterious. The vulgar must not learn of it, and, when it had to be mentioned, exact and explicit description was out of place.

These indications, slight as they are, make it more likely than not that Homer wrote. But he wrote for his own use, not for his poem to be read. The whole art of the *Iliad* implies that it was meant for recitation, not for the library, and, as we shall see, this fact accounts for some of its most remarkable features. A recited poem is bound to differ in character from a poem meant for reading. It must give fewer details; it must keep its story clear and simple; it must employ certain devices to ease the listener's attention. In all these things the *Iliad* shows the marks of recitation. So in the end it is not really of great moment whether Homer wrote or not. The important thing is that he composed for recitation, and whether or not he composed on paper hardly affects the character of the poem as we have it.

[1] 'He gave him baneful symbols, having written in a folded tablet much to destroy life.'

THE HEXAMETER

IN our discussion of the origins of the *Iliad* we have said nothing of the hexameter and its history. The metre should give us good evidence for the beginnings of the epic, but the problems it presents are so special that they need separate consideration. Here we are on slippery ground. The loss of pre-Homeric poetry deprives us of the only conclusive evidence, and there is no sphere of Homeric study where we are more dependent on general considerations.

At the outset we are faced by a fundamental problem. Was the *Iliad* composed for singing or for recitation? The bards in the *Odyssey* sing their lays and accompany them on the φόρμιγξ (θ 67, 332). This form of art agrees with conditions elsewhere. Slavonic bards accompany their narrations on a single-stringed fiddle, and the French *jongleurs* of the Middle Ages intoned their epics to a musical accompaniment. On the other hand the popular bards of Russia use no such accompaniment but content themselves with declamation.[1] To which of these classes does the *Iliad* belong? Was the φόρμιγξ of Demodocus used by Homer, or was it known only to tradition and put into the *Odyssey* just because it belonged to the past? And was Μῆνιν ἄειδε, θεά, a genuine invocation of song or a conventional formula which had lost its real meaning?

When the poems first appear in history there is no trace of the φόρμιγξ. The bard has not a lyre but a baton. Pindar, a careful and reverent observer of ancient custom, attributes such a method to Homer:

> ἀλλ' Ὅμηρός τοι τετίμακεν δι' ἀνθρώπων, ὃς αὐτοῦ
> πᾶσαν ὀρθώσαις ἀρετὰν κατὰ ῥάβδον ἔφρασεν
> θεσπεσίων ἐπέων λοιποῖς ἀθύρειν. (*Isthm.* iv. 37–9.)[2]

No doubt he draws his picture from the rhapsodes of his own time and their method of performance, but the use of the

---

[1] Drerup, *Homer*, p. 146.
[2] 'But Homer has honoured him (sc. Aias) among men—he who set aright all his excellence and told it to the wand of his divine songs for others to sing of.'

baton instead of the lyre is older than Pindar. Hesiod
(*Theog*. 30) speaks of a σκῆπτρον of laurel-wood which the
Muses give him with the power of song, and says nothing of
a lyre. On the Greek mainland from the earliest times the
poems seem to have been performed without the lyre, by a
poet who simply declaimed them.[1] On the other hand
Homer's own picture is invariably of the poem being sung
by the bard to the accompaniment of his own lyre. Which
conditions suit the *Iliad* better?

At the outset it is important to notice that Homer's account
of the performance of lays is not only explicit but entirely
consistent. Of the use of the σκῆπτρον by bards he says not a
word. Elsewhere when he archaizes he betrays himself
sooner or later by mentioning the practice of his own day.
But in this he gives one picture and only one. The natural
conclusion is that recitation to the lyre was the method of
recitation known to him and practised by him. If so, it
follows that Pindar is describing the methods employed by
rhapsodes but not by Homer, and Hesiod those practised
on the mainland in his day but not in Ionia in Homer's.
Hesiod sang for the country populace, not for princes or
festal gatherings; and his method of performance may well
have been the traditional method of Boeotia.

That Homer chanted, and did not recite, seems to follow
from certain characteristics of his hexameter, particularly
from his use of hiatus[2] and from some apparently unmetrical
features. The epic differs from much Greek poetry in two
marked uses of hiatus. First, it often keeps a final long vowel
unshortened before another vowel, as in the first line of the
Iliad Πηληϊάδεω Ἀχιλῆος, and secondly it shortens a long
vowel or diphthong in hiatus before another vowel, as in
χρυσέῳ ἀνὰ σκήπτρῳ or ἑκηβόλου Ἀπόλλωνος. The important
point about these forms of hiatus is that they occur anywhere
in the line and so cannot be explained by a pause in the
recitation. Nor are they common in other Greek verse. The
keeping of a long final vowel before another vowel is very
rare outside Homer, and is hardly found at all except in

---

[1] Cf. E. Bethe, *Homer*, i, p. 15.
[2] Cf. A. Shewan, 'Hiatus in Homeric Verse', *C.Q.* xvii. 1923, pp. 13–20.

Archilochus and Sophocles.[1] The second is commoner in
lyric poetry and the tragedians, but in time it too is superseded. Wilamowitz regards these two forms of hiatus as a
licence admitted in the early days of the hexameter when
poets were not strict masters of their material; their survival
was due to their usefulness, although they were alien to the
nature of the Greek language, which is shy of hiatus.[2] But
against this we may argue that choric poets, who were
complete masters of their material, used them, whereas in
the simple vernacular verse of Sappho they are avoided.[3]
We can, however, find another explanation in the fact that
once the epic was sung. Sung poetry is naturally less shy of
hiatus than spoken. Sophocles, for instance, allows it in his
lyric passages but not in his iambic. And this is easy to
understand. A sung or intoned verse relies only partly for
its effect on its scansion, but a spoken verse entirely. The
writers of Elizabethan songs were able to take great liberties
because they composed for music. Who, for instance, can
say what is the metre of 'O mistress mine'? Where the metre
might not be clear when merely recited, the tune made it
clear enough. So too, in a different way, with Homer.
In recitation the hiatus would have been obvious and intolerable, but when sung or chanted the difficulty would no
longer be felt.

The licence allowed by music may also explain the Homeric
treatment of metrical quantities. Athenaeus (xiv. 632 d)
notices that Homer differs from Xenophanes, Theognis,
Solon, and others by admitting certain forms of hexameter
which they do not. In him we find what are called ἀκέφαλοι,
λαγαροί, and μείουροι στίχοι. The στίχος ἀκέφαλος is the line
which begins either with an tribrach like

διὰ μὲν ἀσπίδος ἦλθε φαεινῆς ὄβριμον ἔγχος   (Γ 357),

or with an iamb like

ἐπεὶ δὴ νῆάς τε καὶ Ἑλλήσποντόν ἵκοντο.   (Ψ 2).

---

[1] e.g. Archilochus, fr. 74 τοῖσι δ' ἡδὺ ἦν ὄρος, Sophocles, O.C. 1453 ὁρᾷ ὁρᾷ
πάντ' ἀεὶ χρόνος.   [2] Griechische Verskunst, p. 99.
[3] Lobel, 'Ἀλκαίου Μέλη, p. xi.

The στίχος λαγαρός is the line which begins with a trochee like

Αἶαν Ἰδομενεῦ τε, κακοῖς, ἐπεὶ οὐδὲ ἔοικε (Ψ 493),

while the στίχος μειουρός gives an apparent iamb instead of a trochee in the sixth foot as in

Τρῶες δ' ἐρρίγησαν ὅπως ἴδον αἰόλον ὄφιν (M 208).

In nearly all these cases the line could be made by a little alteration to conform to the usual scansion, but the tradition seems to have allowed such licences, and there is no need to reject or alter them. But this freedom with quantity goes farther than Athenaeus noticed, and is not confined to the beginning and end of the line. Words, which would not otherwise fit into the line, were made to fit by having their recalcitrant syllables lengthened or shortened as necessity demanded. On the one side we find ἀθάνατος, προθυμίῃσι, συβόσια, and on the other εὐρύχορος for εὐρύχωρος. A learned attempt has been made by W. Schulze[1] to show that in this artificial lengthening, which is extremely prevalent, the poet was guided by definite rules, but his theory breaks down. The poet seems to have been guided entirely by convenience. He scans ἄορι both as an anapaest (K 489) and as a dactyl in the space of six lines (K 484). He is equally free with his treatment of εἰλήλουθα and ἐλήλουθα, of Οὔλυμπος and Ὄλυμπος. Schulze's rules do not cover all the exceptions, and he fails to fit them in to his plan.[2] The natural conclusion is that a considerable number of words could be scanned either long or short, and in many cases the difference of scansion was represented by a difference of spelling. We have ἔλλαβε and ἔλαβε, οὔνομα and ὄνομα, ὑπείρ and ὑπέρ. But the different spelling represents not so much a real difference of form as a difference of scansion. That the same word could be scanned differently need not surprise us. Before quantities were finally fixed by literary use, many must have been half-way between short and long, and had their precise value fixed by their position in the verse. So in English accentual verse the accent of a word may vary with its position in the line. But

---

[1] *Quaestiones Epicae.*
[2] Cf. Leaf's searching criticism in *Iliad*, i, pp. 590–8.

the real determining factor in a doubtful quantity would be the musical accompaniment, which would give its accent where the long syllable should occur, and so turn a doubtful sound into a long.

These considerations indicate that Homer was right in speaking of the hexameter as sung. Of course we do not know how it was sung. But the problem arises whether its musical accompaniment was similar to that of the dactylic poems written by the lyric poets of the seventh and sixth centuries. If it could be proved to be similar, there would be a good case for deriving the hexameter from a lyric measure, and indeed for Bethe's view that the epic narrative has developed from the sung lyrical lay. We have some specimens of dactylic hexameters written by Sappho, Alcaeus, Corinna, and Alcman, and they differ notably from the Homeric hexameter in two important respects. First they show a much smaller use of spondees than the Homeric verse. Even when we have got rid of a large number of apparent spondees in Homer and turned them into dactyls, e. g. transformed μίμνειν ἠῶ δῖαν into μίμνεμεν ἠόα δῖαν, there still remains an enormous number which cannot be removed. In the lyric writers it is quite different. Of eight dactylic hexameters preserved in Sappho's name five are purely dactylic: so are all the five preserved from Alcman and the one preserved from Corinna. In the remainder very little variation is allowed. Alcaeus uses a spondee in the first foot in his only example, so does Sappho twice, and she once uses a spondee in the third foot. In these examples, then, the proportion of spondees is much smaller than in Homer, and they are confined to the first and third feet. When we look at the dactylic hexameters written by the tragedians the lesson is similar. In his *Philoctetes*, 839–42, Sophocles writes dactylic hexameters without any admixture of lyric metres. Of the four lines one is purely dactylic, of the others one has a spondee in the first foot and three have a spondee in the third. Equally remarkable is the use by Euripides in his elegiac lines in *Andromache* 103–16. Here in a total of seven hexameters four are purely dactylic. Of the remainder two have a spondee in the second foot, and one has a spondee in the first. His practice is not quite that of the early lyric poets, but like them he eschews a large admixture of spondees. The conclusion to be drawn from this difference between the Homeric hexameter and the hexameter of the lyric poets must be that the lyrical hexameter was hampered by stricter rules because it was sung to a fixed tune. The Homeric verse with its great variations of rhythm and scansion can only have been intoned or sung to a very simple chant.

This difference becomes clearer when we examine the two types in their treatment of the caesura. The lyric writers employ both the male and female caesura in the third foot without much distinction. So too does Homer, but he also employs a caesura in the fourth foot in lines like

$$\delta\iota o\gamma\epsilon\nu\grave{\epsilon}s \ \Lambda\alpha\epsilon\rho\tau\iota\acute{\alpha}\delta\eta, \ \pi o\lambda\upsilon\mu\acute{\eta}\chi\alpha\nu' \ 'O\delta\upsilon\sigma\sigma\epsilon\hat{\upsilon} \quad (B \ 173 \ \&c.),$$

and this form the lyric poets do not use. Their abstention from it must have been decided by musical considerations. No doubt the accompaniment demanded a pause in the third foot and made one in the fourth foot impossible. Homer laboured under no such restriction and could employ either caesura as he pleased. This liberty too points to his being much freer in his musical accompaniment than were the singers of lyric hexameters.

The conclusion then is that the epic was intoned or chanted, but not sung to what we should call a tune. This did not prevent musical reformers like Terpander from taking selections from it and setting them to music in the strict sense.[1] The same was done to verses ascribed to Orpheus.[2] But such a musical setting only became possible when the simple chant gave place to the piece of music. As Bethe says, 'the citharodic nomos was full of its own content, it shattered the old form and changed it into a new kind, a composed piece of music with changing forms of verse following the temper of the contents'.[3] This change was of vast importance for Greek music and for lyrical verse, but it did not affect the epic, which preceded it and had no real connexion with the type of music used for strictly sung poetry. The tradition of epic

---

[1] Plut., de Mus. 1132, c; Proclus, Chrestom., p. 320 B 6; cf. Wilamowitz, Timotheos, p. 89 ff.   [2] Plut., de Mus. 1132, c.   [3] Homer, i. p. 39.

recitation persisted and gradually became mere recitation. Such at least it seems to have been to Pindar.[1] What had once been intoned was now simply recited. And such the epic clearly was when it first appeared in recorded history, but it still carried the traces of its sung character, and there is no reason to think that Homer's own practice was in this respect different from that which he ascribed to Demodocus.

The hexameter in Homer's day was then an intoned verse. The question next arises whether we can trace its origin farther back and see from what sort of verse it developed. Such an inquiry is quite legitimate. Some Greek metres are of great antiquity and might give a hint of what helped to make the hexameter, and the hexameter is so long a measure that it is unlikely to have come into existence in its present form.

In the last century a popular view of its origin was based on the presence of a caesura in the third foot.[2] This was thought to mark not a pause in a single line but a division between two lines. Thus the original form would be either

μῆνιν, ἄειδε, θεά,
Πηληϊάδεω Ἀχιλῆος

or

οὐλομένην ἣ μυρί'
Ἀχαιοῖς ἄλγε' ἔθηκε.

Such a division of the lines presents us with elements familiar in Greek lyric verse. The first half, both in its longer and its shorter form, whether we call it hemiepes or prosodiac, is a fundamental element in the dactylo-epitrite metres of Pindar and can be found in the choruses of the tragedians. The second half, both in its longer and shorter form, is equally familiar as the paroemiac. Thus in Tyrtaeus we find

κοῦροι πατέρων πολιητᾶν[3]

and in Archilochus

Ἐρασμονίδη Χαρίλαε.[4]

[1] Hence his use of ἔφρασεν in *Isth.* iv. 38.
[2] Bergk, *Uber das älteste Versmass der Griechen*, 1854.
[3] Bergk, *P.L.G.* ii, fr. 15, l. 2.   [4] Ib., *P.L.G.* ii, fr. 79.

From a combination of these two ancient forms the hexameter is thought to have come into existence. Usener, who took this theory from Bergk, developed it even farther.[1] He showed that Homer often neglects the digamma in the third foot caesura and often fails there to lengthen a short vowel before a mute and a liquid. From these observations he deduced that the hexameter had a fundamental division at this point. He then connected these separate portions with the primitive form of Indo-Germanic verse, which has four stressed syllables regardless of the number of unstressed syllables and survives in the Latin Saturnian, in the long German verse, and in Celtic and Slavonic verse. This theory may satisfactorily account for the development of some lyric metres, but really it leaves the origin of the hexameter unsolved. In the first place the other Indo-Germanic metres are not quantitative but accentual. Some primitive Greek metres may have a semi-accentual character. For instance, in the song:

ἄλει, μύλα, ἄλει
καὶ γὰρ Φίττακος ἄλει

the metre may possibly be determined by accent.[2] But of such an accentual metre there is no trace whatsoever in the epic. It is fundamentally quantitative and as such differs from other Indo-Germanic metres. Secondly this theory allows much more elasticity in the verse than we find in the hexameter. In other systems of scansion the number of syllables may not matter, provided we have the right number of stresses, but in Homeric verse the number of syllables is determined strictly by rules, and pre-eminently by the rule that one long syllable takes the place of two short syllables, so it seems that the hexameter is only remotely connected with the primitive form of Indo-Germanic verse.

There might still be truth in the view that it is formed from the combination of two simple and primitive song-measures. But here too the theory is based on a misapprehension. The paroemiac and the prosodiac survive in Greek lyric and

---

[1] *Altgriechischer Versbau*, 1887.
[2] But cf. Wilamowitz, *Griechische Verskunst*, p. 401.

choric poetry. They may ultimately be derived from the primitive *enoplion*, the measure of the war dance. This primitive form permitted great variety and accounts for the enormous range of surviving Greek lyric metres, but there is no reason to believe that the epic is derived from the μολπή, the song and dance. As we have seen, narrative poetry stands apart from this, and its metre too seems to stand apart from early lyric metres. This distinction becomes clearer as we examine the facts. The most notable feature of the Homeric hexameter is the way it preserves its dactylic rhythm. A long syllable may be substituted for two shorts, but two shorts may not be substituted for a long. It allows spondees but not anapaests. In this it differs from some other Greek verse. Anapaestic verse, for instance, allows the use of dactyls and spondees as well as anapaests, and so achieves a very varied character which is often far from anapaestic. But the hexameter keeps its dactylic character throughout. If it were developed from the original *enoplion* there is no reason why it should not freely allow anapaests, and yet it forbids them. Secondly, such views account for groups of sound far more complicated than any found in the hexameter. The lineal descendants of the *enoplia* are the odes of Pindar and Bacchylides. Each ode has a metrical system of its own, though most can be reduced to certain elementary rhythms. The advantage of these forms was the variety they allowed in rhythm, and consequently in music and dancing. But the hexameter has no such variety. Such variety as is it allowed is confined to the substitution of spondees for dactyls. Nor is there any trace of the hexameter being developed differently in works outside Homer. The metre of Hesiod is the same as his. So are the metres of the Epic cycle, the Hymns, the Delphic Oracles, and all the fragments of early narrative verse. And yet if narrative verse were really developed from this highly elastic and adaptable form we should expect as great a variety in the metres of different epics as we find in the odes of Pindar.

The origins of the hexameter must be found elsewhere than in the metres of early songs. Its source must be a primitive type of narrative poetry whose unit was not the stanza but the line, and whose character was mainly dactylic. Other forms of dactylic verse existed in Greek literature. The Lesbian poets employed a dactylic tetrameter, as in Alcaeus'

ἄλλοτα μὲν μελιάδεος, ἄλλοτα
δ' ὀξυτέρω τριβόλων ἀρυτήμενοι   (fr. 132)

and a pentameter such as in Sappho's

ἠράμαν μὲν ἔγω σέθεν, Ἄτθι, πάλαι ποτά.   (β 5 App.)

These poems are, however, lyrical and not narrative, and so their evidence must not be pressed too far. But in the *Wedding of Hector and Andromache*[1] an imitator of Sappho has written a narrative poem in dactylic pentameters not divided into stanzas. Presumably this poet, who may have been an Athenian, was following some reputable Lesbian precedent, and there is a good probability that the dactylic pentameter was used for narrative verse. If so, the dactylic tetrameter may equally well have been used, and when Alcaeus and Sappho used the two forms for personal lyric, perhaps they borrowed them from the simple rhythm of narrative verse instead of from the mixed rhythms of the μολπαί. If such a shorter form of dactylic verse existed, it may well have been the parent of the Homeric hexameter.

In the first place it seems likely that the original dactylic metre was not a long metre like the hexameter. As Wilamowitz says, 'on the analogy of all surviving Greek metres it is hard to believe that so long a verse of sixteen or seventeen syllables should have been a complete unity from the beginning'.[2] In other words, just as the long στίχοι of Pindar grew from a short *enoplion* or *aiolikon*, so we should expect the hexameter to grow from a shorter line. In the second place, as Wilamowitz also points out, we should expect it to be purely dactylic. This is possible, but more open to question. The dactylic rhythm is so elementary that the earliest poetry may easily have employed it by itself, just as the French epic employs an iambic and the Finnish a trochaic metre. On the other hand early poets are not always masters of their materials, and the Greek language is not ideally fitted for the

---

[1] Lobel, Σαπφοῦς Μέλη, β 2.   [2] *I. und H.*, p. 352.

writing of pure dactyls. But whether purely dactylic or not, the early form must have been mainly dactylic. Otherwise the epic would not have its remarkably consistent dactylic character. Bearing these considerations in mind we may look for traces in the epic of a shorter, dactylic verse. The Homeric verse shows a strong predilection for a break after the fourth foot. There are many lines like

ἐννῆμαρ μὲν ἀνὰ στράτον ᾤχετο κῆλα θεοῖο   (A 53),
or like

οἵδ᾽ ἐπὶ δεξία, οἵδ᾽ ἐπ᾽ ἀριστερὰ νωμῆσαι βῶν.   (H 238)

Not only do these lines have a remarkable break after the fourth foot but their caesura is often merely formal, coinciding with no real pause in the voice. From this K. Witte has deduced with much reason that the original form was a dactylic tetrameter followed by a dactylic dimeter catalectic.[1] This view receives further evidence in Homer's dislike of spondees in the fourth foot. In the *Iliad* there are only 280 spondees in the fourth foot, a small proportion in so long a poem. Of these some 86 should be resolved into dactyls by the substitution of uncontracted for contracted forms. In the remainder there are very few examples of single spondaic words occupying the fourth foot. They are usually closely connected with what precedes by a preposition or by καί. Moreover, the poet seems to avoid this scansion as often as possible. For instance,

μειδιόων βλοσυροῖσι προσώπασι· νέρθε δὲ ποσσίν   (H 212)[2]

contains the rare προσώπασι instead of the common προσώποις because the poet wants to avoid the spondee in the fourth foot. A similar avoidance is found in Hesiod and in the *Homeric Hymns*. This evidence seems to confirm Witte's view of the existence of the dactylic tetrameter as a separate unit and to indicate that it was purely dactylic or anyhow had to end in a dactyl.

This tetrameter had probably no need of a caesura, and certainly no need of a caesura in the third foot. The Homeric caesura is due to the two original elements being formed into

[1] In Pauly-Wissowa, *Real-Encycl.* s.v. 'Homeros'.
[2] W. R. Hardie, *Res Metrica*, p. 18.

a single hexameter. Such a formation is easily understood. The second, subsidiary line was closely connected in thought with the main line and, as metres tend to become more interdependent with use, it would eventually become one with it. But it left traces of its original independence in the pause after the fourth foot and the avoidance of the fourth foot spondees. When the two became one, the Homeric hexameter came into existence, and with it came the caesura. A long line cannot be recited or intoned unless the reciter has a slight pause for breath. The natural place for this pause is somewhere in the middle of the line, though it does not exactly matter where. Thus in Homer the commonest pauses are after the first long syllable in the third foot, as in

μῆνιν ἄειδε, θεά, Πηληϊάδεω ᾿Αχιλῆος

or after the first short syllable as in

οὐλομένην, ἣ μυρί᾿ ᾿Αχαιοῖς ἄλγε᾿ ἔθηκεν.

Sometimes, though rarely, the caesura is not till the fourth foot, or rather there are two caesurae, in the second and fourth feet, as in:

οὐκ ἀγαθὸν πολυκοιρανίη· εἷς κοίρανος ἔστω.   (B 204)

The rarity of this form is due to the desire for a break which is really more or less constant, and therefore easily suited to the exigencies of rhapsody. We find similar breaks in other epic verse. The iambic pentameter of the *Song of Roland* has a pause after the second foot, and simple forms like the verse of the *Edda Poems* or of *Beowulf* require a pause in the middle. The pause is essential because it gives the rhapsode time to take breath, and so we find it in the Homeric hexameter.

Such may have been the origins of the hexameter, but in the *Iliad* it is a fully developed entity and has marked characteristics of its own which owe nothing to the earlier form. It is no longer two verses, but one. Each line must be an obvious unity separated from preceding and succeeding lines and complete in itself. In a metrical system which lacked stanzas, rhyme, or assonance, the character of the line had to be emphasized and preserved. In consequence we find the hexameter possessing characteristics which can only have developed when it was already a complete line and were designed to preserve its character as such. The epic poet learned certain rules, and he adhered to them. First, he had to make it clear that the line ended when it did, and not before. This was all the more necessary if the forerunner of the hexameter was a dactylic tetrameter. So the Homeric line avoids the division after a trochee in the fourth foot, the so-called τομὴ κατὰ τέταρτον τροχαῖον. The reason for this is obvious. To have such a pause sounded too like the end of a line, and might suggest that the verse was shorter than it actually was. There are a few cases where the rule is not obeyed, as in:

ἄγχι μάλ᾽, ὡς ὅτε τίς τε γυναικὸς ἐϋζώνοιο   (Ψ 760)

or in

πολλὰ δ᾽ ἄρ᾽ ἔνθα καὶ ἔνθ᾽ ἴθυσε μάχη πεδίοιο   (Ζ 2).

Such examples are very rare. Their main justification is that they are sometimes the only way in which the line can be made to hold certain words of five syllables. Their rarity was noticed by the ancient metricians, and a learned writer like Apollonius Rhodius never employed the licence at all. In choric stanzas, however, which employ dactylic hexameters mixed with other metres, this licence is much more freely admitted. Bacchylides provides

ἀμφί τ᾽ ἰατορίᾳ ξείνων τε φιλάνορι τιμᾷ   (Ode i. 39–40)

and Pindar

αὐτίκα δ᾽ ἐκ μεγάρων Χίρωνα προσήνεπε φωνᾷ.   (Pyth. ix. 29)

For them not the line but the stanza was the unit, and there was no need to emphasize the length and character of the single line, which was only a subordinate part of their main scheme.

For the same reason the Homeric hexameter could not be hypermetric, nor could it allow a new or subordinate clause to begin near the end of a line. Sophocles, writing tragic hexameters, could pass

πάντων Ἑλλάνων ἀδικώτατοι ἀνέρες, οὓς δή   (Trach. 1010)

but the epic gives no parallel to it. It does not on the other hand object to carrying over a word to the next line, as this leaves the structure of the hexameter comparatively clear, even if the word carried over is a spondee, as in

τότε δ' οὔ τι δυνήσεαι ἀχνύμενός περ
χραισμεῖν, εὖτ' ἂν πολλοί κ.τ.λ. (A 242-3)

This consideration for the end of the line accounts for another characteristic in the hexameter. Originally the last foot seems to have been a trochee, that is a dactyl deprived of its final short syllable to give a pause and allow the music to mark time. But in the *Iliad*, as we have it, only one line in five ends in a pure trochee such as ἔθηκε or ἐρίσαντε. The origin of the final trochee is forgotten and its place is often taken by a spondee. This shows that the original pause was not thought enough, and the line was fully completed with a spondaic ending before the next line began.

Finally the hexameter shows some repugnance to the division of the line at the end of the third foot. Such a division would make a hexameter into two dactylic trimeters and was therefore avoided. One case is:

ἤ οὐ μέμνῃ ὅτε τ' ἐκρέμω ὑψόθεν ἐκ δὲ ποδοῖιν. (Ο 18)

But in this, too, the choric poets show no such respect for epic rules. Pindar could write lines like

ὅς τότε μὲν βασιλεύων κεῖθι νέαισι θ' ἑορταῖς (*Nem.* ix. 11),
and

ἀνδροδάμαντ' Ἐριφύλαν, ὅρκιον ὡς ὅτε πιστόν (*N* ix. 16)

but he was writing two prosodiacs and was not bound by the rules that governed the epic hexameter.

In practice then, though the hexameter shows traces of its origin, it adheres firmly to certain rules which keep it intact and separate. If such rules had not been made, the epic might have lost much of its simplicity and rapidity. It existed too early for any elaborate structure of lines to be used, such as, for instance, we find in Virgilian hexameters. Instead it evolved a few rules which maintained its character and differentiated it from the quite different measures of choric poetry.

IV
SOME PRIMITIVE ELEMENTS

IN our attempt to reconstruct the origins of the Greek epic we have drawn freely on parallels in other literatures, and so long as we are considering not the *Iliad* but its forerunners, the comparison with other primitive poetry is legitimate. For early poetry is usually recited, and is therefore conditioned by its hearers and their desires. The bard who composes for recitation faces much the same difficulties wherever he is, and for this reason comparisons drawn from other languages are both legitimate and valuable. But, when we consider the *Iliad* in its present form, these parallels from other early poetry may prove delusive. The complete *Iliad* has passed beyond the domain of primitive poetry, in that it has a character of its own and must be considered as a whole. In this it differs from traditional epics like the *Kalevala* or the *Mahabharata*. They draw their long length along with little thought for anything but the individual episodes. The *Iliad* aims at a unity and achieves it. So it is not a primitive epic as the others are, even if it was still recited and developed from similar origins as theirs.

Because it is a unity, the *Iliad* cannot be called primitive, and can claim to be a work of art. But it is developed from primitive poetry and it shows marks of its origin. In it simple elements are mixed with elements far more sophisticated, and because of this mixture it holds a special place in literary history. It marks a transition from early recited poetry, composed in accordance with strict conventions, to a more sophisticated poetry where the conventions are put to new uses. Its transitional character may perhaps be seen better if we compare it with other poems composed under rather similar conditions. The *Song of Roland* is a development of a simple song sung at Hastings, but the poem in the Oxford manuscript is structurally not primitive. It is constructed with masterly skill, and it is a unity. It tells of one main action only, the betrayal of Charlemagne's army by Ganelon. Outside this it hardly strays, and it leaves us with a satisfying sense of completeness. But in its details it seems far more primitive than the *Iliad*. The characters are only sketched, there is little or no description, the turns of action are produced by simple, if magnificent, expedients. Compared with it the *Iliad* is highly complicated both in art and in temper. Nor is this surprising. The *Song of Roland* represents not the ripe product of a literary type but its youthful hey-day. The *Iliad* belongs to a later stage of development and is definitely more complicated. On the other hand, it presents remarkable similarities in temper and method to some stories in *The Canterbury Tales*. And this too is easy to understand. Chaucer, though he wrote in English, was really the last exponent of French medieval poetry. He took some of its stories and many of its mannerisms, and he turned them to uses entirely new. Some of his tales had been told often before, while others were fresh with the first breath of the Italian renaissance. So, too, Homer told of an age-old quarrel, but told it in a way that was strange and unexpected. But even more precise parallels may be found than this. Both poets were confronted with a mass of conventions which had come to be regarded as the very stuff of poetry. In Chaucer's time conventions had stupefied the French Romance and made it wearisome beyond words.[1] But the 'grant translateur' did not entirely abandon them. Perhaps that was bad form, or perhaps he enjoyed using them. For he used them in new and surprising ways. Sometimes he was just cynical and made the daisy surpass all flowers in odour, though he knew as well as Shakespeare that the daisy was *smell-less*. His excuse was that the daisy was the type of the lady and must have all the attributes of beauty, including smell. But in other ways he was more adventurous and made experiments. The French tradition had a stock description of the perfect woman whom all knights loved. Chaucer gives us such a description complete in every detail from 'hir nose tretys' down to her ring inscribed 'Amor vincit omnia'—but the woman is a nun and all the stale inventory takes on a new life in its almost mocking surroundings. Thus the old conventions, the complete embodiment of the age of chivalry,

[1] I owe what follows to J. L. Lowes, *Convention and Revolt in Poetry*, pp. 62–7.

are made to live again in a world which is beginning to know the Renaissance. In Homer's art we may trace a not dissimilar use of traditional elements taken from early recited narrative. His forerunners have unfortunately perished, and we cannot say with certainty that this or that is definitely primitive. But there are so many cases where he employs expedients common in early poetry that we may assume that he too uses the mannerisms and methods of early narrative verse for a poetry which was passing into a different phase. He is, it is true, less a master than Chaucer of these traditional elements, but their use is an important and integral characteristic of his style.

The most primitive poetry is useful poetry. So we find it in early Latin where verse consists mainly of hymns and incantations. Of such there is little trace in Homeric art. Homer wrote to please and not to secure crops or to avert disease. But of narrative poetry he shows traces in its most elementary form. Early audiences found pleasure in simple things. Consequently in most early poetry we find passages which seem to us dull or unpoetical but were highly valued in their day. And some of these survive to perplex us in the *Iliad*.

Early poetry likes lists, whether of ancestors, or men gathered for battle, or men slain. The list, of course, had a use. In days when written history did not exist, one of its functions was taken by a versified list of names. By such means record could be kept of the past. Being in verse it could be memorized and passed on to posterity with less danger of corruption than if it were in prose. Such a list, too, carried authority. It could be called in as a criterion for disputes over ancestry or religion. Into it accumulated tradition was crystallized, and it carried the weight of the inspired word. Originally no doubt such lists existed unadorned, like the genealogies in *Genesis*, but at a later stage they were slightly expanded. Notes were added on the characters, and we get the Hesiodic lists of women. But the form survived and remained essentially primitive, and it is typical of early literature that it clings to this form after it has lost its usefulness. Thus in one of the *Edda Poems*, the *Voluspo* or

Prophecy, a long list of dwarfs is inserted in the account of the gods' doings before the making of man. It is certainly interpolated, but its presence shows how strong a hold such lists had on the popular imagination that they could find their way into a famous poem in defiance of the context. The reason of course is that they provided history, geography, and theology, and possessed an importance far beyond their literary merits.

In the *Catalogue of Ships* the *Iliad* has preserved such a list from Greek antiquity, and its presence is remarkable and rather embarrassing. Whether the *Catalogue* is a correct account of the troops who sailed for Troy need not immediately concern us. The question is : Why is it here incorporated, and what purpose, if any, does it serve in the construction of the *Iliad*?

Taken by itself the *Achaean Catalogue* forms a complete poem. It is introduced by an address to the Muses and a statement of the greatness of the theme. It is constructed on a simple but satisfactory arrangement by which the various contingents are enumerated on a geographical system of concentric circles. It gives an unbiased and comprehensive picture of what heroic Greece was thought to be. In all this it resembles other primitive poems which aimed only at recording facts. And this consideration alone might justify us in claiming it as an independent poem, incorporated in the *Iliad*. On closer examination it is found to be slightly discordant with the rest of the poem. It tells in fact not of the tenth year of war but of the gathering at Aulis. Such is clear from phrases like ἄγε νῆας, νέες ἐστιχόωντο.[1] It describes characters such as Protesilaus and Philoctetes who have no place in the *Iliad*. It mentions many minor characters who are known only from here and play no further part. Its impartial description of the Achaean states, though not greatly discordant with the account given by the *Iliad*, gives quite a different idea of the relative importance of the heroes. No one could tell from the *Catalogue* that Odysseus was a hero of the first rank or that the Boeotians were militarily negligible. The Arcadians have their sixty ships, but their part in the rest of the poem is nothing. So too in the localiza-

[1] *B* 557, 516.

tion of heroes the *Catalogue* is explicit, where the poem leaves us vague. Elsewhere Diomedes is just an Aetolian, here his kingdom is described. The facts of the *Catalogue* may indeed on the whole be squared with the facts of the *Iliad*. But there is an enormous difference of emphasis. Instead of directing attention to a few salient persons and places, the *Catalogue* floods us with details and obscures the leading heroes in a welter of names. It is true, too, that even Philoctetes and Protesilaus are adjusted to the date of the *Iliad*. The one languishes on his island and the other is dead, but why are they mentioned at all? Why has the poet troubled to provide a list of warriors which is not the list required by his plot?

The only satisfactory explanation of the *Catalogue* is that it was held in high esteem and worth including even at the cost of some loss to the narrative. That the poet of the *Iliad* composed it himself is improbable. If he had, it would fit better into his general plan. On the other hand, he took steps to incorporate it by devising a reorganization of the Achaean forces before it. He meant it to be here. He felt that he owed it to his patrons. Even in post-Homeric Greece the *Catalogue* was the 'golden book', and appeals to it were made over disputed territories. When the Athenians claimed Salamis, they argued that the *Catalogue* set Aias among the Athenian troops.[1] In earlier days such authority would have been greater still, and this accounts for its inclusion. Homer's audience perhaps knew of the *Catalogue* and expected it in any poem dealing with the Trojan War. They revered it as an authentic account of the men who fought, and were doubtless able to claim ancestors among them. For them it was history, sanctified by tradition, and they demanded it from their poet. By including it Homer conformed to the ancient traditions of poetry, and gave his hearers what they felt entitled to get. For his art the result was not entirely fortunate. The *Catalogue*, however interesting, disturbs the plot, and Homer has not completely surmounted the difficulties caused by its presence. But in one or two ways it helps. First, it gives us the numbers of the Achaeans present at Troy. This was most essential to the *Iliad*, which

[1] Cf. T. W. Allen, *The Homeric Catalogue*, p. 56.

gives in a synoptic and selective manner the history of the siege. The number of ships is 1,186, and Thucydides' estimate of the crew (i. 10) would mean an army of about 100,000 men. The greatness of this figure showed what a great affair the Siege of Troy was and how worthy of a poet's song. Heroic ages demand large numbers of fighters in their sagas, and by this means Homer gave it them, without having to detract attention later from the few important characters whom his poem celebrated. From rather similar motives the *Song of Roland* tells of the ten columns of the army of Charlemagne, each of 10,000 men under its own leader. Numbers and size were essential to any heroic undertaking, and from them the audience could see what a great king Agamemnon was. Secondly, as we have seen, Homer is at pains to introduce his hearers to the circumstances of the war. Gradually he reveals the characters of the opposing armies and their leaders. The *Catalogue* helps him in this. It can be used as a work of reference for the Achaeans, but more than this it gives us a background, perhaps not ideal but still useful, for the persons and events which are to follow. Its presence prevents us from thinking that the Trojan war was a minor affair of single combats. This detailed account of the great army is almost unavoidable if we are to see the Achaean heroes as the foremost warriors in a great undertaking. No doubt tradition knew of the Trojan war as one in which vast hosts were engaged. Homer had to repeat this. It was simplest to state the fact clearly, and then to get on with the story regardless of it.

The *Trojan Catalogue* which follows is not quite in the same case. For a Greek audience a list of Trojans could never have the same sacred importance that belonged to a list of Achaeans, and perhaps that is the reason why it is shorter and less detailed. Even if some of his Ionian patrons claimed descent from Trojan heroes, and that is likely enough, still the Trojans were enemies and therefore not worthy of the same reverence. The *Trojan Catalogue* may also have been an independent poem, called into existence by a society which liked facts and insisted on getting them. It too is arranged on a simple geographical plan of four routes centring on

Troy, it too has a formal introduction, it too differs somewhat from the rest of the *Iliad*, notably from the list of Trojan allies in *K* 428 ff. Several of its characters do not reappear, and though it says that Ennomus (*B* 858) and Amphimachus (*B* 874) were slain by Achilles in the river fight, the actual account of the fight does not confirm this. So it seems to be a separate poem like the *Achaean Catalogue*, and the motives for its inclusion must be similar. Once the poet has decided to enumerate the Achaeans he was bound to enumerate the Trojans. The *Trojan Catalogue* gives a contrast to the Achaean and assists the poet's plan of showing the different characters and numbers of the opposing armies before he introduces the leading persons on the Trojan side.

In these two cases Homer is closely bound by tradition, and though he makes some attempt to fit what it demanded into his general scheme, he is not really successful, and the inclusion of the catalogues is a concession to primitive elements in his art and circumstances. But in other cases he employs the same ancient device with more effect. In the touching scene where Achilles hears of the death of Patroclus, his mother comes to comfort him and we are prepared for unrelieved pathos. But before the talk begins, ten lines are devoted to a list of the Nereids who accompany Thetis.[1] The list has no relevance to the story and delays the action. Its character is quite primitive, and the lines have been excised as Hesiodic from the days of Zenodotus and Aristarchus. But they are certainly genuine and the poet's own invention. The melodious names—Cymodoce, Galatea, Callianeira, and the rest—are full of poetry, and, as Wilamowitz well says, 'the enumeration, sounding like the ripples of a quiet sea, soothes our agitation, turns us away from the agitating scene, and makes us ready for the calm of the words between mother and son'.[2] Thetis, the divine sea-nymph, comes to comfort her son in his agony, and she brings with her these nymphs whose names are fragrant of beauty and happiness. The old device is completely mastered and subordinated to the tragic story.

In two other places Homer uses rather similar lists with

[1] *Σ* 39–48. [2] *I. und H.*, p. 135.

full significance, though hardly to achieve pathos. The famous catalogue of Zeus' love-affairs (*Ξ* 315–28) has something in it of those lists of fair women which we find in the *Eoiae* of Hesiod or the *Νέκυια* of the *Odyssey*. But though its origin perhaps lies in an inventory compiled for the devout worshipper, its presence in the *Iliad* is entirely comic. Zeus solemnly enumerates his loves to Hera with the self-satisfaction of an experienced philanderer. The comedy is enhanced by the trap into which the old boaster is being led by his wife; the father of the Gods, who is so proud of his conquests, is being caught on his favourite ground. Here the list, so far from being solemn or traditional, recalls the enumeration of her husbands by the Wife of Bath. Something of the same mocking spirit enters into the list of indignities suffered by the gods from men with which Dione comforts Aphrodite after Diomedes has wounded her (*E* 383–404). The sad adventures of Ares, Hera, and Hades are paraded with evident relish and no sense of respect for the divine sufferers. No doubt these comic affairs were derived from some solemn original where they and similar sufferings were set forth with Hesiodic completeness. But here they are comedy, aimed at making rather ridiculous the sad plight in which Aphrodite finds herself.

Another primitive type of poetry is the genealogy. It reaches its fullest form in Hebrew literature, but the *Theogony* is a good example of it applied to the gods. A genealogy was a sacred matter to any family proud of its ancestry, and the best way to preserve it was to have it in verse. Even so children learn simple rhymes giving the names of the Kings of England. The literary interest of such genealogies is small, and they belong to the deplorable class of useful poetry. Yet Homer, who meant to please, includes genealogies in the *Iliad*. The descent of Agamemnon is given through the account of the sceptre (*B* 101), Aeneas gives Achilles a full account of his descent from Zeus (*Υ* 215 ff.), Glaucus tells Diomedes how he traces his ancestry back to Sisyphus the son of Aeolus (*Z* 153 ff.). The first of these is contributed by the poet himself, the last two are put in the

mouths of heroes engaged in fighting, and come with some
surprise in their context. They are a primitive indulgence
which the *Song of Roland* does not permit itself. Why then
does Homer break his narrative to include them? The
answer must be that his audiences claimed to be descended
from the heroes of Achaean days and demanded accounts
of their ancestries. In Strabo's time the Penthilidae of
Mytilene and other great families of Cyme and Tenedos
traced their descent back to the time of Orestes,[1] and it seems
to have been natural to the nobles of Aeolis and Ionia to
regard themselves as the legitimate heirs of Agamemnon's
army.[2] In Homer's day, when aristocracy was still supreme
and the heroic age was nearer, there must have been many
families who claimed such descent, and for these he added
his family-trees. They flattered pride of race and strengthened
tradition with the sanction of verse. But in their context they
do more than this—they assist in the story. The Descent of
Glaucus is a frame for the thrilling story of Bellerophon, the
Descent of Aeneas tells of the horses of Dardanus. They also
serve a part in the plot. The Descent of the Sceptre is given
at length because it explains the peculiar position of Agamemnon in the Greek camp, and makes us understand why
the Greeks listen to him even after the extraordinary affair of
the pretended retirement from Troy. His power comes from
Zeus, and in the end he must be treated with respect. Because of it his decisions are accepted, and the reviler Thersites
is treated with brutality. Glaucus' story of his ancestry
provides a chivalrous interlude in the battle. Diomedes is
afraid that he is a god, and asks him if he is. Glaucus answers
that so far from being a god he is a man of Achaean descent.
The two find they have family ties, and part in friendship.
The scene comes near to the heart of chivalry with its picture
of ancient hospitality and generous enthusiasm. It breaks
the horrors of fighting and takes us to the bright side of the
heroic age. Without the genealogy this would have been
impossible. The descent of Aeneas is important for the contrast it makes between him and Achilles. Part of the glamour
and glory of Achilles is that he is the son of a goddess. He

---

[1] Strabo, ix. 401, xiii. 582.   [2] Cf. G. Busolt, *Griech. Gesch.* I p. 274.

himself is very proud of it and taunts those who are born of mortal mothers. His pride makes him address Aeneas with scorn, and the long answer which Aeneas gives him is a criticism of his pride and boastfulness. Aeneas is the first opponent met by Achilles whose parentage is as good as his own, and the occasion is important. So through Aeneas the poet gives us the story of the House of Dardanus to show that at last Achilles has met an opponent who too is the son of a goddess. The story implicitly censures Achilles' arrogance, and the moral is driven home by Aeneas' final words, where he compares his adversary's boasting to the wrangling of old women in the street, and bids him get to his fighting.

There is, too, another type of list in the *Iliad* which causes some embarrassment to critics and hardly gives much pleasure to modern readers—the lists of men slain in the ἀνδροκτασίαι of different warriors. Such lists exist elsewhere than in the *Iliad*. They may be found to some extent in the *Song of Roland*, but nowhere are they so obvious as in the *Iliad*. Their presence needs explanation. Even in primitive saga they suggest difficulties, and in the *Iliad* their presence is a problem. It is of course natural that in early poetry a great hero should be celebrated by a list of the men he has slain. In his lifetime such a song would be essential, and after his death his descendants might still find pleasure in it. The songs would of course be extremely simple, like the epitaphs of the Scipios, and content themselves with a list of names. But why should Homer give such lists in his epic? To his audience most of the names must have been meaningless, and there seems little object in retailing them. The answer must be that these, like other lists, were part of the epic tradition and demanded by the Ionian princes who claimed to be descended from the heroes whose exploits they recorded. So much is clear, but then the problem really begins. Are these lists inventions of the poet or are they directly inherited from the past? And what truth, if any, lies behind them? Of all the traditional elements in the *Iliad* these look the most ancient, and if we could trace them to their origin, we might see into Homer's workshop.

The bareness of some of the lists seems to indicate that the poet intended them to be taken for history. But it is too much to hope that they can be literally true. The epic art is not so scrupulous of historical accuracy as to make this probable. Nor is it likely that they are all pure invention. If they are, the poet has done poorly not to make their presentation more pleasing, or to curb their numbers. Being an ancient form of poetry they must have some history behind them, and Homer cannot have entirely composed them out of his own head. Hence an explanation put forward by Cauer and Bethe has found supporters.[1] They consider that these lists of single combats are the echo of wars and battles once fought in Greece. The tendency of the unsophisticated is to crystallize a war into a battle and to remember peoples only by their protagonists. So when Idomeneus kills Phaestus (E 43–7) Bethe thinks that we have 'the last remains of an old Cretan heroic song', and that the fight is really between the men of two Cretan towns, for the warrior Phaestus is simply the eponymous hero of the town of the same name. The theory is specious and would carry weight if it were based on firmer foundations. But Bethe[2] is unable to find many other cases so useful as that of Phaestus, and is reduced to asserting that Hector was originally a Boeotian hero and that the lists of men he slays are the echo of tribal warfare on the Greek mainland. That is why he kills a man called Αἰτώλιος and another man who comes from the banks of Cephisus (E 706 ff.). But it is highly improbable that Hector is a Boeotian by origin, and in most cases the men he slays have nothing to do with Boeotia. In other places than this they have often no given home. If there is truth in this theory it must be stated differently.

The truth seems rather to be that Homer without doubt bases many of his obscure heroes' names on the names of places. His method can be seen if we go beyond his list of slain and examine the general principles on which he names his minor characters. First are the eponymous heroes who look like inventions, and are more likely to be called

---

[1] P. Cauer, *Grundfragen*, p. 234 ff. Bethe, quoted by Drerup, *Homerproblem*, p. 305.   [2] *Homer*, iii, pp. 79–83.

after their tribes than their tribes are to be called after them, although there is no assurance that the derivation of the name was made by Homer and not by his predecessors. Of these there are many examples on the Achaean side.[1] Thessaly presents a number. Γουνεύς (B 748) from Γόννοι,[2] Λῆθος (P 288) from the Ληθαῖον πεδίον,[3] Τρῆχος (E 706) from Trachis, Φόρβας (Ξ 490) from the city of the same name,[4] and above all Θεσσαλός (B 679), the eponymous hero of the whole country. From Leucas comes Odysseus' comrade Λεῦκος (Δ 491); Κόρωνος (B 746) comes from Coroneia in Boeotia, 'Αζείδης (B 513) from the 'Αζᾶνες[5] in Arcadia, Πειραΐδης (Δ 228) from Πειραί[6] in Achaea, and others may with equal probability be located in the same way. So far as Achaean names were concerned, it is likely enough that Homer followed the family traditions of Aeolic and Ionic colonists, who claimed descent from places on the mainland, and traced their genealogies back to the heroes of mainland tribes. For the Trojans things must have been more difficult. But Homer names his minor Trojans on the same principle. Above all their names come, as we might expect, from the Troad. The two Adresti (Z 63, Π 694) come from 'Αδρήστεια on the Propontis,[7] Αἴσηπος (Z 21) from the river of the same name,[8] Εὔηνος from a river near Miletus (B 693),[9] Θηβαῖος (Θ 120) from Andromache's home at Thebe,[10] Θυμβραῖος (Λ 320) from Thymbra, 'Ιδαῖος (E 20) from Ida, Κεβριόνης (Π 781) from the river Κεβρήν,[11] Πήδαιος (E 69) from Πήδαιον under Mount Ida,[12] Σιμοείσιος (Δ 488) from the Simois. But the Troad seems not to have had enough names to go round, and Homer goes beyond it for his Trojans. From Phrygia come 'Ασκάνιος[13] (N 792), Μυγδών[14] (Γ 186) and Φόρκυς[15] (P 318). The traditional connexion of Troy with Thrace justifies the presence of Αἴνιος (Φ 210) from Ainos.[16] But the poet goes even farther than this and takes his Trojan names from the Greek mainland. Thessaly provides Orthaios (N 791) from Orthe,[17] Ormenos (Θ 274, M 187) from

[1] H. H. Roer, de Nominibus propriis quae in Iliade inveniuntur, 1914.
[2] Steph.Byz., s.v. Γόννοι.   [3] Theognis l. 1216.   [4] Step. Byz., s.v. Φόρβας.
[5] Ib., s.v. 'Αζανία.   [6] Paus. vii. 18, 1.   [7] B 828.   [8] M 21.
[9] Strabo, xiii. 614.   [10] Z 397.   [11] Apollodorus iii. 154.
[12] Schol. T. in N. 172.   [13] Steph. Byz., s.v. 'Ασκανία.   [14] Ib., s.v. Μυγδονία.
[15] Cf. Roer, l.c., p. 27.   [16] Steph. Byz., s.v. Αἶνος.   [17] Strabo, ix. 440.

Ormenion,[1] and Pyrasos (Λ 491) from the place of the same name.[2]

This derivation of Trojan names from Greek places has naturally caused some stir, and Bethe sees in their presence an argument for his view that the fights recorded by Homer were originally fought on the Greek mainland between Greek tribes. But this theory is improbable. That Homer knew enough history even for this distorted view is unlikely. It is much more likely that out of deference to the tradition which demanded lists of warriors, and especially of men slain, he and his forerunners found their names where they could, and when the Troad ran out, they did not scruple to borrow from Greece.

So far as the Greek names are concerned, it is remarkable that a large proportion comes from Thessaly. Thessaly was the original home of the Aeolic colonists of Asia Minor, and the use of Thessalian names points to the poet employing old family traditions which existed among the families of Aeolis. By so doing he would flatter family pride, and no doubt such a motive prompted his use of these names. Some such reason may also account for the presence of Thessalian names among Trojans. No doubt some families in Asia Minor claimed descent from Trojan princes, and the long genealogy given to Aeneas looks as if it were drawn from a family tradition. It was only natural that such families, absorbed in the Greek colonization, should adopt Thessalian names while still claiming a Trojan origin.

But whether Homer invented or not in this, it seems clear that in other cases the names he gives are inventions. Among the Trojans killed by Odysseus we find:

ἔνθ' ὅ γε Κοίρανον εἷλεν Ἀλάστορά τε Χρομίον τε
Ἄλκανδρόν θ' Ἅλιόν τε Νοήμονά τε Πρύτανίν τε. (E 677–8)

Hardly one of these names does not betray its origin in the poet's brain. They are suitable titles invented for the occasion. Every one of them can be readily translated and they are all quite suitable for soldiers. The same fictitious air hangs over other lists of Trojans. Aias kills Πάνδοκος, the welcomer of all; Λύσανδρος, the releaser of men; Πυλάρτης,

---

[1] Hesychius, s.v. Ὄρμενος.   [2] Steph. Byz., s.v. Πύρασος.

the gate-keeper, (Λ 490–1). Achilles kills Θερσίλοχος, the bold in ambush; Ἀστύπυλος, of the city gate; and Θρασίος, the bold (Φ 209–10). Patroclus kills Ἀμφοτερός, Τληπόλεμος, Ἰφεύς, Εὔιππος, and Πολύμηλος (Π 415–17). These names are inventions as much as the names of Thetis's Nereids or the Phaeacians in the *Odyssey*. They are just suitable labels for soldiers slain in battle.

With the Achaeans things are not so simple. There are fewer lists of slain Achaeans than of slain Trojans, and what there are, are less easily accounted for. Of nine men slain by Hector in one place (Λ 301) only Ἱππόνοος and Αὐτόνοος look like pure invention. Their names seemed to be formed from other sources. There are those formed from places, as we have seen. There are, too, others given to obscure men and known better from more renowned holders such as Orestes, which is given to three different men who are only mentioned when killed (E 705, M 139, 193), or Oenomaus (E 706, M 140). On the Trojan side the best example of this class is Deucalion, slain by Achilles (Υ 478). These names have, of course, no connexion with their better-known holders. They are taken at random by the poet from the wealth of names preserved by the saga. But outside all these there still lies a mass of Achaean names which cannot be derived or explained. Many of them are preserved in the *Catalogue*, and may be of very ancient origin. The tradition must have clung to them simply as names, because their enumeration was part of poetry, and so they survived when the histories attaching to them were largely, if not entirely, lost. Homer used these names as he used those he invented, to satisfy convention and to give probability to those lists of deaths which his profession forced on him.

The simple lists of slain have hardly any aesthetic merit, and in this state Homer is often content to leave them. But occasionally he varies the slaughter with some little detail, and the passage becomes beautiful and significant. He calls up a picture of men otherwise obscure and uninteresting, of Oresbius who lived by the banks of Cephisus (E 707), of Axylus who kept hospitality by the road-side (Z 13 ff.). These cases show that even this intractable form was made

to yield at times to his sense of style and construction, to add
a sudden and unexpected beauty or pathos in the middle of
the horror of battle.

Another primitive trait in the Homeric epic is its use of
stock or conventional epithets. This trait it shares with
other early poetry. In the Russian epics simple adjectives
are attached to certain characters.[1] In the *Song of Roland*,
France is always 'France dulce', Oliver's sister is 'Aude au
vis cler', Charles is 'l'emperere magne'. Similar uses are
to be found in the Serb and Finnish epics. In these the epithets are simple and on the whole monotonous. In the *Iliad*
the use of the stock epithet is so successful that no praise of it
is necessary. Its origins are hard to discern, but they seem to
lie in the need to distinguish one man from another. So one
Aias is Τελαμώνιος and the other is Οἰλιάδης. But there is also
a simple pleasure in attaching an epithet to a great name.
Early history and literature abound in such cases, and examples spring at once to the mind like Richard 'cœur de
lion' or Berthe 'aux grands pieds'. The epic tradition inherited by Homer had gone far beyond this, and had its
stock epithets not only for men and gods but for the sea and
animals and the wonders of nature. These justified themselves by their beauty, and they remain the wonder of posterity. But they served another purpose. They eased the
listener's attention by their repetition, and helped to give the
epic that looseness of texture which saved its hearers from
too much concentration. As Homer uses them they are
usually both appropriate and beautiful. It is right that
Achilles should be called ποδάρκης when he leaps to seize
Hector from Apollo (Υ 445) or when he pursues the River
God (Φ 265). It is right that Hector should be called
κορυθαίολος just before he takes his small son in his arms and
frightens him with his horse-hair plume (Z 440). It is right
that the boar sent by Artemis to ravage the fields of Calydon
should be called σῦν ἄγριον ἀργιόδοντα (I 539). Far more often
than not the epithet adorns without delaying the story. But
in a few places the tradition has been too strong for Homer,

---

[1] Drerup, *Homerproblem*, p. 461, n. i.

and from carelessness he falls a victim to it. Ancient custom demanded that Athene should be γλαυκῶπις and Hera βοῶπις, because once Athene was an owl-goddess and Hera a cow-goddess. For Homer they were anthropomorphic, but he used the old adjectives. Perhaps he did not know their real meaning, and just repeated what he had learned. And so far as goddesses were concerned this might pass as an excuse. But he seems to have given some new meaning to the words; for he calls a mere mortal, Clymene, by Hera's title of βοῶπις (Γ 144). It may be that his audience understood the words to mean 'bright-eyed' and 'mild-eyed', and that he so understood them himself. But their natural meaning was 'owl-headed' and 'cow-headed', and if they had not been sanctified by tradition, they would not have found their way into his verse and been used in this rather inappropriate way. Here Homer may be excused on the ground that he thought the words meant something different from their real meaning. But in some cases he has not this excuse, and uses his epithets inappropriately. The Alexandrian critics complained that Hector should not call himself δῖος (H 75) or Menelaus call his unscrupulous antagonist, Antilochus, διοτρεφές (Ψ 581). But such might be explained as examples of heroic pride and heroic good manners. The real failures are where the epithet contradicts the conditions described in the context.[1] There is no point in Achilles being called ποδάρκης when he is in council (A 121) or in his tent (Π 5). There is no point in ships being called ὠκύποροι when they are drawn up on the shore (A 421, H 229). There are not many cases like these, but these are sufficient to show that Homer sometimes found the traditional epithet so convenient that he fell into it without much thought for its meaning. But he was too good a poet to do this often, and it is instructive to see how on the whole he manages the old artifice and makes a new use of it. Often where he might use the stock word he substitutes another which is more appropriate. When Priam sees Achilles from the wall or when Hector waits for him, the Achaean warrior is no longer 'fleet of foot'. That would be

---

[1] So in the Slavonic epics the epithet 'white-handed' is applied even to the Moors.

appropriate, but Homer uses a still more appropriate word and calls him πελώριον instead of πόδας ταχύν (Φ 527, X 92), thus delineating the great strength and stature against which Hector is soon to pit himself. So, too, the Trojan Polydamas is called rightly ἐγχέσπαλος in battle (Ξ 449), but in council πεπνυμένος (Σ 249).[1] Both words scan alike, and the poet's decision is based upon the appropriate sense. When Menelaus throws his spear at Paris it is ὄβριμον, and well it may be, for it pierces most of Paris' armour (Γ 357), but when with its bronze tip it hits the hand of Helenus it is χάλκεον, and as the wounded man draws it out by the ashen shaft it is μείλινον (N 595, 597). Zeus is often called νεφεληγερέτα and it is usually right for the god of the sky and storms, but in a simile he clears away the clouds from a mountain and so νεφεληγερέτα would be wrong, and he is called instead στεροπηγερέτα (Π 298). The change may not be perfect but it shows some regard for the context. More skilful is the treatment of Pandarus. Athene addresses him conventionally as Λυκάονος υἱὲ δαΐφρον (Δ 93), and we do not wonder at it, though Pandarus is not a very heroic figure. But the point of the epithet comes later. Athene persuades Pandarus to break the truce and shoot an arrow at the Achaeans, and then we see why the poet has called him δαΐφρον. For his comment is:

ὣς φάτ' Ἀθηναίη, τῷ δὲ φρένας ἄφρονι πεῖθεν.   (Δ 104)

The epithet was needed to lead up to this comment by contrast, and shows how Homer can, if he chooses, subordinate this ancient usage to his own purposes.

A similar mastery of the stock epithet is seen in those places where Homer employs it so surprisingly that at first we think he has blundered, but later realize that the surprise is intended to give an effect of pathos or irony. Diomedes is often called βοὴν ἀγαθός, and the title holds well for him, the bravest of the younger Achaeans. Once only is he afraid for a moment, and that is when he sees Ares ready to protect Hector. Then, we might have thought, Homer surely would forgo the epithet, but at this moment of fear we are told

τὸν δὲ ἰδὼν ῥίγησε βοὴν ἀγαθὸς Διομήδης   (E 596)

---

[1] Cauer, *Grundfragen*, pp. 449 ff.

and at first we feel that if Diomedes were really βοὴν
ἀγαθός he would not shudder at the sight of Ares, or anyhow that this is hardly the moment to mention his courage.
But the effect is deliberate. Diomedes is a brave soldier, but
even he is frightened by Ares. The epithet, so far from being
superfluous or inappropriate, gives exactly the right idea of
a brave man being for once afraid. Even more remarkable is
the use of the conventional φυσίζοος to describe the earth in
which Helen's brothers are buried. In this beautiful scene
Helen does not know of her brothers' deaths, and we are
told it by the poet after she has looked for them in vain
among the Achaeans. They are not there:

τοὺς δ' ἤδη κάτεχεν φυσίζοος αἶα
ἐν Λακεδαίμονι αὖθι, φίλῃ ἐν πατρίδι γαίῃ. (Γ 243-4)

Surely, some have thought, the epithet is wrong. Why call
the earth 'life-giving' when it is thought of as a tomb? And
yet the effect is pure pathos. The earth, which gives birth, is
still a grave. The thought is simple and ancient and perfectly
just. No doubt Homer had it in his mind when he wrote
these lines. The unexpected use of the epithet may, too, serve
for anger or complaint. Achilles fills the river Scamander
with dead bodies, and the river cries out in complaint:

πλήθει γὰρ δή μοι νεκύων ἐρατεινὰ ῥέεθρα. (Φ 218)

And here, too, objections have been raised that ἐρατεινά is out
of place. But of course it is quite right. The river's water
should be beautiful, and was, until Achilles filled it with blood
and bodies. The god has every right to plead its beauty as
a reason for not defiling it.

Another early trait in the *Iliad* is its love of diversions. Any
reader must at once be struck by the way in which the action
is delayed by apparently irrelevant narratives told by the
chief heroes even in moments of great emotional excitement.
A similar method is employed in *Beowulf* and the fragments
of *Waldere*. The Greek epic, like the Anglo-Saxon, selected
from a great mass of saga, and in these diversions referred to
earlier history which lay outside the immediate plot. But
these episodes are not always irrelevant. Some serve a purpose,

and if we examine them we see how the epic achieves part of its fullness and richness.

In the first place some of these episodic passages, though strictly speaking irrelevant, contribute to our understanding of the characters. When Beowulf tells of his great swimming-match with Breca, we realize his enormous strength and capacity for submarine adventures—qualities which are to stand him in good stead in his struggle with Grendel. So, too, when Zeus tells Hera of his earlier loves, we understand why he is so quickly caught by Hera's artful trap. But more commonly the episodes are illustrative of the main narrative. When Hrothgar's noble sings of Heremod, the slayer of monsters, he gives a good parallel to Beowulf. And in the *Iliad* this same method is often pursued. Particularly it is used to point a moral. When Agamemnon finds Diomedes slacking before battle, he tells him a story of Tydeus, how his rapidity of movement circumvented his enemies in the siege of Thebes (Δ 371–400). The reproof comes with all the more force because the lesson is drawn from Diomedes' father. When Diomedes tells the story of Lycurgus and Dionysus to Glaucus, he gives a good reason for his not attacking at once. He is afraid that Glaucus is a god, and the story of Lycurgus warns him against fighting with gods (Z 128–41). When Agamemnon makes up his quarrel with Achilles he tells a long story of how Heracles was from his birth the victim of Ἄτη. The story is a piece of self-justification. Agamemnon apologizes for his infatuation, but he gives as his excuse this story which shows that even a man so good as Heracles suffered from the same curse (T 95–133). But perhaps the best example of this type is the story of Meleager which Phoenix tells to Achilles. Meleager, like Achilles, persisted in his anger and only abandoned it when it was really too late. The story is a warning. If Achilles too persists, he may live to repent it (I 529–99).

On the other hand, some of these stories are almost irrelevant and claim attention more for their own interest than for any addition they make to the story. The tale of Finnesburh in *Beowulf* is really an interlude and no more. So in the *Iliad* are most of Nestor's garrulous reminiscences. When

Patroclus goes anxiously to hear news of the battle, Nestor detains him with a long story lasting over a hundred lines. The only point is that Nestor is not the man he once was, and that Peleus behaved better than his son (Λ 668–790). Nor is there any more relevance in Nestor's harangues to the Achaeans before the duel of Aias and Hector (H 125–57) or to his son after the chariot-race (Ψ 629–50). Homer seems to have liked Nestor and to have taken a pleasure in his garrulity. But though these episodes are really irrelevant, they are not inexcusable. They are all drawn from the Heroic Age, and one of the poet's functions was to recall this age to his audience. By such expedients as Nestor's reminiscences he widened the limits of his subject and gave a short glimpse of the rich and varied stories of the great past.

In these cases we can see Homer using the traditional forms of early poetry and changing their character as he fits them into his epic. The *Iliad* is in most ways so much more advanced and mature than most early epics that these primitive traits come as a surprise to us. They may of course mean that the Greek epic grew up rapidly and reached maturity while it still preserved some of the traits of its childhood. Or perhaps they mean that Homer preserved some ancient devices of verse and chose to see what he could do with them, just as Virgil used with masterly skill the old Latin trick of alliteration which he had learned from Ennius and earlier poets. These primitive traits do not constitute the bulk of the *Iliad*, and we must not, because of them, treat the *Iliad* as if it belonged to the first beginnings of poetry. But they are, at least, a warning that Homer was much nearer to the origins of poetry than was Milton or Virgil or even Dante. Because of this he must not be judged entirely by the standards we apply to them. The Greek epic created its masterpieces when the poetic art was still hampered by the earliest forms into which poetry falls. Homer emancipated himself from the chilling influence of these archaic formulae, but he was still nearer the sources of poetry than most great poets, and he could profit little by the precedent of mature, flawless masterpieces. To this we may ascribe some peculiar features of the *Iliad* which we must consider next.

REPETITIONS AND CONTRADICTIONS

EARLY epic poetry begins with improvisation, and traces of this survive long after their real uses are forgotten and the practice itself has ceased. The improvising bard has under his control certain useful artifices which help him in his work and lessen the labours of creation. In particular he has stock lines which may be repeated whenever he has to deal with speech and answer, with the return of night or day, with the approach of death or the throwing of a weapon. Such themes recur constantly in all heroic poetry, and the poet who treated of them was helped by stock lines which he learned when he learned his art. Such repeated lines exist in most early poetry. In *Beowulf* eight out of thirteen speeches made by the hero begin with the same words: *Beowulf mapelode bearn Ecgpeowes*,[1] and the *Song of Roland* gives its scene more than once in the line: *halt sunt li pui et li val tenebrus*.[2] These lines are not in themselves evidence for improvisation, but originally such repetitions can only have arisen from the poet's need of help if he was going to make a new song every time. Being a recognized part of poetry they survived into the age of more considered composition, and as such we find them in Homer.

In practice, however, they performed a function quite different from that for which they were originally intended, and this was based on a sound knowledge of psychology. No one can listen for long with rapt attention to any recited poem. Sooner or later the fancy will wander, and the thread of the story will be lost. Under other conditions this may not matter. Modern readers may doze over a novel, but if they want to know what they have missed they have only to turn back and see. The Homeric poet could not allow for such a solution to the difficulty, and with perfect insight into the conditions he used the expedient of repeated phrases and lines. Any reader of the *Iliad* notices at once the enormous number of

---

[1] 'Beowulf, son of Ecgtheow, replied'. Cf. Chadwick, *The Heroic Age*, p. 320.
[2] 'High are the mountains and dark the valleys.'

verbal repetitions. They become so familiar that we fail to regard them in reading and take them as read. But to the original listeners their effect was different. When the first audiences heard a line like

ὣς οἱ μὲν τοιαῦτα πρὸς ἀλλήλους ἀγόρευον[1]   (E 431 etc.)

or

ὣς ἔφαθ᾽, οἱ δ᾽ ἄρα πάντες ἀκὴν ἐγένοντο σιωπῇ[2]   (Γ 95 etc.)

most of their attention could lie dormant: they were rested for a moment and the more prepared to hear something new and exciting when it should come. These stock lines are not even very important for the story, which pursues its way largely in spite of them. But they were quite necessary if the audience was to listen to the whole poem with greater ease and less exhaustion of the faculties. The appearance of such a line meant that both the ear and the mind slackened some of their effort, and the listener was momentarily rested. For this purpose the poet largely confined himself to those lines which deal with the machinery of the story, and we can see how many these are when we realize that out of the total 27,853 lines which make up the *Iliad* and the *Odyssey*, about one-third, 9,253, are repeated or contain repeated phrases. The repeated phrase had another use. When, for instance, we find seven times in the *Iliad* the line

ἀνέρες ἔστε, φίλοι, μνήσασθε δὲ θούριδος ἀλκῆς[3]   (Θ 174 etc.)

it is not a mere piece of machinery. It helped the audience to know what was going to follow, acting as a signpost and thereby relieving the mind of some effort. The value and function of these repeated phrases are revealed more clearly when we compare them with the different method employed by a sophisticated poet like Virgil. Virgil repeats lines, even passages, but quite differently from Homer. For the coming of dawn or night or for death in battle he is at great pains to vary his expression and resorts to many kinds of periphrasis. The result is a loss of spontaneity. He was writing for men who could read and examine his poem in detail, and he did

[1] 'So they spoke such words one to another.'
[2] 'So spake he, and they all became silent and still.'
[3] 'Be men, friends, and remember your impetuous might.'

not care for rapid movement. For him the poetry is always more important than the story, and like a conscientious artist he avoids anything savouring of slackness or lack of polish. When he repeats, it is usually for other reasons, to recall some earlier passage or to emphasize some moment of pathos.[1] The result is a gain in the texture of his work. It can be read with far closer attention than Homer's, but it loses in life and vigour; his varied ways of opening or closing speeches degenerate into rhetorical artifice. Homer knew that he often had to describe similar events happening, and he was not afraid of describing them in the same words. This is simple, unsophisticated art, like the repetitions in the Old Testament, but it has its origin in a real sense of how to recite poetry to an audience who must not be expected to listen continuously without some rest or guidance.

Homer, however, does not merely repeat phrases and single lines. He repeats sets of lines, either with or without alteration. For instance four lines (Γ 334–7) in which Paris arms for battle are repeated word for word when Patroclus arms (Π 135–8), and there are many other cases of such wholesale repetition. It is true, indeed, that the poet usually varies the theme sooner or later. Thus while Paris fits on his brother Lycaon's breastplate, Patroclus puts on that of Achilles, and while Paris takes only one spear, Patroclus, a more redoubtable warrior, takes two. But the repetitions remain, and they must be accounted for or excised. In antiquity the method was to mark them as spurious, though they have managed to survive in our texts. The scholia are full of such cases, and neither Zenodotus nor Aristarchus nor Aristophanes seems to have had the slightest compunction about marking repeated lines. Their method was to regard as dubious any set of lines which had appeared before and was not organically necessary in its place. This method is open to criticism. Even allowing that some such lines are spurious, it is by no means certain that the first place is the genuine place and the second the spurious. The earlier might as easily be interpolated from the later as the later

---

[1] Of course many of his repetitions may be temporary stop-gaps, which he would have removed if he had lived to finish the *Aeneid*.

from the earlier. Again, the test that the context does not suffer by the removal of a line or lines is not an adequate test of genuineness in Homer. Of all poets he writes the loosest and least periodic style, and even a large number of his unrepeated lines may be removed without any great damage to the context. Lastly, the repetitions are so numerous that their presence must be explained, before they can be excised, and this the Alexandrians failed to do. And naturally, for there can be no explanation of an interpolation so wholesale as this. In modern times the repetitions have been treated in a different way, and in particular they have formed a corner-stone of the Higher Criticism. When one passage reproduces another, one or the other of the passages tends to be considered as a later imitation of the first, and by the vigorous application of such a test, efforts have been made to distinguish later from earlier passages in the poem. To the sophisticated mind this argument carries force. Just as later Greek poets imitated and robbed Homer, so may the writer of a later part of the *Iliad* have robbed the writer of an earlier part. The ancients had small conscience about literary plagiarism and no law of copyright. So wholesale imitation and borrowing of lines is perfectly possible. But in practice the test is not easy to apply. Which of any two similar passages is the earlier? On the one hand it might be maintained that the simpler is necessarily the earlier. The tendency of imitators is often to expand. Just as Virgil adds to Homer, so the later writers of the *Iliad* may have added to the earlier. This at least would explain the repetition. The newer poet would feel that he was improving on an earlier treatment of a theme, and therefore feel justified in his imitation. This was Seeck's view. He proclaimed the axiom that 'the copy must surpass the original in beauty'.[1] On the other hand, some critics treat the repetitions in quite a different way. The less beautiful of any two similar passages must necessarily be the later, because it is the work of a copyist, and copyists are proverbially incompetent. This point of view is often pressed, but a typical example will help to make it plain. Leaf is a great advocate of it, and applies it firmly in dealing

[1] *Quellen der Odyssee*, p. 354.

with two passages where the same simile is repeated. The simile is famous. In *Z* 506–11 Paris going to battle is compared to a well-fed horse breaking away from the stable to the pasture. In *O* 263–8 precisely the same words are used of Hector after Apollo's words have encouraged him to go to battle again. Which is the earlier passage? Leaf is quite clear that the passage is aesthetically far more appropriate to Paris than to Hector and supports Aristarchus in his athetizing of the Hector passage. By Seeck's test precisely the opposite result would be obtained. The Paris passage must be the later because it is more beautiful. Clearly any such *a priori* tests as these are futile, and Hermann, who started them, ought to have known better. There is no natural law to govern the goodness or badness of imitators, and time does not necessarily bring either improvement or decay. But the attempts to date different portions of the *Iliad* by the character of their repeated passages are anyhow open to grave objection on the ground of ordinary logic. In the first place no internal test can be applied. Nearly all the passages are relevant in their context and may be genuine. In themselves they provide no test for dating. Hence the editors have to decide by other means, and the existence of a repetition is no evidence at all. But in the second place this too is unsatisfactory. The repetitions are so numerous that mere rewriting is not an adequate account of them. They are deeply embedded in the text of the poem, and have been part of it ever since the poems took their present shape. What is needed really is an explanation of what part they play in the poems as they now stand. If we can find that, we can with greater assurance proceed to explain their origin.

The repetitions consist roughly of three classes, the repeated phrases and single lines, which we have already considered and found functional in the poems; the groups of lines repeated with or without differences; and finally passages in which the same or a similar event is repeated under different circumstances or with different persons. The first group is so essential to the poems that it hardly needs any further thought. Not only are the familiar repeated lines entirely necessary, but so too are the familiar titles such as γλαυκῶπις Ἀθήνη or πολύμητις Ὀδυσσεύς.

Of these there is no more need to speak, but the groups of lines present more difficulty. The question is: how could one poet repeat a set of lines in one context after using them in another, more appropriate context, and how, having found a suitable mode of expression, could he alter them in unimportant points of detail? An example of each will show the difficulty. For the first, there are the two similes for the arming of Hector and of Paris, where certainly that concerning Hector, which comes later, loses much of its interest because we have had the other lines before. But on closer examination there is more in it than this. When Paris arms, he is acting rather against his character as a frivolous and none too courageous fighter. He puts on the heroic panoply of war, and we are interested to see how the new part will suit him. The details of the arming help to stir our curiosity about his behaviour in his new role, and make us wonder how he will acquit himself in it. Hector is the antithesis of this. His prowess and character are proved. We know that whatever happens he will acquit himself like a man. So when he arms himself, our feelings are quite different. Each runs into the fight like a stallion broken loose from its stall. In identical words the cowardly Paris and the 'preux chevalier' Hector advance to their different fates. The conclusion must be that the repetition is deliberate. It is too bold to be the work of an imitator, too remarkable to be mere textual corruption. When in O 263–8 the same words describe Hector as described Paris in Z 506–11, we can only remember Paris, and contrast the two in our mind. So far the two were similar. It is in what follows that they differ. Paris cuts no important figure in the fight. Hector is the pillar of the Trojan attack. But for a moment they are similar. Such is the repetition in its present position, and such was the intention of whoever put it in its present place, whatever the original use of the lines was.

The second type, in which slight alterations were made, is well instanced in the repetition of another famous simile. In Θ 555–8 the camp-fires of the Trojans are compared to the stars on a windless night:

ὡς δ' ὅτ' ἐν οὐρανῷ ἄστρα φαεινὴν ἀμφὶ σελήνην
φαίνετ' ἀριπρεπέα, ὅτε τ' ἔπλετο νήνεμος αἰθήρ,
ἔκ τ' ἔφανεν πᾶσαι σκοπιαὶ καὶ πρώονες ἄκροι
καὶ νάπαι· οὐρανόθεν δ' ἄρ' ὑπερράγη ἄσπετος αἰθήρ,
πάντα δὲ εἴδεται ἄστρα, γέγηθε δέ τε φρένα ποιμήν.

When the poet comes later (Π 297–300) to describe the relief
of the Achaeans after the Trojan retirement, he uses a similar
simile:

ὡς δ' ὅτ' ἀφ' ὑψηλῆς κορυφῆς ὄρεος μεγάλοιο
κινήσῃ πυκινὴν νεφέλην στεροπηγερέτα Ζεύς,
ἔκ τ' ἔφανεν πᾶσαι σκοπιαὶ καὶ πρώονες ἄκροι
καὶ νάπαι, οὐρανόθεν δ' ἄρ' ὑπερράγη ἄσπετος αἰθήρ.

The comparisons are quite different, but two lines are common to both. We might of course excise the two offending
lines from the first simile, as Aristarchus and Zenodotus did,
and so get rid of the difficulty. But why did the lines get in?
There is nothing in the context to suggest them, and if we
excise here, we must excise elsewhere and the difficulties are
only multiplied. The lines are more likely to have been here
early. We cannot here treat them like the repeated simile
of the stallion. The likeness is too little for the later passage to
recall the earlier, except at one small point. The first tells of
the Trojans camping before the Achaean Camp, the second
of their retirement from it, and there is a connexion of this sort
between the two. But the repetition is too slight for this to
be immediately obvious to any listener. We must seek for
another explanation, and if we look at other poetry we soon
find one. In *The Knight's Tale* Chaucer wrote the famous
and lovely lines in the last speech of Arcite:

> What is this world? what asketh men to have?
> Now with his love, now in the colde grave
> Allone, with-outen any companye.

Here, if anywhere, we might think, is the final, inevitable
language of great art, and if any modern poet had written
this, he would be content with it and leave it. But Chaucer
for his own reasons did not leave it. In *The Miller's Tale* he
repeated the last line in an utterly different context, of the
gay clerk Nicholas.

> A chambre hadde he in that hostelrye
> Allone, with-outen any companye,
> Full fetisly y-dight with herbes swote.

If we think of this the Homeric repetitions are more intelligible. The conclusion would be that early poets felt no qualm about repeating a line if it was good enough. Its mere excellence was in itself sufficient claim to repetition. This is not a modern view of poetry, but it is an intelligible view. It implies simply that when a theme has found its perfect expression, it needs no variation. This was not the view of Dante or of Milton, who were at great pains to vary even the description of the simplest themes. But it is a common practice of poetry in the youth of the world.

The third kind of repetition is not of words but of situations. In such the *Iliad* abounds. Sometimes the same thing happens to the same character, sometimes the action is repeated under different circumstances with different characters. In the first class we may notice the following. In *B* 110 ff. Agamemnon suggests as a trick that the Achaeans should take to their ships and go home. In *I* 27 ff. he makes the same suggestion, but this time seriously, and in *Ξ* 74 ff. he repeats the suggestion. Similarly in *E* 720 ff. Athene and Hera get ready their chariot to go and help the Achaeans, and they do the same in different words in *Θ* 381 ff. The second class, in which the characters are changed, is even more common. An outstanding instance is the way in which the indecisive duel of Paris and Menelaus in *Γ* is soon followed by the indecisive duel of Hector and Aias in *H*. But there are other cases less marked than this of one action repeating another. For instance, in *E* 432 ff. Diomedes attacks Aeneas, who is defended by Apollo. Three times he attacks without success and the fourth time Apollo warns him off. So too in *Π* 698 ff. Patroclus tries to scale the walls of Troy, which are under the protection of Apollo. Three times he tries, and the fourth time Apollo tells him to give up the attempt. In the *Odyssey* much play has been made over similar themes treated differently. Thus Kirchoff thought that the story of Calypso belonged to an old epic, the story of Circe to a more recent.[1]

---

[1] Cf. Drerup, *Homerproblem*, p. 183.

He presumed both to be variations on an old folk-tale, in which the hero is detained by an immortal enchantress on a remote island. The identity of origin is accepted by Wilamo-witz who reverses the method and says that Calypso is clearly an invention and therefore later than Circe. The repetition of incident cannot be dealt with so light-heartedly as this. Like that employed with the repetition of lines, this method is vicious as it is based on utterly unproved assumptions. The whole theory of repeated themes must be treated differently. Like repeated lines, they too are a feature of early poetry. Scholars in comparative literature assert that they occur in all primitive folk-epic, in those of the Tartars, the Slavs, and the Russians. So too in the *Song of Roland* the speeches of the knights are often repetitions of the same theme. In modern literature repetition of this kind is dead. Shakespeare repeats the substance of his scenes hardly at all, and Dante never. The Renaissance, fed on the critical and self-conscious literature of Rome, had no use for such simplicity. But in simpler poetry things are different. Even Chaucer thinks nothing of making the heroine of *The Man of Law's Tale* go through two sets of almost identical adventures, first in Syria and then in Britain. In so doing he followed the prolixity of the medieval epic and forgot the lessons he had learned from Boccaccio and the new poets of Italy who guided their art by stricter classical rules.

If we consider the matter, an age when poetry was recited could endure repetition more easily than we can. It is un-likely that a long epic was often recited at full length. Selec-tions, as we have seen, were made, and consequently any-thing in the nature of repetition was less likely to be noticed than if the poem had been read in the quiet of the study where minute criticism and back references are possible. The poet not only distributed his jewels, he repeated some that they might not be lost in the preference of his audiences for certain popular passages. In small matters this explana-tion is adequate and probably correct. It does not, however, explain such a repetition as that of the duel. The audience would know that there were two duels and would ask for one or the other, but neither could easily be sandwiched in if the other was not asked for. Here he must have had other reasons for the repetition. The two duels are ultimately different, though in some ways they are surprisingly similar. In both the technical victory falls to the Achaeans. Paris is spirited off by his guardian Aphrodite, and Hector is wounded by Aias but saves further fighting by an appeal to the approach of night. But for the purposes of the story both are essential. The first is the fight of the two real makers of the war, Menelaus and Paris: the second the fight of the two best soldiers then in the field, Hector and Aias. The second duel shows how the war has ceased to be for Helen's sake and has become war to the death for Hector and for Troy. Thus in their separate ways they show what the war was which for motives of injured pride Achilles had for the time abandoned. They too have other aesthetic differences. They concern four principal characters of the story, and they help to bring out their individualities in a way impossible in the crowded narrative of the general fighting. The slap-dash methods of Paris are contrasted with the more confident soldiership of Menelaus, and the rather unimaginative courage of Aias is contrasted with the real heroism of Hector who knows exactly his own worth in fight. To a generation used to fighting, these details would bring home at once the several personal characteristics of the combatants and justify the repetition of two otherwise rather similar episodes.

The three types of repetition are important features in the epic structure. Each has a function calculated for a listening audience, but the poet has turned this function to other uses. With his recurring lines and epithets he can not only rest the mind, he can prepare an atmosphere. With his recurring passages, he can give one emotional colour here and another there, and by reminiscence of an earlier scene he can im- plicitly point a contrast. With his recurring themes he puts his material to many uses, and gives an old story new life in new and different forms. His art is greater than the art of primitive epics where repetition tends to be wearisome. Here, too, Homer took the primitive formulae of epic writing and turned them to new uses.

Herodotus says of Homer that he only once contradicts

himself (ii. 116). His judgement has not been accepted, and since Alexandrian days critics have found contradictions plentifully in the *Iliad*. The scholars of antiquity were usually unitarians so far as Homer was concerned, and their cure for contradictions was to blame the text rather than the poet. So either, like Aristophanes, they marked the offending passages or, like Zenodotus, they omitted or emended them. Others tried to find an explanation which avoided the inconsistency. A good example of their work may be seen in the notorious case of Pylaemenes, King of the Paphlagonians, who is killed by Menelaus in *E* 576 but mourns for his son's death in *N* 658. The ancients saw the difficulty. Aristophanes obelized. Aristarchus thought that perhaps the poet referred to another Pylaemenes, and Zenodotus wanted to emend from Πυλαιμένεα to Κυλαιμένεα. In fact they treated Homer as modern scholars treat most classical authors, and devised means to get over the difficulties. There were, however, a few eccentrics, regarded as unimportant in scholarly circles, who attacked the difficulties from a different angle. οἱ χωρίζοντες, as they were called, tried to show from internal inconsistencies that not only were the *Iliad* and the *Odyssey* written by different persons, but that neither was written by any single person.[1] Their reasons, which survive in the scholia, are often unconvincing, and they made no impression on the great. Clearly they were thought to have been routed in Aristarchus' 'Reply to the Paradox of Xenon'. For centuries the question of contradictions lay quiet. The author of Περὶ ὕψους knows or says nothing about it in his long discussion of Homer. Seneca (*de Brev. Vit.* 13) dismisses as an example of Greek logomachy their foolish question: 'Did the same poet write both poems?'. Even in more critical times the arguments of the Separatists were late to be revived. They did not occur to the critical mind of Wolf, who admired the literary unity of the poems, whatever their origin was. The doubt was first raised by Kirchoff and Lachmann, and where they set the lead, countless others have followed, till to-day contradictions

---

[1] Cf. J. G. Kohl, *de Chorizontibus*, Giessen, 1917. For internal inconsistencies in the *Iliad* cf. Schol. ad Γ 124, N 365, Φ 550, O 77, Θ 371–2.

play an important part in any theory of the authorship of the poems.

It is natural that this should be so. Any work of art is expected to be self-consistent, and, the critics argue, if it is not reasonably self-consistent, it is more likely to be the work of many than of one, because a single author can carry the details of a story in his head better than a crowd can. But at the outset this procedure stirs doubts. All authors contradict themselves, many contradict themselves violently. An example or two in notably careful writers will suffice. Dante is rightly regarded as a man of highly critical intellect with an overpowering absorption in his theme. Yet in dealing with the prophetess Manto, the eponymous enchantress of Virgil's own town and therefore a woman of considerable importance, he contradicts himself flatly on a point dealing with so vital a matter as life after death. In the *Inferno* (Canto xx. 55) she is placed in Hell with the false prophets, but in the *Purgatorio* (Canto xxii. 113) she is placed in Purgatory. For Dante the difference was of fundamental importance: yet he failed to notice the contradiction. So, too, in other poems there are parallels to the case of Pylaemenes, who is killed and later lives again. In the *Kalevala* Kullervo's family is blotted out (31, 65 ff.), only to be living a little later (34, 125 ff.), and if the *Kalevala* is thought to be too primitive to be good evidence, there is a case in a poem of the full Renaissance, the *Orlando Furioso* of Ariosto. In 18, 45 Ballustrio is killed, but in 40, 73 and 41, 6 he is numbered among the living. There is no need to enumerate other such cases. They abound everywhere, even in poets like Virgil who are regarded as models of critical and sophisticated art. But it might well be claimed that the contradictions are more numerous and more violent in Homer than in any other poem which is admitted to be the work of a single man. This claim has been pressed and would be of great force if all, or nearly all, the contradictions claimed in Homer were there. But on close examination the evidence is less satisfactory than we might have expected from so many distinguished scholars, who have devoted years to tracking the inconsistencies down. There is no need to recapitulate here the blunders of great men like

Fick, Bethe, and Wilamowitz. When they approach the question, a great blindness has too often descended on them, and they have utterly mis-stated the evidence. They have been adequately routed by Professor Scott in his book *The Unity of Homer*,[1] and there is no need to repeat his arguments here. But there are other claimed contradictions, which on closer analysis are not contradictions at all. They may appear to be, but on closer inspection they can be seen to be an essential feature of the epic style as Homer practised it, and they are due, like the repetitions, to the exigencies of recitation, and the difficulties of making a recited poem both interesting and easily intelligible.

There are, of course, a few inexplicable and unquestionable contradictions, as obvious and as unimportant as the case of Pylaemenes. Thus in *B* 45 the sword of Agamemnon is called ἀργυρόηλον, whereas in *Λ* 29–30 we are told ἐν δέ οἱ ἧλοι χρύσειοι πάμφαινον. And no doubt many other such cases could be unearthed. Aristarchus regarded such inconsistency as the poet's right. Just as Virgil makes the wooden horse of three different woods,[2] so too Homer seems to have been poetically inexact about the studs on the sword of Agamemnon. But these cases are not germane to the present issue, nor are they those on which the Higher Criticism has thought fit to dilate. They are instances of Homer nodding. The critics have preferred to seek out cases of a different nature, where the inconsistency is less obvious, and it is from studying these that we get light on how the poet worked.

Recited poetry differs from read poetry in requiring a less exact attention. At all costs it must make the story clear, and at times it has to make sacrifices in the interests of clarity. In particular it cannot be encumbered by tiresome details. Hence of the omissions in Homer many are meant to keep the hearers from worrying. These omissions have often been seized as examples of inconsistency, and it has been thought that they betray the unskilful hand of the late editor who ultimately failed to harmonize different poems because he

---

[1] pp. 137–71.

[2] *Aen.* ii. 16, sectaque intexunt abiete costas; ib. 112, trabibus contexlus acernis, ib. 258, pinea claustra.

did not pay enough attention to the story. The facts are quite different. The poet could not afford to encumber his story with details, no matter how exact and necessary, if they were going to stop the free flow of the narrative. He had to omit what he thought unessential, and leave the supplying of it to the intelligence of his audience. By this means much wearisome redundancy, and even anti-climax, is avoided. The poet describes in detail what he thinks significant, and leaves out many minor results and consequences. Thus in *N* 23 ff. the arrival of Poseidon on the field of battle is described in full detail. The poet lingers lovingly over his gold chariot and gold-maned horses. But that is enough. There is no need to repeat all the same details when the god leaves the battle, and his departure is economically described in the words:

> ὣς εἰπὼν λίπε λαὸν 'Αχαιϊκὸν ἐννοσίγαιος
> δῦνε δὲ πόντον ἰών.   (*O* 218–19)[1]

So, too, with Athena and Hera, who turn their horses out to graze when they come to help the Greeks (*E* 775). Once their work is done, there is no need to pile on details, and they are moved off with the simple stage direction:

> αἱ δ' αὖτις πρὸς δῶμα Διὸς μεγάλοιο νέοντο.[2]   (*E* 907)

In *Φ* 17 Achilles lays down his spear on a tamarisk bush that he may the more easily display his skill in swordsmanship. In l. 67 he has his spear in his hand again, though we are not told that he has taken it up. This action has to be supplied by the hearer. Once the variation made by the sword is finished, the poet reverts to his original narrative without troubling to pick up all the threads he has left. So, too, in *X* 97 when Hector soliloquizes about his coming fight with Achilles, he lays down his shield against a projecting part of the city wall. Thus does he recover what strength he can for the forthcoming encounter, and thus, too, we get an intimate touch which lends light to his absorption in his thought. Later he has it again,[3] but we are not told that he takes it up. The significance of his putting it down is over, and there is

---

[1] 'When he had so spoken, the Earth-Shaker left the Achaean host and went and sank in the sea.'   [2] 'They went back to the house of great Zeus.'
[3] This is not stated explicitly, but follows from *X* 111 ff. and from the absence of any statement that Hector is not fully armed.

no need to add details. The story takes its course in a new direction and leaves what is said alone. In these cases the omissions, which might seem to amount to contradictions, are part of the poetic economy. By leaving out unimportant details, emphasis is laid on what really matters for the story. To insert them would be to weaken the emphasis and to take away some of the listener's attention when the story takes a new turn. So, too, Virgil omits to tell us that Ascanius comes back from his charmed sleep on Mount Ida after Cupid has done his work in his shape. There the essential point is that Dido should fall in love with Aeneas. Once that happens, everything else is unessential, and even so vital a detail as the return of Ascanius and the departure of Cupid are not mentioned. They might take our minds off Dido, if they were mentioned early, and once Dido is in love there is no point in recovering themes which have lost their significance.

The hearer's attention must not only be treated lightly, it must also have its excitement, and some of the apparent contradictions are really a rhetorical device for providing the unexpected. A simple fact is stated, and then we find that it was not really quite what we thought it was going to be. Thus at the end of *A* we are told that Zeus went to his bed:

ἔνθα καθεῦδ᾽ ἀναβάς παρὰ δὲ χρυσόθρονος Ἥρη.   (*A* 611)[1]

So are the slight disagreements in heaven ended, as the quarrels on earth have also been temporarily ended, by sleep (*A* 476). This gives a close to a chapter, and here no doubt the rhapsode could stop for a rest and refreshment if he wanted. But the sleep of Zeus is only a device. The opening of the next book shows this at once. It begins with the words:

ἄλλοι μέν ῥα θεοί τε καὶ ἀνέρες ἱπποκορυσταὶ
εὗδον παννύχιοι, Δία δ᾽ οὐκ ἔχε νήδυμος ὕπνος.[2]   (*B* 1-2)

The poet is not here contradicting himself. His point is that the other gods slept all night long—παννύχιοι—while the sleep of Zeus was neither untroubled, νήδυμος, nor was it unbroken—the imperfect ἔχε does its work exactly. A similar

---

[1] 'Thither he went up and slept, and golden-throned Hera by him.'
[2] 'The other gods and men with horse-haired helmets slept all night long, but Zeus was not subdued by sweet sleep.'

effect is produced in *K*, where at the beginning we are
told that all the Achaeans slept except Agamemnon, and
then a few lines later we find that Menelaus too (l. 25) is
passing a sleepless night. Another example of this unexpectedness is to be found in the account of the burning of the body
of Patroclus. The whole host waits for the burning and the
Myrmidons bring up the body, set it down, and heap up the
wood for the fire. Thus we are prepared for a great public
funeral, but the result is otherwise. The host is scattered to
its tents, and only a few kindred mourners wait behind to
heap on more wood, and the cremation takes place in quiet
and solitude (*Ψ* 140–83). Thus does the poet bring home the
intimate quality of Achilles' affection for Patroclus. He
wants at first to do honour to him in great splendour and
publicity, but he changes his mind and knows that in these
last rites he must be left alone with his dead friend. There is
no need to excise *Ψ* 140–63. It is true that without them the
story is still a story, but it misses the delicate art of the hero's
last farewell to Patroclus. Here the unexpectedness is used
for pathos. In the battle with Scamander it is used almost
with irony. There the river out of its depths calls to Achilles
to stop filling his channel with corpses, and Achilles answers
that he will stop:

$$\text{ἔσται ταῦτα, Σκάμανδρε διοτρεφές, ὡς σὺ κελεύεις.}\quad (Φ\ 223)\text{[1]}$$

But the river is not content with his promise and calls on
Apollo, telling him that he has not kept Zeus' orders that he
is to help the Trojans. This enrages Achilles, and he leaps
into the stream and fights it. There is no contradiction here.
We are led by the poet to think that Achilles will stop filling
the river with dead, but the character of Achilles is too proud
to endure insults, and when the river prays to Apollo, he
resents it fiercely, and the great battle with Scamander begins.
This is not incompetence but art. In these cases, and in
others like them, the poet leads us to expect one thing and
then provides another. This is of the very essence of story-
telling, and there is no need to doubt its deliberate and conscious craftsmanship.

---

[1] 'This shall be, Scamander cherished by Zeus, as you order.'

This quality of unexpectedness comes out especially in some movements of the gods. In the first book we are told that Zeus and all the gods have gone to the Aethiopians (*A* 423–4), but this does not prevent Apollo sending down the arrows of plague on the Achaeans (*A* 44–52), or Hera prompting Achilles to get an assembly of the Achaeans called (*A* 55), or Athene from coming down οὐρανόθεν (*A* 195), to stop the anger of Achilles. Here the difficulty is different. The poet is confronted, as elsewhere, with the task of combining two almost contradictory features in the gods. They must be anthropomorphic, or else their part in the story is sadly mutilated. Homer makes no attempt to reduce their human characteristics. On the other hand they are still gods, and as gods they answer prayers and interfere in human action. So in *A* when it suits the story, Zeus can be kept away at the end of the world, but that does not prevent Hera, Apollo, and Athene from playing their part in the quarrel of Achilles and Agamemnon. They come from their undefined Olympus or from heaven—no distinction is maintained between the two —and start the story. There is a contradiction here, but it is a contradiction inherent in most religion. To the eye of faith a god may have his special home in which he is pre-eminently present, and yet exist everywhere. Even so does Glaucus call on Apollo, whether he is in Lycia or Troy, because he can listen from anywhere to a man in trouble (*Π* 514–16).

A particular form of this unexpected effect is perhaps due to the poet employing a familiar saga. He was able to create a new thrill by leading his audience to expect a well known ending and then suddenly giving them something new and quite surprising. A poet dealing with traditional material may treat it much as he will, provided that he keeps some resemblance to his authority. The Attic tragedians were not blamed for giving different versions of the stories of Philoctetes or Orestes, and no doubt some new invention was expected from a poet. Only under such conditions could poetry keep its liveliness. But when Homer employs his resources to give a new turn to an old tale, he is accused of being self-contradictory, simply because we think that he is going

to say one thing and he says another. The lesson drawn from
these cases has too often been that the poem is a hotch-potch
and has no story. But if we examine the leading cases, we
shall see that as Homer uses it this method does not in-
volve any real contradictions. It employs surprise tactics
and takes us unawares. We are led to expect one thing, and
we get another. This is an old device of fiction, and it should
not shock us in the *Iliad*. Moreover, if we examine cases of
this treatment we see how Homer works. Employing an old
story he gives it a new character, and vastly increases its
human and dramatic significance. In particular he seems
to take an old, rather painful or barbarous episode, and to
transform it into something more profound and more
pathetic. Two cases will be sufficient to show this side of his
art. The first is the so-called contradiction involved in the
death of Achilles, which is often announced and is still outside
the scope of our *Iliad*. We are led to expect it, and it does not
take place. Here, it is claimed, is not precisely a contradiction,
yet an awkwardness which would not exist if the poem were
the work of a single man. But if we look into the case, the
difficulty disappears. Over Achilles hangs the threat of an
early death. So no doubt the saga told of him, and so Homer
repeats the saga. As Achilles is drawn back into the story,
his impending doom is often mentioned. While he waits for
his armour to be made, he knows that he will not see his
home or his father again, but will be buried in Trojan soil
($\varSigma$ 329–32). In his refusal of mercy to Lycaon he speaks of
his own early death:

ἔσσεται ἢ ἠὼς ἢ δείλη ἢ μέσον ἦμαρ,
ὁππότε τις καὶ ἐμεῖο Ἄρῃ ἐκ θυμὸν ἕληται,
ἢ ὅ γε δουρὶ βαλὼν ἢ ἀπὸ νευρῆφιν ὀιστῷ.   ($\varPhi$ 111–13)[1]

He even knows that it will be at Apollo's hand, for so his
mother has told him ($\varPhi$ 277–8), and he learns from the dying
Hector that it will be by the Scaean Gates at the hands of
Paris and Apollo (X 359–60). Even when Hector is dead the
threat continues, and the ghost of Patroclus tells him that his

---

[1] 'There will be a dawn or an evening or a mid-day when one shall take my
life from me in war, striking me with a spear or with an arrow from the bow-
string.'

fate is to be slain under the walls of Troy (Ψ 80–1). The reiterated menace is so striking that we are surprised that the *Iliad* ends before the death of Achilles. Wilamowitz is so impressed by it that he concludes that the original *Iliad* ended with his death on the day after the death of Hector.[1] He thinks that the present ending from Ψ 257 to Ω 804 is the work of a later poet which superseded the original story of the mutilation of Hector and the death of Achilles. Achilles knows that his fate is coming. The bones of Patroclus are to be kept unburied until his own death. 'Do we not feel how the shadows of death gather ever thicker over the hero's head? Even his heroic strength grows feeble. In the first night after Hector's death he at last falls asleep from weariness with watching the body, but only that the ghost of Patroclus may appear to him in a dream.'[2] The conclusion is that on the next day he tried to take Troy, and was killed in the attempt.

Of the tragic fate awaiting Achilles there is no question. He knows it as well as his mother or Hector knows it. And yet it may be questioned whether the *Iliad* ended quite as Wilamowitz suggests. If such was the real end of the *Iliad*, why was it lost and the present ending substituted? Wilamowitz seems to think that the original end, which included the mutilation of Hector, was too barbarous, and was removed to suit the more sensitive feelings of a later age. Such a motive might well account for the alterations in the treatment of Hector, but it would not account for the change in Achilles' story. That he should himself die would be entirely right and fitting. Why then should it be altered? Such a theory ignores the close relation between the end of our *Iliad* and its beginning. It postulates that the poet of Ω cannot be the poet of the *Achilleid* and therefore of *A*. But *A* and Ω are so closely related that they must be the work of a single man. The first tells of the outbreak of the wrath, the second of its healing. In both, the tragedy of Achilles is not the brief season of his splendour but his uncontrollable temper and the shame to which it brings him. The choice of such a tragedy instead of a more obvious tragedy based on the shortness of his life is indeed remarkable. And it means that

---

[1] *I. und H.*, pp. 68–79.   [2] ib., p. 78.

both books, and the design which depends on them, are the fruit of a single, sensitive morality, of a single creative brain. To detach *Ω* from *A* is not merely to deprive the *Iliad* of an ending which, on Wilamowitz's admission, is probably more beautiful than the original ending, it is to mutilate the whole structure of the story of Achilles, which is sketched in the opening of the poem and worked out in detail in the last books. It is not enough to say that *Ω* is the work of a gifted poet who knew his *Iliad* well. If the poem had ended with the death of Achilles, the tragedy would have been quite different, a tragedy of death and not of moral failure. But the *Iliad* shows that what the poet was most interested in was precisely this moral failure. It is emphasized at every turn, and because *Ω* tells of the healing of the wrath of Achilles it must be the authentic close.

Still the fact remains that Homer emphasizes in words of great pathos the shortness of Achilles' life and the nearness of his doom. That he does so, is no doubt due to the saga. Achilles is the type of the short-lived hero, and the poet, faithful to the tradition, depicts him as such. But in so depicting him he naturally leads us on to expect that Achilles will die, and yet he does not. Here is perhaps a difficulty, which needs some explanation. Homer seems to fall between two stools, his desire to reproduce a faithful version of the saga and his desire to develop his theme of Achilles' wrath. But the apparent awkwardness is due to his wish to keep a surprise for his audience. They knew the story of Achilles and expected the *Iliad* to end with his death. To keep up that illusion Homer often refers to the death, and then in the end he gives them a nobler, quite unexpected ending. But his forecasts of Achilles' death are not mere baits to put off his audience or mere tributes to the authority of the saga. They are not only of great beauty in themselves —the words to Lycaon are among the sublimest in all poetry— but they also enhance the tragedy of Achilles. His foremost tragedy is that he loses his only friend and outrages the laws of god and man, but his story is all the more tragic because of this shadow of doom which lies over him. Because of it he has no time to wait. He hurries from one thing to another, feeling that he has not long to live. There is no time for consideration or for mercy when his life is short. He wants to make the most of it, and he is frustrated first by Agamemnon and then by Hector. He knows he must die soon, and he feels that he is losing something unless he acts at once. His sense of coming doom acts as a spur to his pride, and his pride is his undoing.

The second case is of rather a similar nature. It is claimed that Achilles threatens Hector with worse treatment than he actually gives him, and that this involves some awkwardness and a feeling of anti-climax. It may well be that in the original saga Achilles treated the body of Hector worse than he does in the *Iliad*. Homer says that Achilles devised ἀεικέα ἔργα[1] (X 395) and dragged the body behind his chariot to the Achaean camp. And a little later (Ψ 24) when he laments for Patroclus, the same words are used, with a hint at the wish of Achilles to throw Hector's body to the dogs, and at his subsequent dragging of the body round the tomb of Patroclus. That the poet so understood the ἀεικέα ἔργα is clear from this last case where he recalls the words and says:

$$\text{τοῖο δ' Ἀπόλλων}$$
$$\text{πᾶσαν ἀεικείην ἄπεχε χροῒ φῶτ' ἐλεαίρων} \quad (\Omega \ 18\text{--}20)[2]$$

and two lines further he says:

$$\text{ὡς ὁ μὲν Ἕκτορα δῖον ἀείκιζεν μενεαίνων.} \quad \text{(ib. 22)}[3]$$

Clearly then by ἀεικέα ἔργα he meant the dragging of Hector's body and the unsuccessful attempts to throw it to the dogs. There seems some anti-climax in this, and critics have tried to show that in earlier versions of the *Iliad* Hector was subjected to greater indignities. Professor G. Murray thinks that originally Hector was dragged alive.[4] Certainly some such story survived, and Virgil made use of it when he spoke of Hector as *perque pedes traiectus lora tumentes* (*Aen.* ii. 273). And perhaps there was such a detail in the saga. But in the *Iliad* there is no trace of it. Hector is dead, and as he dies

---

[1] 'Shameless deeds.'
[2] 'From his skin Apollo kept all dishonour away, pitying the man.'
[3] 'So he dishonoured god-like Hector in his anger.'
[4] *Rise of the Greek Epic*, pp. 126-7.

he foretells the death of Achilles. This is so integral a part of the story that it eliminates any possibility of his being dragged alive later. Wilamowitz develops ἀεικέα ἔργα on other lines. He thinks that in the original end of the *Achilleid*, Achilles, after dragging the body to the camp, cut off the head and threw the trunk to the dogs to eat.[1] He bases this view on two main considerations. First, when Achilles prepares to kill Hector he addresses the dead Patroclus and says:

οὔ σε πρὶν κτεριῶ, πρίν γ᾽ Ἕκτορος ἐνθάδ᾽ ἐνεῖκαι
τεύχεα καὶ κεφαλὴν, μεγαθύμου σοῖο γονῆος. (Σ 334–5)

And secondly, he threatens to throw Hector's body to the dogs (Ψ 183 ff.). But neither threat is carried out. Of the first nothing more is said. The second is frustrated by the intervention of Apollo and Aphrodite, who keep off the dogs and miraculously preserve the body. But here Wilamowitz claims that the text is wrong. It gives:

181 δώδεκα μὲν Τρώων μεγαθύμων υἱέας ἐσθλοὺς
τοὺς ἅμα σοὶ πάντας πῦρ ἐσθίει· Ἕκτορα δ᾽ οὔ τι
δώσω Πριαμίδην πυρὶ δαπτέμεν, ἀλλὰ κύνεσσιν.

And he shows that a verb is wanting in 181. An anacoluthon is out of place in a formal address to the dead such as this. He considers that the text has been tampered with. Its original sense was 'Hector I cannot burn, but I will give him worse treatment'. Then the poem went on to say how Achilles took the body and threw it to the dogs. What follows in our *Iliad* is the work of a later poet who wished to save the poem from so barbarous a conclusion.

Such may well have been the story in the original version. Achilles' failure to carry out his threats needs explanation, and something seems wrong in the story as we have it. But not too much weight must be given to the argument based on the corrupt passage Ψ 181 ff., where not the poem but the manuscripts seem to be at fault. In one of the earliest papyri,[2] dating from the fourth century B.C., the passage runs differently and there is no difficulty. The papyrus gives:

δώδεκα μὲν Τρώων μεγαθύμων υἱέας ἐσθλοὺς
τοὺς ἅμα σοὶ πάντας πῦρ ἀμφέπει, Ἕκτορα δ᾽ οὐχί·

---

[1] *I. und H.*, pp. 73–9.   [2] p[12] in T. W. Allen's list.

τόνδε γὰρ οὐ δώσω πυρὶ κάεμεν, ἀλλὰ κύνεσσι
ὠμησταῖς φαγέειν· τόσα γὰρ κακ᾽ ἐμήσατ᾽ Ἀχαιούς.

This shows at least that there were other readings of the
passage early in antiquity, and it makes sense if we take τοὺς
as a demonstrative which contrasts the twelve victims with
Hector. Indeed, so far as sense goes, it may be the correct
text, and if so, Wilamowitz's point breaks down. But still a
serious difficulty remains. Why does Achilles make threats
which he fails to fulfil, although there is nothing to prevent
him fulfilling them? Why does he not cut off Hector's head,
as he has said he will? The explanation lies on the same lines
as that of the threatened death of Achilles. The saga, let us
admit, told of some such mutilation done to Hector, and the
audience expected that Homer would repeat the old horrors.
But he gave them a new and quite different conclusion.
Achilles is prevented by the gods from mutilating Hector's
body. Aphrodite keeps the dogs away and anoints the
corpse with ambrosia to save it from decay, while Apollo
sheds a dark cloud over it in case the sun's beams should
breed worms in it. For Homer's own purpose this preservation was fundamental. If the body was destroyed or mutilated
beyond recognition, the beauty of the ransoming by Priam
would be spoiled. At all costs the body must be saved, and
no doubt this treatment was dictated in the first case by the
thought that the body had to be ransomed later. But by
avoiding the mutilation Homer achieves another success.
He redeems the scene from what must have been an intolerable brutality. The Greeks of his age thought it im-
pious to maltreat the dead, and though Achilles wanted to
throw Hector to the dogs, our feelings are far less outraged
when he fails than they would be if he succeeded. Then
indeed he would be an inhuman monster beyond endurance.
As it is, he is on the verge of inhumanity, but still he is
human. Nor could we tolerate that Hector, whom Homer
has made such a pattern of chivalry, should be treated in
such a way. He has behaved so well in life that it would be
intolerable if in death the gods should abandon him to such
horror.

But in all fairness it must be admitted that Homer is not always equally successful in adapting the saga to his present purpose. In other cases his problem has clearly been similar and he has not solved it with equal success. This is particularly noticeable in certain scenes in *B* and *Γ*, which must take place in the tenth year of the war, but would much more probably have taken place in the first. The three most noticeable cases are the organization and marshalling of the Achaean army in *B* 336 ff., the duel of Paris and Menelaus in *Γ*, and the τειχοσκοπία in *Γ* 121–244.[1] All this would certainly have been more in place in a poem that describes the first year, and yet they are put in here. They must therefore be carefully considered.

In *B* it is perfectly clear that the war is in its tenth year. Agamemnon says that nine years have passed and that the ships' timbers have rotted and their cables decayed (*B* 135). This is emphatic and clear. But soon after this Nestor suggests that the Achaean army must be organized by battalions and companies, and Agamemnon accepts the idea gladly. This we might expect to have been done earlier, but perhaps by itself it may just pass. Then we have a full account of the marshalling of the Achaeans, ending with a review of their forces in the *Catalogue*. The problems presented by the *Catalogue* are so special and complicated that they cannot be considered here, but the whole account of this mobilization smacks of the beginning of war, not of a late stage. It is no matter for wonder that here the critics have found traces of another epic which told of the first years of the war. Why this late organization, and why this marching to battle as if for the first time? The solution must be that Homer is certainly using the saga here, and repeating a traditional account of the first Achaean advance. His motives for using this are clearly important, and must be guessed from the part played by this scene in the poem. And perhaps they were these. The first book has acquainted us only with the Achaean leaders. Of the mass of the fighters we as yet know nothing. We have sooner or later to get acquainted with them, and for this purpose Homer hit on the expedient of incorporating an old

[1] Cf. Van Leeuwen, *Commentationes Homericae*, pp. 17–34.

poem giving the list of the troops who gathered at Aulis. This was not altogether a happy expedient, but it serves its purpose. Henceforward we have an authoritative list of Achaeans and cannot complain that we do not know who any one is. To introduce this catalogue he needed some device, and his device is the simple plan suggested by Nestor of reorganizing the army. Once such a reorganization is mentioned it is easy to give a list of the troops concerned in it. And perhaps he had another motive. The abstention of Achilles had left the Achaeans in a bad position. Their first duty was to see if they could win the war without him, and so after some trouble they decide to do. To win it they must put forward their greatest effort and mobilize every man. This is reasonable and not to be disputed. So there is a natural motive for this advance and the high colours in which Homer paints it. It shows that despite the absence of Achilles the Achaean army is still full of fight and likely to do damage to the Trojans. There is then some excuse for the scene, but the fact remains that it is rather awkwardly constructed and that if Homer had clung less closely to tradition he might have given us something which fitted better with his plot.

The duel of Paris and Menelaus also seems to belong naturally to the beginning of the war. If such a duel were likely to stop the general fighting, then we should expect it to be tried earlier. Only when it failed to produce a satisfactory result would both armies resort to universal war. As the story is told there is no flagrant contradiction, but the time of the duel is odd, and a little later another indecisive duel is to be fought between Hector and Aias in *H*. The position of the duel here may, however, be justified. It introduces Paris, the cause of all the trouble, and it shows us Menelaus in the field, where he cuts a better figure than he did at home. Both these are characters of the first importance, and it is well that we should know them soon. The contrast is brought out most skilfully in the scene that follows, where Helen chides Paris for his cowardice. In this we see the struggle that goes on in Helen's heart, and it is one of the poet's finest flights. The duel is really an introduction to it.

By contrasting the two claimants for Helen Homer makes way for the discord in her, her love of courage and her love for the flighty Paris. Without it that contrast could never have been so well made, and it is essential for the delineation of Helen. We might perhaps add that the duel is necessary in Homer's scheme of the Trojan guilt. It emphasizes the cowardice of Paris, and it leads up to the treacherous action of Pandarus for which Agamemnon prophecies that Troy will be destroyed.

The third case of the τειχοσκοπία is a scene of such beauty that it might almost stand on its own merits and transcend criticism. But as Leaf says, 'it assumes an ignorance on the part of Priam unaccountable, according to prose or logic, after ten years of war'. It is certainly odd that the King of Troy should have waited ten years to ask the names of the chief men beleaguering his city. The scene is so simple that it may well have been part of the tradition, and this may account partly for its inclusion here. But once it was put here it served excellent purposes despite its intrinsic improbability. In the first place it presents the chief personalities on the Achaean side at close view. Hitherto there has been no opportunity for any such review. This scene makes it possible, and from Priam and Helen we hear of the ways and appearance of Agamemnon, Odysseus, Aias, and Idomeneus—certainly a representative selection. And in the second place it develops with great skill the position of Helen. In Troy she is still a stranger, and she feels her guilt and her loneliness. But she is equally severed from her own people, from her first husband's brother, εἴ ποτ' ἔην γε (Γ 180). Her loneliness is made more painful by the end of the scene where she looks for her brothers, Castor and Polydeuces, and cannot find them, not knowing that they are already dead in Lacedaemon.

These three cases show a peculiarity in the methods of Homeric narrative. It is so deeply concerned with the moment and its immediate future that it neglects some features which we regard as essential. It does not often do this, and, when it does, the loss is often well concealed and the gain great. But it is fundamentally a fault, and if we cannot entirely excuse it, we can perhaps explain it. The Homeric audience expected a full and fair share of traditional stories. Perhaps, if they did not get enough, they felt defrauded and blamed the poet. It was his business to produce the familiar traits as well as his new inventions, and at times he could only do so at some cost to his general design. In themselves the scenes have great beauty, and sometimes they are relevant in their immediate context. To the stern eye of criticism they violate the probabilities of time. Perhaps Homer did not mind this. Or perhaps, reciting his story, as he did, in sections, he concentrated on the passage before him and gave it his full attention, not caring vastly whether it entirely agreed with what he had sung on other days, which was by now largely forgotten.

THE SIMILES

IN European literature the simile is so familiar a feature that we do not often trouble about its use and origin. It has justified itself by its intrinsic beauty; it sheds a new light on its subject by comparing it to something in a different order of things. The simile of Milton or Dante is drawn from Virgil, and Virgil drew his from Homer. So what we take for an essential part of poetry has derived life and strength from a single source. It is therefore important to examine Homer's use of the simile, and see from what he derived it and how he employs it. We have seen that in other ways he takes a primitive form and adapts it to his own uses. Can the same be said of the simile? Is it too a survival, put to new uses? Or is it largely his own invention? In most primitive narrative poetry similes are very rare. In the *Song of Roland* for instance they are few and simple. The most adventurous is that which compares the whiteness of Baligant's complexion to that of a flower in summer (l. 3162). Of the full-dress simile there is no trace. The seven similes in *Beowulf* are no more elaborate than this. In the *Kalevala* and in the *Nibelungenlied* they hardly exist. On the other hand they are found at certain great moments in the *Edda* poems. When Gudrun weeps for Sigurd, in the *First Song of Gudrun*, she celebrates his greatness in comparisons:

> So high stood Sigurd over Gjuki's sons
> As the spear-leek over the thirsty grass,
> As the glittering diamond outshines the gold,
> The pale circlet of the chieftain's crown.

This has something akin to the Homeric practice, but the *Edda* poems are more songs than epic. On the whole, early narrative verse seems to eschew the simile, and for obvious reasons.[1] The story has at all costs to be made clear, and the simile of any length tends to distract the listener and break the thread of the narrative. In a song which concentrates

---

[1] In the later French epics and in Layamon's *Brut* similes are quite frequent, but their presence is probably due to imitation of classical models.

on some single aspect of a story there is not the same objection, and perhaps that is why similes are found in the *Edda* poems and not in the early epics. But in Homer we find the simile fully developed, and this is almost unique in early narrative poetry.

The simile has its origin in an identification of one object with another, and traces of this form are not unknown in the *Iliad*. When Thetis rises out of the sea ἠΰτ' ὀμίχλη—like a mist (A 359), or Apollo descends νυκτὶ ἐοικώς—like the night (A 47), or when Hera and Athene walk τρήρωσι πελειάσιν ἴθμαθ' ὁμοῖαι—like shy doves in their gait (E 778), the poet is hardly using a simile.[1] For his audience, and almost for him, Thetis might be seen as the mist, Apollo as the night, and Hera and Athene as birds. Such in the earliest stories they may have been, and such the poet may have meant them for the moment to seem, though a little later they have taken human shape, when Thetis speaks to her son, Apollo shoots his shafts at the Achaeans, and the goddesses take part in the battle. In Homer the identification between the two objects has almost disappeared, but it is the original form of the simile. Two things are not compared, but identified. This identification accounts for the simplest of the genuine similes. In these one object is compared with another, but in such language as the original identifications must have been made. This simple type is common. Aias carries a shield ἠΰτε πύργον— like a tower (Λ 485), and a warrior is βροτολοιγῷ ἶσος Ἄρηϊ— like Ares the bane of men (Λ 295). These are real similes of the simplest kind, like those in the *Song of Roland*. Identity has given place to comparison. They are at the same level of language as metaphor. A thing is compared to something else, but it does not lose its own character in the comparison. Such a use is natural in young and vital speech. Its meaning is seen at once, and it adds to what the poet has to say. It is much the same when he simply uses metaphor without any word of comparison and gives us a phrase like ἅμα δὲ νέφος εἵπετο πεζῶν (Δ 274).[2] Such phrases are so natural and simple that they can hardly be reckoned as poetical devices.

---

[1] Cf. Thomson, *Studies in the Odyssey*, pp. 5–7.
[2] 'And with them followed a cloud of foot-soldiers.'

They can be found wherever language is lively and fond of illustration.

The real simile is developed from this, but it is different. Instead of one simple thing being compared to another, one composite action is compared to another composite action. In other words, there is more than one item in each side of the comparison. Similes of this sort are not common in colloquial speech. They belong essentially to poetry, and especially to that kind of poetry which seeks to illuminate what it is describing by comparing it to something else. At its worst such a comparison adds nothing and is due to a love of decoration for its own sake or to a perverse desire for variety. When Timotheus calls teeth 'white-shining children of the mouth'[1] he does nothing but titillate our appetite for obscurity. Homer's similes aim at illuminating the narrative. Whether they always succeed is perhaps more questionable, but they are always perfectly straightforward and honest. For him the simile is still a living device, no matter what its origins.

It is natural that efforts have been made to trace back Homer's use of the simile, and to try to distinguish earlier and later elements in it. The question is important. If Homer can be shown to use his similes inappositely or not to be master of them, then it is probable that he has taken over the form from predecessors.[2] He may even have taken over stock forms of words and used them without full consideration of their new context. Thus in one place the Myrmidons going to war are compared to wolves tearing a deer to pieces and then slaking their thirst at a fountain (Π 156–63). The simile, though full and beautiful, is not entirely apposite. The Myrmidons are still arming, and therefore to compare them to wolves at work is premature. Still less are they like glutted wolves going to drink. Hunger, not satiety, is their main characteristic. Here Homer seems to have taken a stock simile meant for an army coming home from battle and applied it to an army going out. The point of comparison is of course the fierce temper of the Myrmidons and of the wolves.

---

[1] *Persae*, 102–3. στόματος . . . μαρμαροφεγγεῖς παῖδες.
[2] G. Murray, *The Rise of the Greek Epic*, pp. 245–9. But cf. A Shewan, 'Suspected Flaws in Homeric Similes', *Classical Philology*, vi, 1911, pp. 271–81.

But even this is based on a mistake, as glutted wolves are notorious cowards.[1] Again in another passage Asius compares the waiting Achaeans to wasps waiting in their nests to attack hunters, but he seems to be concerned only with two men, Polypoetes and Leonteus, and the notion of the swarm is out of place (*M* 167–72). In these, and in some other cases, the comparison is often inexact, and one explanation is that these similes belonged, like some repeated lines, to the common stock of epic poets. It is quite true that they are not grotesquely inapposite. The thirst of the Myrmidons for blood is like the wolves' thirst for water, and if we forget the exact context, the waiting Achaeans are like waiting wasps. The similes serve their turn, but they have not the exactness we expect from a poet who is anxious to make his picture clearer. On the other hand their presence is quite explained if they were part of tradition and used to meet a need. It does not, of course, follow that critics are right in blaming Homer for the inexactness of these supposed traditional comparisons. They assume that the simile must be exact at more than one point. In highly developed poetry this is true.[2] When Keats compares the fallen gods to Stonehenge, or Thea's comforting words to Saturn to the 'one gradual solitary gust' amid the dreaming oak-trees, the simile presents several points of comparison and the whole scene is enriched and enlivened. Homer, it is true, is capable of such similes, as when the Greek host led by the two Aiantes is compared to an advancing tempest which drives the shepherd into a cave (*Δ* 275 ff.). But ordinarily he is content with a single point of comparison. If Dante's similes 'make us see more definitely the scene',[3] Homer's make us feel one particular aspect of it. And in this perhaps lies the true explanation of his use of these similes. They emphasize one thing and one thing only, but the thing emphasized is of first importance to the story. The fierce temper of the Myrmidons is like the fierce temper of wolves at work, the angry Achaeans are like angry wasps waiting for their opportunity to attack. Homer lived nearer the beginning of the simile than Dante or Keats and had not fully explored all its possibilities. He

[1] Cf. Leaf, ad loc.   [2] Cf. W. P. Ker, *Form and Style in Poetry*, pp. 254–5.
[3] T. S. Eliot, *Dante*, p. 24.

must not be blamed because he used the form without a full sense of all its possibilities.

The influence of tradition may be seen in certain repeated similes. These are few, and their rarity shows how well Homer freed himself from the shackles of tradition, but they existed and cannot be ignored. Thus the comparison of a stallion leaving his stall and running to the pasturage of mares is used both of Paris and of Hector going to battle (Z 506 ff., O 263 ff.). When Aias is pressed back by the Trojan advance (Λ 548), and when Menelaus leaves the battle to look for Antilochus (P 657) with the news of Patroclus' death, both are compared in the same words to a lion being driven from a steading. When Asius and Patroclus are killed, both fall like a tall tree which is felled to make a ship's timber (N 389–91, Π 482–4). When Ares is wounded by Diomedes, and Poseidon calls on Agamemnon to fight, the voices of both are compared to nine or ten thousand men shouting in battle (E 860, Ξ 148). When such a repetition of similes is found, one of the two is often more appropriate than the other. Aias, pressed hard by Trojans, is more like a retreating lion than Menelaus going to find Antilochus with the news of Patroclus' death. Paris may be more like a stallion galloping after mares than Hector. The agonized cry of the wounded Ares is perhaps more likely to suggest an enormous shout than the encouraging words of Poseidon to Agamemnon. On the other hand the falling tree is appropriate both to Asius and to Patroclus, nor can we see how their deaths could be described without it. The natural conclusion is that in the more inappropriate cases the text and not the poet is to blame, and we can solve the problem by excising the offending similes as the Alexandrian scholars excised them. For this there is much to be said. Excision is a recognized cure in other poets, and we should expect it to be legitimate in Homer, whose text, being older, must have contained many deep-seated corruptions. But perhaps the similes are not entirely inappropriate. Hector runs to battle, like an eager horse. Poseidon, being a god, has a tremendous voice. Menelaus moves slowly because he has bad news and the battle is pressing round him. None of these

cases are sufficiently inapposite to merit wholesale omission.
It follows that here Homer shows the traces of his tradition.
The epic poet learned some similes as he learned other stock-
lines, and, if these were less appropriate in some places than
in others, that was because for the moment he relied more on
his training than on his judgement.

The simile then seems to be part of the epic tradition. Just
as in details of armour he recalls the Mycenean Age and is
clearly drawing on ancient material, so, it has been thought,[1]
in his similes he draws on early material dating back to many
centuries before his own time. Such a world Homer cannot
himself have known and must therefore have taken over from
an earlier tradition. In other words, here are 'relics of the
poetry of the Mycenean Age itself'. This view is attractive,
and, if true, most important for the understanding of Homer's
art. It is based on the indubitable resemblance between some
of the similes and certain scenes depicted in Mycenean art.
The life shown on the dagger-blades from Mycenae and on
the Vaphio cups is very like the scenes described, for instance,
in Π 156 ff., where wolves go to a mountain spring, or P 133 ff.,
where a lion protects its young, or Y 164 ff., where a lion
gathers its courage against hunters. These scenes are sketched
in detail and show a real knowledge of the wild life they
describe, just as the Mycenean artists had a keen eye for
noticing the traits of wild beasts. On the other hand, it is
claimed, there are similes in which no such real knowledge
of wild nature is shown, and these must be imitations or
adaptations of the earlier similes. For instance in Π 352 ff.
wolves raid a herd of lambs or kids, taking them out of the
flock. Here the poet is thought to have no real experience in
his mind, but to be drawing on literary precedents, just as
the artists of late Mycenean and post-Mycenean days looked
for their subjects not to nature but to art, and made mistakes
in consequence. By giving an alternative of lambs or kids
the poet is accused of deserting nature for art, of sacrificing
description for ornament. So too in N 389 when Asius falls
like 'an oak or a poplar or a tall pine' the poet is said to

[1] F. Winter in *Einleitung in die Altertumswissenschaft*, ii (1910), pp. 161–87
Cf. P. Cauer, *Grundfragen*, pp. 472–6.

have no definite picture in his mind. There is then an important distinction between those similes in which the picture is precise and exact, and those in which there is a vagueness caused by the presence of alternatives. Next, the theory maintains, in the same book two descents of goddesses to earth are compared to very different things. In *O* 170 ff. Iris descends like a cold cloud of snow or hail, in *O* 80 ff. Hera descends like thought. Here, too, a difference of date is presumed. And lastly, in the description of Agamemnon, where he is said to have the head and eyes of Zeus, the waist of Ares, the chest of Poseidon (*B* 478–9), it is claimed that so anthropomorphic a picture must be much later than the Mycenean Age when gods were not seen in the likeness of men nor men in the likeness of gods. In other words, the criterion of date provided by this theory is that those similes where nature is faithfully represented date from Mycenean days, but if the description is vague, or if some other subject is found, the simile dates from some later period.

This criterion is worth consideration more than most criteria of date, because similes seem to have been part of the traditional stock-in-trade of the poet, and there certainly is a resemblance between some of the scenes in the similes and some scenes in Mycenean art. Homer has reminiscences of the Mycenean Age in other parts of his poem: so there is no *a priori* objection to his having such in his similes. But there is one grave objection to believing that the similes are a direct heritage from Mycenean art. Elsewhere in the poem Homer describes certain features of art, armour, &c., which may well be Mycenean, but in the similes there is nothing which is incontrovertibly Mycenean. If he had taken over even some of his similes from so remote an antiquity, surely there would have been a trace of life or culture which can only be called Mycenean. But there is none. Instead there are descriptions of nature which are as free as the Mycenean artists could have made them, but nature was probably the same in Homer's day as it was some centuries before, and any lively poet might write of it with accurate understanding without being indebted to an earlier generation which had an understanding similarly lively. But there is a stronger objection to the theory than this. Not only in his similes does Homer avoid mentioning any specifically Mycenean features, he actually describes in many places a world which differs from the rest of his poems and is quite definitely not Mycenean at all. In fact, as the Alexandrian critics noticed, Homer does not mind putting into similes features which he excludes from his narrative.[1] So he speaks of the staining of ivory by a Maeonian or a Carian woman, but elsewhere he hardly makes any mention of either stained ivory or Carians (Δ 142 ff.). In M 421 ff. men quarrel over common land, and such a detail must belong to the poet's own time. In Ψ 712 wrestlers are like the rafters of a house, and the poet can only refer to a gabled roof. In O 679 there is a man who knows how to ride horses, and to vault from one horse to another. With the exception of Odysseus and Diomedes under very peculiar circumstances, the Homeric heroes do not ride horses. In Σ 219 there is a trumpet, which occurs nowhere in the narrative. In Υ 372 the might of Achilles is compared to iron, which is only intelligible if iron is thought of as a metal used for weapons, but in the rest of the poem bronze and not iron is used. In Π 212, walls are made of shaped and closely fitted stones, a style of building not mentioned in the rest of the poem. In each of these cases the world of the similes is not the world of the narrative, and in each the detail described belongs not to the Mycenean Age but to a much later time. The conclusion can only be that while in his narrative Homer maintained a close and consistent archaism, in the similes he allowed himself more rein and freely borrowed from the life he saw about him. It is quite true that he also used images drawn from mythology and from the timeless phenomena of nature, but so far as the similes give any indication of date, they present a civilization later than that of the Mycenean Age. So, too, Milton in his similes draws not only on nature and classical mythology, but also on novelties of more recent days, such as the telescope of Galileo, and the naked American found by Columbus.

[1] Scholia on O 679 (riding), Σ 219 (trumpet), Φ 362 (boiling meat), cf. A. Platt, 'Homer's Similes', *Journal of Philology*, xxiv, 1896, pp. 28–38.

The simile then does not seem to be a very ancient form, though it belonged to the epic tradition before Homer. And when we examine the case more closely, it will be seen that Homer is nearly always master of the simile and uses it with deliberate effect. It has often been noticed that he uses similes much more in some books than in others. In *A* there is no simile longer than one line, but in *B* there are nine long similes; in *E* there are seventeen and in *Z* only two. This uneven distribution has led to much misunderstanding, and to misguided views of authorship and date of composition. For instance, it has been thought that the fewer the similes, the earlier must be the book.[1] This theory in itself is open to suspicion, as it would mean that *Paradise Regained* is earlier than *Paradise Lost*, or that the *Odyssey* is earlier than the *Iliad*, and the *Hymn to Demeter* earlier than both.[2] And for the *Iliad* itself the view contradicts other views held by its adherents. For it makes *A*, which is thought to have been written to hold the later books together, earlier than they are. Clearly the presence or absence of similes is no test of date in a poetry so homogeneous as the epic. It might, however, seem more reasonable to use this presence or absence as a test of different authorship. A poet may be given to similes or he may abhor them, and if in a great mass of poetry like the *Iliad*, some parts abound in similes while others eschew them, there is some show of reason in claiming that the different sections are the work of different authors. Thus Wilamowitz notes it as characteristic of the author of *A* that, being interested in individuals and not in crowds, he has no need of similes,[3] while the small epic *ΓΔΕ*, being concerned with crowds, shows a fondness for them.[4] His theory rests on the certain fact that similes are much commoner in some books than in others. From this he deduces that the different sections come from different hands. This assumes that any poet uses similes, if at all, regularly throughout his work. But this is not only inherently improbable, it is contradicted by other evidence. Virgil, for instance, in the *Aeneid* uses one simile

---

[1] Bethe, *Homer*, i, p. 31, and p. 342.
[2] Wilamowitz, *I. und H.*, p. 258.
[3] ib., p. 258.   [4] ib., p. 297.

only in Book iii and fifteen in Book xii. Here then we should assume a difference of authorship. Even in the *Iliad* the theory proves awkward in detail. The last book, Ω, which Wilamowitz regards as a late, alternative ending, has only four similes and should therefore be classed rather with A than apart from it. So despite the great ingenuity and authority with which this theory has been advanced, it does not suit the facts, and we must find some other explanation of the irregular placing of similes in the *Iliad*.

The clue is to be found in their absence from a book like A, where there is no fighting, and their presence in a book like E, where there is hardly anything but fighting. If we omit for convenience all the minor similes of three or four words, we find that some 164 similes occur in scenes of battle, while only 38 occur in other scenes. This gives us the kernel of Homer's practice. He uses similes more often in fighting scenes, because fighting scenes have a tendency to become monotonous and therefore need variation. So, too, *Aeneid* iii, which is not concerned with fighting, has only one simile, while *Aeneid* xii, which is, has fifteen. It explains, too, why the *Odyssey* has far fewer similes than the *Iliad*. The *Iliad* with its long battles needs variety, but the *Odyssey* has so varied a plot that it needs much less help of this kind. Homer's audience must have begun to lose interest in the mere details of fighting and to have demanded relaxation. In this they differed from the Normans who listened to the *Song of Roland* and could find interest in its uninterrupted accounts of battle.

The distribution of similes points to a poet who knew his business and his audience, and this becomes clearer if we examine the principles on which Homer places his similes. So far from a haphazard scattering, we find a deliberate use of them to mark pauses and changes in the action. Thus he introduces a new phase of narrative by a simile. When the adventures of Diomedes begin, we are told that the fire on his head is like the bright star of autumn (E 5). When Hector and Paris go out to join the Trojans, they come like a breeze to tired sailors (H 4–6). The embassy to Achilles begins with the Achaeans being divided in mind like a sea driven by contrary winds (*I* 4–7). The fatal adventure of Patroclus begins with his tears falling like a stream from a rock (*II* 3–4). The last duel of Hector and Achilles is heralded by the flight of the Trojans like frightened fawns (*X* 1). Even inside the main sections, similes mark the introduction of new turns in a single stretch of narrative. This can be seen clearly in the ἀριστεῖα of Diomedes. Before he meets Pandarus he is like a swollen river (*E* 87–92). When the Trojans begin to rally after his attacks, they are white with dust like a threshing floor (*E* 499–502). When Hera and Athene intervene in the battle, they are like doves and the Achaeans are like lions or boars (*E* 778–83).

In the same way similes are often used to end scenes both large and small. The adventure of Diomedes ends with the healing of Ares by Paeon, when his drying blood is compared to milk congealing (*E* 902–3). The first section of Achilles' warfare after his wrath ends by comparing him to a devouring fire and to oxen treading corn (*Y* 490–7). Hector's first attack on the Achaeans ends with his watch-fires like the stars round the moon (*Θ* 555–9). The simile, by heightening the effect, prepares for events to come or closes a chapter of events related.

A similar desire to mark a pause or to make an emphasis can be seen in those passages where Homer accumulates similes. In *B* 455 ff. the advancing Achaeans are compared successively to fire, birds, and flies, and immediately afterwards we are told that their leaders sort them out as a herdsman sorts his goats, and that Agamemnon is like the bull in the herd. The three similes which come first and describe the advance have each a separate import. The fire gives the glitter of their armour, the birds their noise and number, the flies the impetus of their advance. The addition of the next two serves a different purpose. They help, in combination with the first three, to mark the occasion as one of great brilliance and importance. The occasion is, for the *Iliad* at least, the first marshalling of the Achaean host. Hitherto we have only had personalities on the scene, now we have a whole army. And it is, moreover, the prelude to the battle which is to absorb so much of the poem. Such an occasion needs emphasis, and it gets it from this rich accumulation. So, too, at other crises of the poem Homer marks the importance by a similar accumulation. In Δ 422 ff. where the two hostile armies first meet we have three similes in thirty lines; the first describes the advancing Achaeans as waves breaking on a promontory, the second the Trojans as ewes in a rich man's stable, the third the meeting of the two armies as the meeting of two mountain torrents in a dell. The next crisis marked in this way is in P 722 ff. where the fighting reaches its climax before the intervention of Achilles. Here there are no less than five similes in the account of the fighting over the body of Patroclus. In such a blaze of splendour ends the last of the large battle scenes of the *Iliad*. Thenceforward we are concerned with Achilles and his personal achievements, not with the clash of great armies. And we are prepared for the change by this heaping on of illustrations just before we see Achilles hearing the news of Patroclus' death as he sits in his tent. Homer, then, accumulates similes for a purpose, to mark some important crisis in the action, and especially in the action of armies, whose massive and disordered movements are best conveyed through figures and comparisons.

In other places Homer uses more than one simile because he wishes to emphasize two different aspects of a single scene, or to point a sudden change or contrast. In Λ 545 ff. Aias is slowly retiring before the Trojan onset. He retires obstinately and unwillingly, and he is compared first to a lion kept out of an ox-steading by men and dogs, and then, most unexpectedly, to an ass strayed into a barley-field whom boys cannot move with their sticks. The juxtaposition of the two comparisons is surprising but brilliantly successful. The first shows the heroic, lion-like courage of Aias, which refuses to admit defeat, and the second shows that his obstinacy lacks something of intelligence, which is true of Aias as Homer delineates him. Compared with the other Achaeans he is certainly rather stupid, and by the device of two similes Homer shows that his courage and stupidity were closely interwoven and both essential to his character. Again when Sarpedon is killed by Patroclus (Π 477 ff.) his death is described in two similes. In the first he is compared to a tall tree cut down to be a ship's timber, and in the second to a great bull slaughtered among his cows by a lion. Both comparisons are perfectly apt. The first gives the fall of this tall, graceful young man, and the second shows that he too was a mighty warrior who fell fighting for his own people. The combination of the two aspects could not have been done better. Or again when Hector leads an attack on the Achaeans and is himself foremost in the fighting, he is compared first to a huntsman urging on his dogs and then to a storm falling on the sea (*Λ* 292–8). In a different way Homer uses two similes in close succession to emphasize a sudden change in behaviour. In *M* 130 ff. the guardians of the Achaean camp, Polypoetes and Leonteus, are compared to tall, deep-rooted oaks withstanding the wind and the rain. As such they resist the attack of Asius, but when the danger comes too near, they rush out and are like wild boars surprised by hunters in their lair. The change of action is so violent that it needs a pair of contrasted similes to do it justice.

So, too, Dante describes the movement of the carnal sinners in the fiery wind by two successive similes.[1] He sees them first as a troop of starlings in the cold season, and then as a long line of cranes chanting their lays. The first simile gives his first vision of them, and the second their appearance as they draw nearer and their lamentations can be heard. His method is substantially not different from Homer's.

The similes then are placed by a man who knew their use, and argue that the poet used them because of the effects with which they provided him. So it seems reasonable to pursue the inquiry farther and to examine the similes themselves. The first point that emerges is that though they are complete in themselves and often of astonishing beauty, they do not provide comparisons so exact as we find in the sophisticated art of Shakespeare or Milton. Their aim is not to provide a series of points in which one thing can be compared to another, but to stress a single common characteristic. This done, the poet follows his fancy and develops the picture without much care for his reason for using it. The blood on

---

[1] *Inferno*, Canto V, ll. 40–98.

the white flesh of Menelaus is just like the scarlet stain put on
an ivory bridle, but it adds nothing to the comparison to say
that the bridle is a king's treasure and desired by many
charioteers (Δ 141–5). The stones thrown by the Achaeans
and Trojans are just like a fall of snow in winter, but the
comparison is lost when we are told that the snow is stopped
by the advance of the waves on the shore (M 278–86). The
normal aim of the simile is to compare one single aspect and
no more. The point of comparison is clear at once, and then
the poet considers himself free to add to the picture. But in
some cases we find Homer reaching towards a further
development of the simile in which more than one detail has
significance. The Achaeans are attacking, but their attack
is suddenly stopped by the appearance of Hector. So, too,
dogs and huntsmen attack a stag or a wild boar in its lair and
are suddenly stopped by the appearance of a lion. Here
there is a double comparison. The attacking Achaeans are
like huntsmen and the sudden appearance of Hector is like
that of a lion. A complicated picture is exactly paralleled by
the scene in the simile (O 271–6). Or again Antilochus tries
to snatch the armour off the dead Melanippus, but Hector
appears and Antilochus retires like a beast with an evil
conscience which retires before men come, whose dog it has
slain (O 586). Here the comparison picks up not only the
sudden retreat of Antilochus but his feelings as well. In
these cases Homer is beginning to use the simile as Shakespeare used it when he compared a lovelorn woman to
Patience on a monument.

Homer's similes then are simple, but masterly. Their influence through Virgil has affected the subsequent history
of European poetry, and this is not surprising. They are
so varied and delightful, so complete in themselves, so apt
and vivid, that they hardly ever fail to heighten the narrative
and to give pleasure for their own sake. To believe that
Homer inherited them all from his predecessors is quite
to misunderstand the nature of a poetic tradition, which can
give rules and devices but not inspiration. They are in most
cases created by the poet himself from the world he saw
about him, and they show how wide his vision was, and how

the strict heroic narrative limited its scope. In them we see his sympathy with humble people unlike his great princes, with the mother who wards flies off her child (Δ 130 ff.), the reapers in the barley (Λ 67 ff.), the child with his sand-castle (O 362 ff.), the fisherman with his line and hook (Π 406 ff.), the woman working at her wool to save her children from poverty (M 433 ff.). They show too his extraordinary eye and ear for natural sounds and sights, for the cry of the birds on the Cayster (B 459 ff.), the wind bellowing into a sail (O 627), the poppy broken by the rain (Θ 306), the ass breaking into the field (Λ 557 ff.), the wasps waiting for wayfarers (M 167 ff.). No one has written better of a snow-storm (M 278 ff.), or of waves breaking on a rocky headland (Δ 422 ff.). He wrote of the world about him as he had seen and heard it. So his descriptions are full of accurate observa-tion and loving detail. His genius compelled him to write of the heroic past and to it he devoted his majestic powers, but he knew too of the immediate present, and this he cele-brated in his similes, spending his great tenderness and love of simple things in these adornments for his heroic tale.

VII

THE LANGUAGE

WE may perhaps never know the original form in which the *Iliad* was composed. In our editions we possess substantially the text which the Alexandrian scholars reconstituted from a great mass of manuscripts after learned and acute examination. But between them and Homer lay a gap of several centuries, in which the text can only have been altered. As the Greek language developed, it was only natural that the language of the *Iliad* should be subjected to changes. So, too, Milton's spelling, so vital to his metre and sense, was accommodated to the varying tastes of the eighteenth and nineteenth centuries. That our text is not exactly what Homer composed is certain. The question is whether it is vastly different or differs only in small points, whether the alterations are superficial as in our texts of Milton, or fundamental as in the later *remaniements* of the *Song of Roland*. Fortunately it is fairly certain that the changes are mostly superficial and may to some extent be detected and removed. The *Iliad* was more a sacred than a popular book. It was vastly well known and commonly quoted, but the dignity in which it was held guaranteed some security for the text and saved it from any complete rewriting. It suffered from considerable alteration on the surface, and in particular from the substitution of Attic for other forms.[1] This was only natural, as Attica was the home of Homeric recitation and the centre of the Greek book trade. But the intrusion of Attic forms can on the whole be detected by the evidence provided by metre. When they spoil the scansion by introducing unmetrical forms or overweighting the line with spondees, we can with confidence restore some more metrical word.[2] In other places the text has been corrupted because Homer used an old word whose meaning was lost and in whose place a substitute was admitted. Even this can often be detected. Modern philology is sometimes better informed

---

[1] Cf. J. Wackernagel, *Sprachliche Untersuchungen zu Homer.*
[2] P. Cauer, *Grundfragen der Homerkritik*, pp. 105 ff.

than ancient and finds a solution where the Athenians and Alexandrians failed.[1] By removing these superficial corruptions we can get a good idea of what Homer wrote. Our knowledge is far from accurate, but on the whole it presents us with the main features of the Homeric text as it must have been before these corruptions assailed it. And such a text must be the basis of any consideration of Homeric language. We must remove the metrical anomalies and the corrupt words, and take the rest as what Homer composed.

The language of the *Iliad* so reconstituted, is the very reverse of primitive. In other ways Homer recalls the art of early epics in western Europe, but his language is utterly dissimilar. Of the ordinary devices of primitive poetical language he shows not a trace. He relies little on alliteration and not at all on periphrasis. His language is simple and clear where most early poetry is contorted and pretentious. There is no mood which he cannot express, no technicality which defies the resources of his verse. His vocabulary is as copious as Shakespeare's, his expression as limpid as Racine's. Though he avoids the periodic structure, and never attempts a correlation of clauses such as Virgil attempted, he never falls into childishness or incompetence. His language is entirely adequate to his needs, and expresses in majestic and lucid words just what he wants it to express. The Homeric style is as great a triumph of the Greek genius as the style of Sophocles. Its syntax is simpler, its nuance less subtle, but when we compare the two poets, we feel that the difference is not between the beginner and the accomplished master, but between one temperament and another. Sophocles had behind him some three centuries of great poetry, from which he was not ashamed to learn. The question that concerns us is whether Homer drew on some similar tradition—whether we can discern in his style any different elements which went to its making.

Homer's language is not primitive, but in some ways it is simple. His syntax, in particular, is more elastic than that of later Greek poetry. He preserves uses which later fell into desuetude. For him the optative still has the force of the

[1] P. Cauer, *Grundfragen der Homerkritik*, pp. 105 ff. and G. Murray, *Rise of the Greek Epic*, pp. 346–7.

remote future, the subordinate moods of the aorist keep their past sense, the article is often demonstrative. Such uses are earlier than most Greek poetry, and they survive vitally in Homer. In other ways he employs a speech which has not yet settled to fixed forms and uses. He makes little distinction between the subjunctive and the future indicative, he is not tied by later rules for the constructions with πρίν or the concordance of moods, he allows himself some latitude in his conditional sentences. This inexactness of function is natural in speech which is still finding itself. The growth of a language means a stricter differentiation of use and the stiffening of grammar, such as we find in fifth-century Attic. Nor are the rules relaxed until the language decays. When Attic passes into the κοινή, something of the early elasticity is regained, but between the two periods lies the age of correct grammar and exact usage. Homer's language has the simplicity and elasticity of young speech. He can say the same thing in many ways because he is not unduly hampered by rules or the complications which time adds to syntax. Nor need he strain after new modes of expression. The words are young and can still be used freely without seeming trite or trivial. The advantages of an immature language are many and various, and they all help the creation of fresh, living poetry. But normally such speech has its disadvantages too. Being drawn from a language meant for everyday affairs it is not well suited for the metrical expression of ideas which are at all out of the common. When Dante formed his *dolce stil nuovo* on the Tuscan dialect of his own time, he was able to emancipate his poem from the burden of weariness which hung over medieval Latin, and to write of simple and profound things in a language of unmatched freshness and power. But when he had to expound his philosophy or even to elaborate some complicated point of geography or astronomy, the resources of his speech were not sufficient for his needs and he fell into obscurity. So, too, the Elizabethans, glorying in a language of unsurpassed vitality, too often lapsed into bombast when they assailed themes more complicated than their usual wont. In Homer we should expect some such price to be paid for the elasticity and adaptability of his speech. But the miracle is that he never falls into obscurity or pretentiousness. Pindar, who owes so much to him,[1] never quite mastered the secret of clarity and fell sometimes into rodomontade and ambiguity, but for this he could not lay the blame on Homer. The Homeric style shows no sign of difficulty anywhere. A complicated question of psychology or an unexpected technicality is mastered with the same ease as the simplest narrative. A style so adequate is indeed astonishing in a language which has not reached its prime, and Homer's achievement becomes the more remarkable when we remember how even so great a poet as Ennius was often frustrated by the intractability of early Latin. So complete is Homer's mastery of speech that he cannot in any sense be called primitive, he can hardly be called a pioneer. The men who provided him with his themes and methods of narration must have contributed also in no small degree to the language which he used. In this as in other ways he recalls Chaucer, who though he was the maker of modern English, was vastly helped in his work by the long tradition of the French *Chansons de Geste*. From them he borrowed many of his words and rhythms, and from them he inherited a confidence that the poet could say anything that he wanted in verse.

The parallel case of Chaucer might well warn us against any light belief that the language of Homer was ever a spoken tongue. Chaucer used the English dialect of the East Midlands into which Wycliffe translated the Bible, but he crossed it with a French stock, and the result, though it lies at the root of modern English, was not in origin anything but an artificially created language. In Homer's case, however, attempts have been made to show that the language which he wrote was the language he spoke and heard in his own island of Chios.[2] In historic times the language of Chios was Ionic with a strong admixture of Aeolic forms. In inscriptions otherwise in the dialect of Herodotus, we find forms like πρήξοισιν and τεσσερακόντων.[3] So, too, the language of

---

[1] Cf. H. Schultz, *de Elocutionis Pindari colore epico*, Göttingen, 1905.
[2] T. W. Allen, *Homer*, p. 103 ff.
[3] E. Schwyzer, *Dial. Graec. exempla*, 688 A 16 ib. c. 14.

Homer is fundamentally Ionic with an admixture of Aeolic. From this it is deduced that the language of Homer is Chian in an early stage. This theory has great advantages. It connects the Homeric poems with Chios, the best authenticated of Homer's many birthplaces. It solves at one blow the difficult relation of Ionic and Aeolic in the poems. It releases us from any further obligation to inquire into the origin of Homeric Greek by limiting it in time and place to the Chian of Homer's day. But unfortunately the whole theory that Homer's Greek is Chian rests on a grave misunderstanding. Whatever its origins, Homeric Greek was not a spoken language. It is too rich and too artificial to have been an ordinary vernacular. The normal test of a homogeneous dialect is that it has one word for a thing and one word only. Words which at first sight appear to be synonyms have in reality slight differences of meaning. For instance, in the Lesbian of Sappho χθών means 'earth' as opposed to sea, while γᾶ means 'earth' in the wider sense including both land and sea.[1] The Homeric poems show no such strictness of use or poverty of vocabulary. They abound in synonyms. Where Lesbian, for instance, has one word for 'house', δόμος, Homer provides at least four, δόμος, δῶμα, οἶκος, and οἰκία. This richness of alternatives can be seen in many other cases and is in itself ample evidence that Homeric Greek was never spoken. We have only to contrast it with the vernacular poems of Sappho and Corinna to see how vastly richer in alternative words it is than they are. Homer too employs different forms of what is virtually the same word. He gives five forms of the infinitive 'to be', in εἶναι, ἔμεναι, ἔμμεναι, ἔμεν, and ἔμμεν. All five cannot have existed in the same dialect, as εἶναι is for ἔμναι, itself a contracted form of ἔμμεναι, while ἔμεν is probably a shortened form of ἔμεναι, itself a variant made metri causâ for ἔμμεναι.[2] It is inconceivable that all these varieties existed at the same time in a single dialect, even if the dialect was mixed like Chian. This variety of forms can be seen in other ways. Among participles we find ὁρῶν as well as ὁρόων, κεκλήγοντες as well as κεκληγῶτες.

---

[1] Cf. E. Lobel, Ἀλκαίου Μέλη, pp. xviii ff., and p. xxxv.
[2] J. Van Leeuwen, Enchiridion dictionis epicae, pp. 247 ff.

In verbs compounded with prepositions we find the same word compounded both with and without apocope. We find καταθνήσκων and κάτθανε, κατέβαλλε and κάββαλε and many other like cases. In the dative plural of nouns there is a like variety. We find ποσί, ποσσί, and πόδεσσι, κυσί and κύνεσσι. These examples might well be multiplied, but for the present it is enough to notice their existence. They are the final argument against the language of Homer being a spoken dialect.

We are led then to conclude that Homer's language was never spoken. It must be an artificial language, used only for literature and created for the purpose. If so, it resembles the language of most Greek poetry. The tragedians employed vocabularies far greater than any provided by the spoken Attic of their time. They culled words from Homer, from other dialects, even from foreign languages like Persian.[1] Other words, notably compounds, they invented with a freedom denied to ordinary prose or conversation. How strange some of these were can be seen from the comic uses to which Aristophanes puts them in his burlesque of the tragic style. So, too, the language of Shakespeare was drawn from many sources. If he did not invent as Spenser and Chatterton invented, he found words everywhere, in old plays, in foreign languages, in adaptations from ancient tongues, in the technical vocabularies of the learned professions. The result is a bewildering variety of words and synonyms. Few poets in Greece or in England have been content to follow Wordsworth's advice and write in the ordinary speech of their time. Such self-conscious simplicity usually comes in the maturity of a literature when poetical language is becoming conventional. Some iambic passages of Euripides, the verse of Racine or of Wordsworth, have much in common with the spoken language of their age, but their simplicity is the result of artifice and even of sophistication. In the heyday of a literature such simplicity is not often found. The poet, glorying in the vast possibilities of words, feels no need to simplify. This is particularly true of poets who write for aristocratic audiences trained to the demands

[1] Cf. A. Meillet, *Aperçu d'une Histoire de la Langue Grecque*, pp. 153-7.

and difficulties of literature. Pindar never wrote in his own
Boeotian, and even the author of *Beowulf* kept to his peri-
phrastic style because his Anglo-Saxon audience knew the
conventions and could understand what he meant. To do
otherwise was to fail in the dignity of a poet. So, too, with
Homer. His language is a poetical language, made of many
elements and intended for men who were used to listening to
poetry and did not expect it to be like everyday talk. But even
if Homer's language is artificial, we have still to decide from
what sources it was formed, and that is an inquiry of particular difficulty. The evidence is hard to interpret, and the
absence of pre-Homeric poetry makes dogmatism impossible,
but on the whole some certainty can be reached.

The Greeks considered that Homer wrote in Ionic, the
dialect of the central portions of the western seaboard of Asia
Minor. They qualified their opinion by calling it Old Ionic
—ἡ ἀρχαία 'Ιάς.[1] The aberrations from Ionic are duly noted
in the scholia, but on the whole they are neglected in any
ancient theory of Homer's language. It was enough for
ancient critics that the bulk of the poem was in Ionic
sufficiently like the language of Herodotus and Hippocrates
to be recognizable as an older branch of the same dialect.
This view, simple as it is, stresses one important side of the
question. The Homeric poems are unquestionably more
Ionic than they are anything else. In the mass of their in-
flections and word-formations they reveal a language which
is recognizably like the Greek of Herodotus. But at this
point the real problem begins. The bulk of the *Iliad* may be
Old Ionic, but there are in it many words and forms which
are not Ionic in any form that we know, but existed in other
historical dialects. This admixture did not entirely escape
the notice of ancient scholars. With sedulous care they
marked the non-Ionic forms and attached other labels to
them. They even attempted to explain the anomaly, saying
that Homer must have travelled all over Greece and gathered
words from the different dialects.[2] Dio Chrysostom noticed

[1] Cf. T. W. Allen, *Homer*, p. 99.
[2] Ps. Plutarch, *Vit. Homeri*, ii, 8. Cf. Kleeman, *Vocabula Homerica in Graecorum dialectis servata*. Colmar, 1876.

that he spoke now in Aeolic, now in Doric and in Ionic, now
Διαστί—in the language of Zeus.[1] Alexandrian scholars
noted with care the fundamental peculiarity of the Homeric
style—the presence in it of Aeolic forms by the side of Ionic.
Aeolic is known to us from the Lesbian vernacular poems
of Sappho and Alcaeus, from inscriptions dating back to the
fifth century, and from a number of glosses preserved in the
scholia and lexicographers. From this emerges the fact that
in historic times Lesbian and, to some extent, Thessalian,
preserved many forms used by Homer. These forms differed
from their Ionic counterparts which are also found in Homer.
The conjunction of the two sets of words and forms in a single
poem is remarkable. Ionic and Aeolic are not closely connected dialects. The distinction between them dates back
before the colonization of Asia Minor, and originally Ionic
was the speech of Attica, Megara, and Epidaurus,[2] while
Aeolic was the speech of Thessaly. They are both descendants
of a common Greek stock, but they were early separated and
differentiated. It is out of the question that Homer's language
belongs to a period before the two dialects had attained
separate characters. Their separation must date back before
the movements across the Aegean at the end of the Mycenean
Age, and Homer is not so ancient as that. When he wrote, the
two dialects must have existed for some centuries as distinct
and highly different branches of Greek speech. What then
are they doing together in the *Iliad*?

In the first place, it is quite clear that many of these Aeolic
words scan where their Ionic equivalents would not, and
consequently we find Aeolic and Ionic forms used as metre
requires. For instance, among patronymics we have the Aeolic
Τελαμώνιος, Κρόνιος, Νηλήϊος, Καπανήϊος, and the Ionic Τελα-
μωνιάδης, Κρονίδης, Νηληϊάδης, Καπανηϊάδης; Aeolic forms like
πίσυρες and πολυπάμων are used as well as the Ionic τέσσαρες
and πολυκτήμων. The apocope of prepositions is used or avoided
according as it suited the poet to follow the Aeolic or the Ionic
practice. Again, Aeolic words are used where metre makes
the Ionic equivalent impossible, and we find ἱππότα instead of

[1] Dio Chrys., xi. 23.
[2] Strabo ix. 392; Paus. ii. 26. 2; Hdt. i. 56; Thuc. vi. 82, vii. 57.

ἱππότης but both κυανοχαῖτα and κυανοχαίτης. So far metre might explain the use of the two dialects. Aeolic was called in to help when Ionic proved recalcitrant. But this does not explain many other of the Aeolic forms. In many places they survive in the text when the Ionic equivalent would have scanned just as well. Thus Homer sometimes preserves the short α where Ionic would have had ε, and we get ὕπαιθα, ἀρίγνωτος, ἀριδείκετος, ἀριπρεπής, ἐπασσύτεροι, though the Ionic form would have had the same scansion, and in similar words we actually find the Ionic form in ἐριβρεμέτης, ἐριβῶλαξ, ἐριούνιος, &c. So, too, Aeolic keeps a long α where Ionic uses η, and in this too Homer is inconsistent. His normal use is the Ionic, but we find λαός, ὁρᾶτο, Μαχάων. This peculiarity was noticed in antiquity, and two reputable writers, Dicaearchus and Zopyrus of Magnesia, said that Homer should be read in the Aeolic dialect.[1] This view is interesting, as it shows that the difference between the two dialects was largely one of pronunciation. A change of voice could change the dialect. There is undoubtedly truth in this, and some Greek poetry was quoted now in one dialect, now in another. For instance, one of the few surviving lines of the *Little Iliad* is quoted in an Aeolic version by Clement of Alexandria[2] as:

νὺξ μὲν ἔην μεσάτα, λαμπρὰ δ᾽ ἐπέτελλε σελάνα

and in an Ionic version by other writers:[3]

νὺξ μὲν ἔην μέσση, λαμπρὴ δ᾽ ἐπέτελλε σελήνη.

But Homer's case is different from this. We have no proved example of any single line being quoted variously in the two dialects, and we find instead a certain consistency of usage. Thus we always have λαός and never ληός, always τιμή and never τιμά. Nor does mere change of the reciter's accent account for those Aeolic forms which differ metrically from their Ionic equivalents. φῆρες might be read at choice for θῆρες, but not πολυπάμων for πολυκτήμων. Mere change of pronunciation would not suit all the cases, and even if it

---

[1] Osann., *An. Rom.*, p. 5 Τὴν δὲ ποίησιν ἀναγιγνώσκεσθαι ἀξιοῖ Ζώπυρος ὁ Μάγνης Αἰολίδι διαλέκτῳ, τὸ δ᾽ αὐτὸ καὶ Δικαίαρχος.

[2] i. 21, 104.   [3] Schol. Lycophron, 344; Tzetzes, *Post. Hom.*, 720, 773.

would, the problem would still be unsolved. What could we make of a language which could be made one or the other of two quite different dialects at will?

The problem then is highly complicated; but in the last half-century a popular theory has held the field in different forms. This theory, put forward by Fick in 1883,[1] held that the Homeric poems were originally written in Aeolic but were later translated into Ionic. With the translation came expansion. This theory has been accepted with modifications by F. Bechtel[2] and C. Robert[3] and still has some popularity. Opinions may differ as to the methods and extent of the translation, but in general it is still commonly held that the *Iliad* was originally Aeolic and later 'taken over' into Ionic. The best argument for the view is the existence of certain forms in the poems which belong to no known dialect, but look like artificial forms made to translate an Aeolic original when the Ionic equivalent would not scan. Thus the Aeolic κεκλήγοντες had to be translated into the invented form κεκληγῶτες because the Ionic κεκληγότες would not fit into the verse. But κεκληγῶτες is an isolated case and not too much must be based on it. Nor is it clear why the translators, who took such pains with κεκλήγοντες, should have left Aeolic forms which could be translated without any loss to the metre like φῆρες or ἐρεβεννός or λαός. Still less is it clear why the poet should have avoided certain Ionic forms and preferred an artificial equivalent of no known origin. For instance Ionic verbs in -εω are commonly written as verbs in -οω. We find not ὁρέω but ὁρόω, and many others like it. Moreover these verbs have o lengthened into ω after o in the present participle, &c., so that we get unreal forms like ὁρόωντες when the Ionic ὁρέοντες would scan just as well. Here surely was a case for the Ionic form, but the Ionic form is sacrificed to a form which seems to occur nowhere except perhaps once on a Chian inscription.[4] Fick's theory assumed that the Aeolisms occurred only in certain books, and this assumption lies behind Carl Robert's elaborate dissection

---

[1] *Die homerische Odysee in ihrer ursprünglichen Sprachform wiederhergestellt.*
[2] *Die Vocalcontraction bei Homer.*   [3] *Studien zur Ilias*, p. 74, pp. 258 ff.
[4] Schwyzer, 693. 14, ·κοπρεόων.

of the *Iliad*. For them there were certain books where the Aeolic element was particularly noticeable, and Fick tried to translate these back into the original Aeolic. His translation is not a success, and it does violence both to the text and to the Aeolic dialect. Nor does his assumption seem to be true that some books are more Aeolic than others. For instance *K*, the most derided and least 'original' of books, has ten dative plurals in -εσσι, ten infinitives in -μεναι, to say nothing of forms like ἄμμι and ἄμμε, ὕμμιν and ὕμμε. In *Ψ* the proportion of Aeolic forms is even higher, and this book too has been gravely suspected, and lies outside almost every *Ur-Ilias* which scholars have constructed. The proportion of Aeolic forms in these books is as great as in *A*, which Fick and Bechtel agree to have been originally Aeolic. And indeed, if we examine the statistics, we shall see that no single book is much more Aeolic than any other. The Aeolic forms are not only deeply embedded, they are scattered all over the poems and forbid analysis into strata by their presence or absence.

The conclusion to be drawn from this is that the language of the *Iliad* is much more homogeneous than some critics have supposed. It is extremely complicated, but the problem of its complication is not solved by adding labels of 'late' and 'early'. There rests, however, an alternative view that the existence of different dialects is due not to the poem being originally Aeolic and later Ionic but to the poet using words in the different dialects of his time.[1] This theory has one great advantage. It explains why in the different books the proportion of Aeolic and Ionic words is maintained—the poet used his own poetical vocabulary and used it consistently. It can claim the authority of parallel cases where single poems combine different dialects and even languages. *Beowulf*, though largely written in Northumbrian, has a considerable admixture of Mercian and even of Kentish words. Chaucer wrote a language formed of the English of the East Midlands and of medieval French. The reason for this mixture in these cases is clear enough. Chaucer wrote for a class who knew both English and French, and for whom his mixed language was intelligible. But it was essentially his

[1] Cf. J. B. Bury, in *Cambridge Ancient History*, ii, pp. 509–10.

own creation. His predecessors wrote in the Anglo-Saxon
tradition, but he created a new language for English verse.
If we press the analogy, it would follow that Homer lived in a
world where different dialects, though existing separately,
impinged on each other and were mutually intelligible. Out
of this situation Homer or his predecessors created a poetical
speech.

Such was probably the origin of the Homeric language,
but such a theory needs more explanation and proof before
it can be accepted. The chief assumption in it is the existence
of a society which was not self-sufficient like the Lesbian
society of Sappho and Alcaeus, but was in touch with other
branches of the Greek race and knew the give and take of
social intercourse outside its own sphere. Now Homer seems
to be writing for such a society. The *Iliad* in no way implies
an audience limited in outlook or experience. Like Pindar,
Homer wrote for men who had wide interests and could
sympathize with events in different parts of the Greek world.
His geographical descriptions of Asia Minor reach from the
Cayster to the Troad. He gives family histories for Glaucus
in Lycia and Aeneas in Troy. His knowledge of geography
may be limited, but what he knows best is the Asia Minor
coast-line held by the Aeolians and the Ionians. Of them he
says nothing specifically,[1] and he makes no direct appeal to
local or tribal patriotism. He writes for a big audience, and
his language therefore is not chosen for local effect. Such
conditions as this requires were probably found in Asia Minor
after the Aeolian and Ionian emigrants had settled down and
made their homes with some sense of permanence and
security. The Ionian settlers lived next door to the Aeolian,
and both must have been united by their efforts against
common foes and their sense of a common origin. Such
audiences, whether in Ionia or Aeolis, would find no difficulty in understanding the language of Homer. These conditions made the creation of an artificial language possible.
The language so created was essentially the product of Asia
Minor. Of Dorian or West Greek Homer shows practically

---

[1] Except possibly in his use of Αἰολίδης in *Z* 154 and his mention of Ἰάονες
in *N* 685.

no traces. But on the other hand he uses words whose origin is not Greek but Asiatic. αἶα seems to be developed from the Hittite 'awa' meaning 'ground', ἰχώρ from 'ishkar' meaning 'red blood', and παρδαλέη from 'parta', 'a leopard'.[1]

So far, then, it seems that the language of Homer is an artificial language created in Asia Minor. But at this point we must consider a serious difficulty which might well impair this theory, if its significance is not properly stated and understood. There are in the *Iliad* many words which look like Attic and nothing else. In most cases they are simply textual corruptions which can easily be emended. For instance the use of π- and ὁπ- in interrogative or relative conjunctions and in personal pronouns (e. g. πῶς, πότερος, ὅπως, ὁππότερος) is purely Attic but it can easily be restored to the Ionic use of κ- and ὁκ-. So, too, the Attic μήν in phrases like ἦ μήν, καὶ μήν, οὐ μήν can easily be restored to the Aeolic μάν or the Ionic μέν as metre requires. The Attic form βοῦν which is found twenty-four times, is clearly a mis-spelt version of the Ionic βῶν which is preserved only once (H 238).[2] In some cases the Attic form is unmetrical and must give place to the Ionic form. Thus many lines begin with ἕως which will not scan and is clearly a corruption of ἧος. But in other places the Attic forms are more deeply embedded and scan where neither the Aeolic or Ionic forms would. Thus in the plural of the imperfect indicative middle we sometimes find the termination -ντο as in:

τὼ μὲν ἄρ' ἄμφω κεῖντο ἐπὶ χθονὶ πουλυβοτείρῃ. (Φ 426)
τοῖοι ἄρα Τρώων ἡγήτορες ἧντ' ἐπὶ πύργῳ.[3] (Γ 153)

Both κεῖντο and ἧντο are genuine Attic. The Ionic forms would be κέατο and ἕατο. Another organic Atticism has been claimed in Ψ 226 where one of the earliest papyri supports the manuscript in giving:

ἦμος δ' ἑωσφόρος εἶσι φόως ἐρέων ἐπὶ γαῖαν.[4]

Here ἑωσφόρος is an Attic word, and if we allow the synizesis of the first two syllables, it would scan when neither the Ionic

---

[1] A. H. Sayce, *Classical Review*, 1922, pp. 19–20.
[2] Cf. J. Wackernagel, *Sprachliche Untersuchungen*, p. 12.
[3] Ib., p. 98.   [4] Ib., pp. 100 ff.

ἠωσφόρος nor the Aeolic αὐωσφόρος would. Such Atticisms are rare in the text, but at first sight they seem to be organic and we cannot remove them without doing violence to the manuscript tradition. So organic are they that they are thought to represent a stage in the history of the poems when they underwent considerable alterations at the hands of Attic editors. Such a view is, however, improbable. If the poems had been Atticized, they would have been Atticized more consistently and more completely than they actually have been. The Atticisms are either superficial, or, if not superficial, they are very rare. The truth seems rather to lie on lines indicated by Wilamowitz.[1] He takes ἑωσφόρος, and shows that it cannot be the genuine reading because ἑωσ- cannot be scanned as a monosyllable. The form is a corruption of some lost monosyllable for 'dawn'. This word existed also in Pindar *Isthmian* 3. 42 where the manuscripts vary between ἀωσφόρος and ἑωσφόρος. Both are unmetrical as the metre demands a trisyllable. The conclusion is that the same word was the original form both in Homer and in Pindar. We do not know what it was, and we must leave it at that. With regard to κεῖντο and ἦντο, Wilamowitz points out that the manuscript tradition is not certain, as at Φ 426 an early papyrus reads θεῖνε. He claims that the original reading was κέατο in Φ 426 and ἔατο in Γ 153. In both the first syllables were contracted, just as τεύχη (X 322) is a contraction of τεύχεα and Τυδῆ (Δ 384) of Τυδέα.

It follows then that the so-called Atticisms are not always Attic. But even if they were, they would not prove that the poems were ever Atticized. Old Ionian and Attic came from the same stem, and forms which survived into fifth-century Attic may originally have survived in old Ionic but have perished before Ionic reached the form we know from Herodotus and inscriptions. But though the case for any fundamental Atticization fails, there are certainly many words in the *Iliad* which are not either Aeolic or Ionic as we know the dialects. For example, there are certain words which survived in the archaic dialects of Arcadia and Cyprus. These closely related dialects differ greatly both from Aeolic

[1] *Die Ilias und Homer*, pp. 506–11.

and Ionic, though they have more similarity to the former than to the latter. The archaic character of Cypriote is shown by the survival of a Cypriote script till the fourth century, whose syllabary of fifty-six signs seems to be the descendant of the Minoan linear script.[1] Both Arcadian and Cypriote preserved to a remarkable degree their ancient character. Despite their wide separation they remained very like, and may for all practical purposes be treated as one dialect. Cyprus was held in Greek tradition to have been colonized from the Peloponnese in the Heroic Age, and so Arcado-Cypriote must be the pre-Dorian language of the Peloponnese, which survived in these two isolated districts of Cyprus and Arcadia, cut off by natural barriers of sea and mountain from the invasions of Doric or Ionic speech. In these two dialects we find many Homeric words. Their meaning has often altered slightly, but that is only a proof of their long and isolated history after they were cut off from their main stock. In Arcadian inscriptions we find the Homeric ἀπύω, ἀσκηθής, ἀρτύω, while the form δέατοι is from the same verb as the Homeric δέατο (ζ 242) and πλός may come from the same adjective as the Homeric πλέες (Λ 395).[2] In Cyprus, where inscriptions are more abundant, we find ἄνωγον, ἀρά in the sense of εὐχή, ἄρουρα, αὐτάρ, ἕλος, Ϝάναξ, Ϝάνασσα, ἔϜερξα, ἴδε, κασίγνητος, νυ, πτόλις, χραυόμενον in the sense of land 'adjoining' (cf. E 138 χραύσῃ, 'graze'). In both languages we find the Homeric αἶσα, βόλομαι, δῶμα, εὐχωλά. In addition to the appearance of certain words found in Homer, Arcado-Cypriote has other words which explain Homeric words whose archaic character would otherwise leave them inexplicable. In Cyprus there was a word οὔνιος meaning 'runner',[3] and in Arcadian οὔνει[4] meant 'run': the root of these two words explains the real meaning of the epithet of Hermes ἐριούνιος. He is simply the 'fast traveller', a suitable title for the messenger of the Gods. The Cypriote ἀκοστή, 'barley',[5] explains the participle ἀκοστήσας used of the well-

---

[1] Sundwall, *Jhrb. des Deutsch. archäolog. Inst.* xxx, pp. 57 ff.
[2] Cf. C. M. Bowra, ' Homeric Words in Arcadian Inscriptions ', *C.Q.*, 1926.
[3] Hesychius, s.vv. οὔνιος and οὖνον.   [4] Ib. οὔνει· δεῦρο, δράμε. Ἀρκάδες.
[5] Hesychius, s.v. ἀκοστή.

fed horse to which Hector and Paris are compared. Such a 'barley-fed' horse would of course be high spirited and make at once for the pasturage of the mares. Cypriote too had a word σμίνθα meaning 'mouse', and this explains why when Chryses prays to Apollo to send plague on the Achaeans, he addresses him as Σμινθεῦ (A 39). Mice were the proverbial carriers of plague, and when Apollo is addressed as 'mouse god', it is as the sender of plague. In another doubtful passage Cypriote may supply to the right words of the poet. When Achilles finally abandons his feud with Agamemnon he attributes his previous passion to Zeus and Fate and, according to the manuscripts, to ἠεροφοῖτις Ἐρινύς (T 87). The epithet ἠεροφοῖτις has not much relevance: what is a fury 'that walks in the darkness'? The Alexandrians found a difficulty in it, and recorded another ancient reading εἰαροπῶτις 'blood-drinking'.[1] The word εἶαρ, 'blood', survived in Cypriote,[2] and the epithet is certainly more to the point than ἠεροφοῖτις. Achilles might well speak of the 'blood-drinking Fury' when he thought of the loss of life which his anger had cost the Achaeans. Another odder, and perhaps less attractive, case is the passage where the hair of Euphorbus is called κόμαι χαρίτεσσιν ὁμοῖαι (P 51), which is conventionally taken as a compendious comparison for 'hair like to that of the Graces'. If so, this is the only example of such a use in the Iliad, and Zenodotus wanted to read χαρίτεσσι μέλαιναι. Cypriote provides an evasion, if we choose to accept it, in taking χαρίτες to mean 'bundles'.[3] The hair of Euphorbus is described by the poet as fastened in ringlets. So the sense is good, even if less lyrical than the ordinary interpretation. In one or two cases Cyprus preserved the rare meaning of a word when it had passed away elsewhere, and by so doing illuminates Homer. The κέραμος in which Ares was imprisoned (E 387) may seem odd till we know that in Cyprus the word survived in its meaning of 'prison',[4] and the θρόνα which Andromache embroidered (X 441) are explained by Cypriote as being 'flowers'.[5] These examples are sufficient to show that in Arcadian and Cypriote we find living traces of vocabulary akin to that of Homer. The rest of the

---

[1] Schol. T. ad loc. [2] Ib. [3] Schol. AB ad P 51.
[4] Bekker, Anecd. Graeca, i, p. 202. [5] Hesychius, s.v. θρόνα.

dialect is quite unlike Homeric Greek, and could never be mistaken for it. So as far as light is thrown from here on Homer, it concerns purely the question of vocabulary.

Other elements of Homer's vocabulary may be found in other dialects, even in so unexpected a quarter as Acarnania,[1] the home of what is called North-western Greek. In the early inscriptions of Crete, too, we find certain words such as the archaic forms ποτί, λαός, ἕρπω, and δένδρεον.[2] But such occurrences are far less common than in Arcadia and Cyprus, and in most cases if a word occurs in West Greek or in Cretan, it usually occurs somewhere else as well.

The existence of these words provides a difficult problem. They help, certainly, to dispose of any view that Homeric Greek was ever a spoken tongue. They show how rich were the linguistic sources on which Homer drew. That Homer himself got the words from Arcadia or Cyprus is improbable. Both districts lay outside his orbit, and he nowhere reproduces the essential characteristics of their dialect. On the other hand they prove that he used a language which was not confined to Aeolis or Ionia. The natural conclusion to be drawn from the presence of these words in Homer is that they belong to an ancient stock of words used by epic poets and dating back to a time when the Greek dialects were not fully divorced and differentiated. As spoken words they may well have already been confined to Arcadia and Cyprus as they were later, but they were part of the vocabulary learned and used by poets. If so, it follows that Homer's vocabulary, unlike Chaucer's, was not really his own creation. He drew on a rich traditional material, and used forms which had ceased to be current in the districts where he wrote, if indeed they had ever been.

This traditional side of the epic style is confirmed by two other characteristics, its treatment of the digamma and of the augment. The digamma has in the past been claimed as a relic of the Aeolic epic, and its presence regarded as

---

[1] e.g. δάπτω, Schol. T ad N 831; ἐνέπω, κῆρ, στείχω, Bekker, Anecd. Graeca iii, p. 1095.

[2] G.D.I., 5168, 15. 4991, x 36. 5040, 38. 4986, 1. Cf. M. Kleeman, Vocabula Homerica in Graecorum dialectis servata. Colmar, 1876.

evidence for the earliness of the passages where it occurs. But even so early as the time of Sappho and Alcaeus the digamma had almost disappeared from Aeolic.[1] It survived only under very limited conditions, in the pronoun of the third person and its corresponding adjective, and in certain words of which the common Greek form begins with ρ. Outside these cases there is no satisfactory evidence for its survival. In Ionic the evidence is harder to interpret, but though the digamma occurs sometimes on early inscriptions, it is certainly not common or usual.[2] On the other hand it is regular in the West Greek dialects and survives in them till a late date. It exists too in Arcadian and Cypriote. Its wide diffusion shows that it belonged to the original Greek speech, even if it was early discarded by Aeolic and Ionic. So when Homer uses it, he may or may not be drawing on an earlier form of either Ionic or Aeolic, but he is certainly using an old Greek sound. In particular he is not using a sound which was in current circulation. So far as the internal digamma is concerned, it is almost impossible to say what Homer's usage was. There are certain words like ταλαύρινος, ἀπούρας, ἀπηύρα where υ has taken the place of the digamma, but it is impossible to say whether the change came before or after Homer's day. With the initial digamma things are quite different. Since Bentley discovered its existence, the digamma has been seen to be essential if the Homeric hexameter is to scan.[3] Its restoration to the text has done as much for Homer as the discovery of scholars that Chaucer could scan has done for Chaucer's poetry. In a line like:

$$\text{ἔψεαι, ἔνθα κε ἔργα ἀεικέα ἐργάζοιο} \quad (Ω\ 733)$$

there are two intolerable cases of hiatus until we restore it to its proper form of:

$$\text{ἔψεαι, ἔνθα κε Ϝέργα ἀϜεικέα Ϝεργάζοιο.}$$

The digammas are essential here, as they are in many places in the *Iliad*. But the problem is made more difficult by the apparent inconsistency which Homer displays in his practice. There are certain words in which the digamma is now

---

[1] Lobel, Σαπφοῦς Μέλη, pp. xxviii ff.　　　　[2] Cf. Cauer, op. cit., p. 152.
[3] Cf. the admirable account in Van Leeuwen, *Enchiridion*, pp. 116–51.

used and now neglected. Normally the scansion requires
Ϝάναξ, but we find ποίησαν ἄνακτι (Ω 449). So, too, we find
both a common Ϝέκαστον and δενδίλλων ἐς ἔκαστον (I 180), both
Ϝοῖνος and παρέστασαν οἶνον ἀγούσαι (H 467) and other similar
cases. The question then is whether we can find any rules
under which Homer uses or neglects the digamma.

The use of the digamma, like the use of Aeolic forms,
cannot be settled by dividing the *Iliad* into early and late
strata. It is sometimes observed in one line, and neglected
immediately afterwards in the same context. For instance, in
A 108 we find εἶπας Ϝέπος, though in A 106 we had κρήγυον εἶπας.
What is wanted, if anything, is a statement of a rule showing when and why Homer neglects or observes the letter.
The single fact that he usually observes it and sometimes
does not, seems fatal to any view that the digamma was part
of the speech about him. If it was still used in speech, it
might easily have fallen out of some words and not from
others, but it would not be used off and on with the same
word. Homer's use of it may be consistent, but his consistency is not such as would be found in a spoken vernacular.
It follows that the use or neglect of the digamma is another
side of the artificiality of Homer's language. A gallant
attempt has been made to formulate Homer's practice, and
this is what we need, if possible.[1] It has been thought that
he observes the initial digamma when it comes after a
syllable in arsis, but neglects it when it comes after a syllable
in thesis. Thus we get εἶπᾱς Ϝέπος where the short syllable -ας
is lengthened before a digamma in the middle of the fourth
foot, but κρήγνὸν εἶπας where the short syllable -ον remains
short before a digamma at the end of the fifth foot. This
theory is based on the sound fact that when Homer neglects
the digamma it is usually in thesis. But his use is not consistent, and we find a case of neglect in full arsis at I 224,
πλησάμενος δ᾽ οἴνοιο. The fact is that as yet no satisfactory
formula for Homer's use has been found, and it looks suspiciously as if he followed his whim and the requirements
of his metre. His neglect of the digamma is rarer than his

---

[1] Hartel, *Homerische Studien*, iii, Vienna, 1874; Solmsen, *Untersuchungen zur griechischen Laut- und Verslehre*, pp. 129 ff.

use of it, and in many cases where the manuscripts give no hint of it, its restoration is a benefit to the text. In other cases we can restore it simply by removing a particle or a paragogic νυ. But still Homer did sometimes neglect it, and this needs explanation. The facts would seem to be something like this. Homer's predecessors used the digamma, probably because it was still a common sound in the Greek dialects of their time. In Homer's time it was passing out of use, and he reflects contemporary speech when he neglects it. But on the whole he followed precedent and observed it. It was part of the poetical tradition, and no more difficult for his audience than his archaic words or artificial lengthenings. On the whole he understood its working and conformed to some sort of consistency in his neglect of it. But in other ways he seems not quite to have understood it, and in particular to have attributed it to words which never contained it. For instance, when he ends a line with μέροπες ἄνθρωποι (Σ 288), the lengthening of the final -ες is only intelligible if Homer believed that ἄνθρωποι began with a digamma. It certainly did not, and Homer was wrong. He was misled by the analogy of other words in the use of a letter which had passed out of use in the dialects spoken round him.

A similar artificiality may be seen in Homer's treatment of the augment. The augment was the original Greek way of expressing the past time of a verb. In its earliest form it was not ἐ- but ἀ-, and as such we find it in early inscriptions at Elis—Κοῖος μ' ἀπόησεν [1]—and in Laconia—Εὔμυθις ἀπόναϝε.[2] As ἐ- it exists consistently in all other early inscriptions and in the vernacular poems of Sappho. In later Greek it was almost universally observed, and when poets neglected it, they were imitating Homer. It was, then, an essential feature of Greek in all its stages, and yet Homer frequently omits it. His reasons are clear enough. If the augment were left out, certain words could be introduced into the verse which otherwise could not. Words like ἐφερόμην, which scanned three shorts and a long, could be reduced to anapaests, words like ἔλαθον, ἔβαλε, ἔφερε, which scanned as tribrachs, could be made into two shorts. So, too, other impossible scansions,

---

[1] G.D.I., No. 476.　　　[2] Schwyzer, Dial. Graec. Ex. 37.

such as ἐκέκαδοντο, ἐβουλεύσατο, ὠλέκοντο, could be reduced to
fit into the hexameter. The omission of the augment had great
advantages. Even words already admissible were made more
elastic by the loss of their augment, and we find both ἆγε
and ἄγε, εἷλε and ἕλε, ὤλεσε and ὄλεσσε. The augment is on
the whole more observed than not, but the poet omitted it
plentifully. Nor do there seem to be any rules which guide
the omission. We find it at the beginning of the line, after
the caesura, after the fourth foot, and after the first dactyl.
Many examples may perhaps be wrongly written, especially
in the case of elided syllables and verbs beginning with vowels.
Perhaps we should read ηὗδον, ηὔχετο, ἤκαζε, not εὗδον, εὔχετο,
εἴκαζε, and μῆρ' ἐκάη, σπλάγχν' ἐπάσαντο not μῆρα κάη, σπλάγχνα
πάσαντο. But the fact remains that in the *Iliad* and *Odyssey*
there are over six thousand cases of the neglected augment,
and this neglect is really a literary artifice employed in the
interests of metre. The licence is employed so confidently by
the poet that it looks as if it were allowed by the traditions of
his art, though on this the nature of the evidence does not
permit us to dogmatize.

In these ways the epic poets took considerable liberties with
language. So it is no surprise to see them taking other liberties in the declension and formation of words. In actual
syntax they seem to have followed the alternatives provided
by spoken dialects. Even the genitive in -οιο is an archaism.
It existed in the fifth century in Thessaly, and is probably a
relic of old Aeolic.[1] The curious verbal terminations in -οωσα
and -οωσι look less like deliberate invention than a misunderstanding of the correct forms. But in the invention of
words Homer and his predecessors seem to have been prolific
and highly successful. Even if we allow that language in
Homeric days was still elastic and malleable, it is unlikely
that it possessed such splendid compound adjectives as we
find in the poems. These seem to be the invention of the
poets—for more than one reason. A large number of them
are admirably suited to occupy the fifth and sixth feet of the
hexameter.[2] The *Iliad* knows of some twenty-five five-

[1] Cf. F. Bechtel, *Die griechischen Dialekte*, i, p. 178.
[2] K. Witte, in Pauly-Wissowa, *Real-Encycl.*, s.v. 'Homeros'.

syllabled adjectives which end the line so well that they look like the creations of art. So, too, the line often ends in compound verbs which occur once and once only, like ἀμφαγέροντο, ἀμφεποτᾶτο, ἐκποτέονται, ἐξυπανέστη. Another part of the line which seems to have begotten new forms was that after the hephthemimeral caesura, where the avoidance of the bucolic diaeresis and the love of a break after the fourth foot excluded many forms otherwise possible. The result is that some words look as if they had been compounded just to meet this metrical need, such as ἀποθύμια, ἀπολυμαντῆρα, ἀποφώλιος, ἐπιδίφρια, ἐπιτάρροθος, &c. In the same way the caesura after the second syllable of the third foot and the preference for the pause after the fourth foot created a number of compound adjectives suited to this part of the line, such as ἀκήρατος, ἀγάννιφος, δυσάμμορος, παλίλλογα, παναίολος, ἐπίδρομον, περικλυτός, &c. No doubt all these compound words seemed natural to an audience whose speech formed them easily, but their existence seems in the first place due to the strict rules which the hexameter placed on the poets and to the adaptations of language which it forced upon them.

The conclusion to be drawn from these cases is that the Homeric language is highly artificial, and its creation seems to be not the work of a single poet but of a series of poets who used old material as well as the different dialects of the Greek world in which they lived. Homer himself no doubt invented as his predecessors had, but he was indebted to them for some at least of the lines on which the vocabulary of the Greek epic was widened and strengthened. Perhaps the nearest parallel is the language of the Elizabethan drama. Here, too, a great tradition of poetry was founded on an elastic speech and enriched by the efforts of successive poets. Shakespeare, like Homer, followed where others had led the way, and though his vocabulary is greater than that of any of his predecessors, he is deeply indebted to them for exploring the possibilities of Elizabethan English and enriching their styles with words drawn from all quarters of speech, new and old.

In a style like this, reaching back through a considerable tradition, we might expect to find traces and survivals of extremely ancient words and uses, and it is pre-eminently its archaic character which separates the poetry of Homer from that of later Greek writers. In particular it preserves words which never survived into the speech or even the literature of historical Greece. There are words in Homer, whose meaning was unknown to antiquity despite the learned guesses of the Alexandrians, and they remain unknown to us. Aristophanes[1] says that in his day no one knew the real meaning of ἀμενηνὰ κάρηνα, and the variety of alternative interpretations show how little is known of the meaning of some Homeric epithets. What, for instance, is the meaning of Ἀργεϊφόντης or ἰοχέαιρα, or even of the familiar εἰλίποδας ἕλικας βοῦς? In antiquity different views were propounded, and more have been propounded since, but any certainty, even ordinary assurance, is far from being attained. At times, aided by an archaic dialect like Cypriote, we can unravel the meaning of a word like ἐριούνιος better than the ancients could, but ordinarily our ignorance is as profound as theirs, and for the same reason. The meaning of the words was lost long ago, and there is no contemporary evidence which can enable us to regain it. Perhaps the deciphering of the Minoan tablets may throw light at least on the titles of the gods, but the tablets remain undeciphered, and after all they may not help. Yet despite our ignorance of the pre-Hellenic language of the Mediterranean, from various little indications we may try to guess how much of Homer's language is strictly speaking not Greek but derived from an earlier, not Indo-European language. To attempt this is not in any way to assume that Homer knew such a language. It may well have disappeared when he wrote, or have been spoken only by slaves and outcasts with whom he had no intercourse. But such a language made its contribution to Greek, and for that reason Homer ultimately draws on it, and it is interesting to assess his debt. The only tests of words belonging to such a language is that they show characteristics which are otherwise not known to any Indo-European language, and are therefore probably of an alien stock. These tests are few and simple. The best assured are words formed

[1] fr. 222, *Daitales*.

in νθ, or with the termination -σος or -σσος, or with an initial
σ. These sounds are not very common in Greek, but they
occur in place-names all over the Aegean. So it is likely
that they belong to a pre-Hellenic tongue. From these
tests we can discover words which date from before the
Greek settlement. In νθ we find words like ἐρέβινθος,
ἄκανθα, ὑάκινθος, ἀσάμινθος, μήρινθος, πείρινθα (acc.); in -σος
or -σσος words like κυπάρισσος, βυσσός, κασσίτερος, χρυσός,
θάλασσα, νῆσος, νύσσα; with an initial σ- we find σίαλος,
σῖτος, σῦκον, σάκος, σύριγξ, σάλπιγξ.[1] The list is a small
one, and most of the words belong to the common heritage
of post-Homeric Greek, but such as they are they show
how the Greeks took over many necessary words from an
agricultural people living by the sea with some knowledge
of the luxuries of life including baths and music. They also
show one of the means by which it was possible for Greek
poetry to have so rich a vocabulary. It had not only its
own extensive Indo-European vocabulary to draw upon, it
had this quite different tradition of words incorporated
from an alien stock and providing, as in σάκος and σίαλος,
synonyms invaluable for poetry.

It would indeed be interesting to know how far the two
stocks had coalesced in Homer's time, and though the inquiry is extremely obscure, the poems give some slight indication of two tongues existing side by side. In four places the
Iliad says that certain things are called one name by the gods
and another by men. Thus a giant is called Briareos by the
gods and Aegaeon by men (*A* 403), a tomb on the plain of
Troy is called the tomb of Myrine by the gods and Batieia
by men (*B* 812–3), the bird whose shape is taken by Sleep is
called χαλκίς by the gods and κύμινδις by men (*Ξ* 291), and
finally the river is called Ξάνθος by the gods and Σκάμανδρος
by men (*Υ* 74). The fact that the poet gives the two names in
each case is remarkable in itself, and the chances are that
when he gives the human name for it he means the old name,
and when he gives the divine name he means the new name.
Thus in the case of Βριάρεως-Αἰγαίων, not only is the divine
name of good Indo-European origin, but the human name

[1] Cf. Glotz, *La Civilisation Égéenne*, p. 441.

Αἰγαίων is unintelligible not merely to us, but presumably was also to Homer's readers, as the poet at once adds an explanation in the words, ὁ γὰρ αὖτε βίην οὗ πατρὸς ἀμείνων. In the second case the divine name is simply the Tomb of the Amazon, Myrine, while the human name Βατίεια is clearly connected with βάτος and means 'Bramble Hill'. Such a name is likely to be older than any attribution of a tomb, has no roots in Indo-European, and is probably pre-Hellenic. In the third case the χαλκίς or 'brass-bird', as the gods call it, has a good origin in the Indo-European words for bronze. On the other hand κύμινδις cannot be derived, and though it survived into later Greek, its νδ is of alien stock, suggesting many pre-Hellenic place-names in the Aegean and Asia Minor.[1] The fourth case is less easy to decide. Σκάμανδρος also is betrayed by its νδ, and we know from Alcaeus that a town with a similar termination Ἄντανδρος had a population of aboriginal Leleges.[2] But Ξάνθος with its non-Hellenic νθ looks as much a stranger as Σκάμανδρος. But though it is hard to decide, the chances are that ξάνθος was early taken into Greek. It is the word used by the poet for his fair-haired heroes, such as Achilles and Menelaus, and has the characteristics of a traditional epithet. Perhaps when the Greeks first came to Greece their fair hair excited the wonder of the dark-haired Myceneans, and they were called ξάνθοι. So the word found its way into Greek early, and by the time that these lines were written was taken for genuine Greek when compared with the unintelligible Σκάμανδρος. In these cases then the language of men is the pre-Hellenic language, while the language of the gods is Greek. That this is so, is confirmed by two other passages where the language of the gods is mentioned, though not contrasted with the language of men. In the *Odyssey* the plant with which Odysseus defeats Circe is called μῶλυ (κ 305) by gods, and the Wandering Rocks are called Πλαγκταί (μ 61). Both words are Greek. μῶλυ is related to other Indo-European words for various kinds of root, such as the Sanskrit mūla-m and the Latin

---

[1] Ἀλίνδοια (Macedonia), Ἄσπενδος (Boeotia), Κάλυνδα and Λίνδος (Rhodes), Σκανδαρία (Cos), Κίνδριον ὄρος (Crete).
[2] Ed. Lobel, No. 98; cf. Ἄνδρος, Φολέγανδρος (Cyclades).

'malva'. The word existed in Arcadia [1] and was no doubt an
old Greek word. Πλαγκταί is so clearly derived from the verb
πλάζω that it needs no further defence. The inference is that
the language of the gods is Greek. Why it should be so called
is a matter of conjecture. The extrusion of an older race and
language by the invading Greeks was no doubt regarded as
the victory of the Greek gods, who took over the seats and
titles of their defeated predecessors. The original inhabitants
must have lived on, even when their gods were dispossessed,
and spoken their own language when the new language was
spoken in the high places. Some such explanation might
account for the distinction between the two sets of names.
For our purpose it is interesting, because it shows that when
Homer wrote there were still traces of another tongue than
Greek spoken, or known of, in the Aegean world. The competing words seem to have been confined almost entirely to
proper names, but such as they are, they show that Greek
had not yet finally absorbed all that it was to absorb of the
language of the pre-Hellenic inhabitants.

From such different sources is the Greek of Homer composed. The intermingling of the different elements is very great,
and it is impossible to separate different sections by tests of
dialect or artificial forms. But we can see how close the inter-
relation is if we take some representative passage and analyse
some of its linguistic characteristics into their origins. Take
the account of the old men sitting on the wall in Γ 149–53:

ἥατο δημογέροντες ἐπὶ Σκαιῇσι πύλῃσι,
γήραϊ δὴ πολέμοιο πεπαυμένοι, ἀλλ' ἀγορηταὶ
ἐσθλοί, τεττίγεσσιν ἐοικότες, οἵ τε καθ' ὕλην
δενδρέῳ ἐφεζόμενοι ὄπα λειριόεσσαν ἱεῖσι·
τοῖοι ἄρα Τρώων ἡγήτορες ἦντ' ἐπὶ πύργῳ.

This is an ordinary piece of Homeric narrative, but it contains several different elements. The bulk is recognizable
Ionic. We should not be surprised to find ἥατο or Σκαιῇσι πύλῃσι or πεπαυμένοι or much else in the Ionic of Herodotus, but
this Ionic basis is varied with other forms. τεττίγεσσιν is an
Aeolic dative and πολέμοιο is an Aeolic form which survived

---

[1] Theophrastus *H.P.* ix, 15, 7.

till the fifth century in Thessalian inscriptions. ἦντ' is Attic and, so far as we know, nothing else, while δενδρέῳ is neither Attic nor Ionic or Aeolic, but an old form which survived in Crete,[1] and is probably Old Peloponnesian. Lastly λειριόεσσαν is a word whose meaning has been lost. The ancients took it to mean 'lily-like', but what that means we do not know. Perhaps it is connected with λειρώς, which Hesychius says means ἰσχνός. But we can only guess.

Almost any passage of the *Iliad* is formed from as many elements as this, complicated often by artificial lengthening or shortening and the treatment of the digamma. The existence of these different elements in so complex a whole is the best evidence for the language of Homer being not a spoken vernacular but a highly developed literary style.

[1] *G.D.I.*, 4986, 1

THE HISTORICAL BACKGROUND

IT is time to turn from Homer's manner to his matter, and to ask where he found his story. The *Iliad* claims to deal with great doings. The fall of Troy before a confederacy of Greek invaders is presented by the poet as a historical event of the first importance. So it is natural that criticism has been devoted to efforts to disentangle truth from falsehood in the story. These efforts perhaps belong more to history than to literary criticism, but they have an interest for the literary critics because they show, or might show, how the poet selects from life and incorporates real, historical elements into a work of the imagination. For history they have a particular interest. The historical Hamlet or the historical Macbeth are known to us from the dull chronicles of an early time, and Shakespeare tells us nothing both new and true about them. But the Siege of Troy is known only from Homer, and if he can be proved to be basing his story on fact, we have added a chapter to Greek history and shed light where there has been a great darkness. That everything he says is accurate is beyond the bounds of hope or possibility, but there may be a central fact around which he constructs his story, and the aim of critics has been to disentangle this. Nor are their efforts unjustified. The Greeks always regarded the Trojan War as a historical fact. For Herodotus it was an early phase of the age-long struggle between Greeks and Barbarians,[1] for the scientific Thucydides it was a political event worthy of close analysis and consideration.[2] But the Greeks had less exacting a notion of scientific history than we have, and their belief in the Trojan War was based chiefly on an acceptance of the inspiration of Homer. Modern critics have tried to go farther and see whether there can be found any good reasons for the Trojan War having taken place. They have more material at their disposal than Thucydides had, and their conclusions have more chance of being final.

The *Iliad* has much in common with the traditional epics

[1] i. 3, 2.   [2] i. 9–11.

of western Europe. It was composed under similar conditions and it employs some of the same devices. They are based on historical events or series of events, and they mention real personages. The *Song of Roland* tells of the wars of Charlemagne against heathen enemies in Spain, *Beowulf* of the Danish King, Chocilaicus, who invaded the Hattuarii at the beginning of the sixth century. The habit has persisted till our own times, and in Cyprus and Herzegovina the Balkan Wars of 1912–13 have become a theme of epic poetry. Combined with real events we find real personages. Roland is the Hruotlandus known to Eginhard's *Life of Charlemagne*, Dietrich of Berne in the *Nibelungenlied* is Theodoric of Verona, Prince Marko of the Slavonic epics ruled over a part of Macedonia and was killed in 1394 in battle against the prince of Wallachia. It follows that epic poems are usually based on historical events and persons, and that by analogy the Trojan War took place and Achilles and Agamemnon existed.

The epics tell of facts to some extent, but they tell of them with a sad disregard for chronology. The *Song of Roland* combines various events into one. In history there were three main events in the story. In 788 Charlemagne's rearguard was attacked by the Gascons and destroyed. In the slaughter were killed, Hruotland, Anselm, and Eggihard. In 793 the Saracens invaded France, and in 812 and 824 the Gascons revolted. All these events are combined in the poem into one. The combination has involved some falsification of facts. The slaughter of Hruotland by the Gascons is ascribed to the Saracens, and the treachery of Ganelon seems to be an invention made to keep the story together. At all events these dates and events belong to the reign of Charlemagne, and so far the epic does not do more than telescope the doings of a single reign. But as the story was developed later characters were added. Geoffrey of Anjou, who died in 987 and Richard I, Duke of Normandy, who died in 996, were added to Charlemagne's following and made to take part in the battle. Fortunately we can control the story of the *Song of Roland* by external sources, and know when it deals accurately with history. But for the *Iliad* external Greek sources are late and derivative. The Greeks merely followed

Homer and had no other authorities to consult. And this coalescing of generations can be found in most early epics. In the *Nibelungenlied* fifth- and sixth-century kings like Attila and Theodoric are put side by side with Gero of East Saxony who died in 965 and Eckehart who died in 1002. The conclusion follows that we must be careful before we believe that Homer's heroes all belonged to the same generation. They may have, but it may equally be doubted. Perhaps the Greek sense of truth prevented Homer from neglecting chronology. Perhaps equally he was a man and a poet like these other poets, and cared little for the dry bones of history. Nor do the difficulties suggested by other epics end here. In some cases they invent characters. Beowulf himself, the 'bee-wolf' or 'bear', is a creature taken from folk-tale and put into history. He keeps some of his traditional characteristics, the terrible grip which tears off Grendel's arm, his gift of swimming under water, but he moves among real Danes in a real Scandinavian world. Even Ganelon seems to be an invention. He may possibly be Wenilo, Archbishop of Sens, who betrayed Charles the Bald in 895. But he may equally be an invention, the type of traitor like Hagen in the *Nibelungenlied*. As such he exists in the tenth century, when the poem on St. Leger makes him the gaoler of its hero. With men events were invented to hold the different strands of story together. In the *Nibelungenlied* the story is held together by an invasion of the Huns' country by the Burgundians, and this invasion is pure invention. So, too, the defeat of the Saracens by Charlemagne in the *Song of Roland* is poetry, not history. Roland's death has to be avenged, and the enemy are destroyed. Yet this episode, which takes up a quarter of the whole poem, has the air of being a record of fact.

These considerations must be borne in mind when we try to find germs of history in the *Iliad*. In the absence of independent records, we cannot say whether the rape of Helen is history, or folk-tale like the rape of Europa by Zeus, or whether the quarrel of Achilles and Agamemnon is not another version of an old story like the wrath of Meleager or the quarrel of Roland and Ganelon. Nor can we say if or when Agememnon existed, until his name appears in some ancient and independent record. Greek history has no early annals by which the truth of its epic may be tested, and we may only form conclusions of a general character. But these we are at liberty to form. We may justifiably ask whether the Trojan War can have taken place, whether there can have been a kingdom such as Homer ascribes to Agamemnon, whether the Achaeans were a real people. The answers to such questions cannot be exact or certain, but such inquiries are legitimate because we have independent evidence drawn from archaeology and historical sources outside Homer.

There was a real Troy: there can be no doubt of it. Or rather there were nine successive Troys on the hill of Hissarlik, and both the Second and the Sixth Cities were rich and powerful, if we may judge by the gold found in the former and by the Cyclopean walls of both. The excavations of Schliemann and Dörpfeld have put it beyond question that here stood Troy. And the Sixth City agrees in some respects with Homer's account of Troy and the Trojan War.[1] It existed in the thirteenth and twelfth centuries B.C., and the most popular date for the Trojan War is that given by Eratosthenes as 1194 to 1184. It shows late Mycenean pottery mingled with its own native ware, and was a place of power and influence. In other ways, too, it agrees with Homer's account of it, as Dörpfeld and Leaf have shown. The epithets of ὀφρυόεσσα and εὐτείχεος well suit its forbidding walls: εὔπυργος and ὑψίπυλος are justified by its bastions and massive gateway: ἠνεμόεσσα is a well-earned adjective, as all travellers witness. Even εὐρυάγυια, which seems at first to be unmerited in a place where the lanes are extremely narrow, has been explained by Dörpfeld to refer to the system of terraces running round the walls inside the ramparts. One of these between the inner face of the rampart and the outer face of the retaining wall has a width from 25 to 30 feet, and so unusual is this feature in the Aegean that the epithet may well be justified. The landscape too agrees with Homer's account. Large natural features like Mount Ida and the distant outline of Samothrace are visible as the poet says, Scamander and

[1] Cf. W. Leaf, *Troy*.

Simoeis may still be identified, the shrubs and plants which were scorched round Scamander in the fight of Achilles and the River God may still be seen in spring growing on the water-courses—elms, willows, and tamarisks, lotus, rush, and galingale.[1] Even smaller details may be identified, such as the θρωσμὸς πεδίοιο in the slightly rising ground of Kum Köi, the Tomb of Ilos in an ancient mound near this, and Kalli-kolone can be found at Eren Köi. All this is very circumstantial and would seem to point to the poet knowing his Troy, or at least knowing some correct account of it. But there are other passages which show that the poet either did not know the landscape, or else he exerted his poetical prerogative and altered it. He describes features which no longer exist, such as the hot and cold springs under the walls (X 147 ff.). There is now no trace of such springs, though there may have been in the poet's day. He makes Troy a big city, capable of holding the Trojans and their allies. He gives their numbers as 50,000—fifty men each to a thousand watch-fires (Θ 562)—but a city of five acres would not hold these and their dependants. But this may be legitimate poetical exaggeration. He may still have known Troy, and yet in the interests of poetic grandeur have enlarged the city to heroic proportions. But this defence cannot be urged in another mistake into which he falls about the course of the Scamander and the Simoeis. It is clear that these rivers did not follow their present course, and there are two alternatives for understanding Homer's account of them. Either, as Schliemann and Dörpfeld hold, the Scamander flowed along the course of the present Kalifatli and In-Tepe Ismaks to the sea. Its course then lay entirely between the camp and the town, and had to be crossed at a ford by any one going from the one to the other. This ford lay where it was joined at right angles by the Simoeis. This theory would make the battle-field extremely small. If it is correct, the poet did not understand the country, as from Θ onwards, when the fighting sways from the Greek camp to the walls of Troy, we should expect to find the armies crossing at the ford, but we hear no mention of it at all. The only acceptable alternative is Leaf's view that the

[1] Φ 351.

Scamander flowed then as now along the western edge of the plain and was nowhere joined by the Simoeis.[1] The road led along the river but did not actually cross it. This fits well with accounts of the river from classical times, but in the *Iliad* it is otherwise. The poet speaks clearly of the Simoeis joining the Scamander under the walls of Troy, ἧχι ῥοὰς Σιμόεις συμβάλλετον ἠδὲ Σκάμανδρος (E 774).[2] Under Leaf's view this is frankly impossible. So far then no view explains Homer's geography of these rivers. Perhaps the landscape has altered more than we think, and some newer and bolder theory must be devised. Or perhaps Homer never saw the Troad and relied on saga which gave him names and some details, but no more.[3] Where he did not know he invented, as Shakespeare invented the cliffs of Elsinore. After all the circumstantial details which he does give correctly are not very circumstantial. He knows the general outlines of the country, but the rest would apply to any walled city on any plain of Asia Minor. And there we must leave it. There was a real Troy, and the poet knew something about it, either from personal observation or hearsay or tradition. In some points, too, he was wrong, but he was a poet and he had the right to invent. There was indubitably a real Troy, and at the right date, but is this sufficient warrant for a Trojan War, and does it mean that this Troy was sacked by a great Achaean Confederacy?

The Sixth City certainly existed and came to an end in the Late Mycenean period. The question is whether it was the Achaeans who destroyed it. The answer to this question must depend on very general considerations. We have Homer's word that the Achaeans burned Troy, and we have the evidence of archaeology that the Sixth City was effectually obliterated. Homer, being a Greek, is perhaps more accurate on historical facts than the writers of the early German or French epics, and perhaps he is more to be trusted. But that is only a possibility. What if, like the author of the

[1] *Troy*, pp. 34–7.   [2] 'Where Simois and Scamander join their streams.'
[3] Cf. Wilamowitz, *I. und H.*, p. 210: 'Über Ilios liess sich sicherer fabulieren; das war nicht nur zerstört, sondern lag in feindlichem Gebiete, wo so leicht kein Hellene hinkam.'

Nibelungenlied, he has confused the dates and made into one story two very distant events? Thus the Second City was actually burned about 2000; it was rich in gold, as the 'treasure of Priam' shows. What if Homer combined the story of this with that of a quite different power of some nine hundred years later? The answer to such doubts cannot at present be final, but if we survey what is known of the history of the time we shall find that an important Achaean power existed, and that it may well have sacked Troy.

The historicity of Homer may be tested by three factors, the historical records of foreign peoples, Greek traditions independent of epic influence, and certain deductions from archaeology. None of these tests are final or entirely satisfactory, but they are all we possess at present and we must make use of them.

So long as the Cretan and Mycenean tablets remain undeciphered, the only contemporary evidence comes from Egyptian and Hittite records. The first are satisfactory in that Egyptian chronology for the period is fairly well established, and that the texts may be read with some accuracy. On the other hand the Egyptian transliteration of proper names is extremely inaccurate and leaves too much room for guessing. The Hittite records, though numerous, are still only partially deciphered. The language, despite some superficial Indo-European characteristics, contains many unknown elements, and all translations are full of guesswork.[1] Fortunately the Hittites used the cuneiform system of writing, in which names of persons and places are indicated by prefixes, and so we know at least when we have to deal with proper names. Allowing for these great limitations these two sources still give us valuable information, and provide the best evidence for the state of the Eastern Mediterranean after the fall of the Minoan Empire.

Both series of records present the same general impression of a number of tribes, some identifiable, some not, moving from one place to another, now as raiders, now as mercen-

[1] Cf. J. Friedrich, 'Alt-kleinasiatische Sprache', in Ebert, *Real-Lexicon der Vorgeschichte*, Band i, pp. 127–37.

aries or tributaries of the greater powers. The first glimpses
came from the Tell-el-Amarna Letters (c. 1379).[1] In these
we find on the one hand raiders called Lukki or Luka
raiding and spoiling the Phoenician coast and Alashiya,
which is possibly Cyprus. The Lukki or Luka are most
probably the Lycians, the Greek Λύκιοι, whom language and
customs show to have been an indigenous race of Asia Minor.[2]
On the other hand Egypt is already employing mercenaries
in North Syria drawn from the same stock of peoples. Among
them are two who reappear later, the Shakhlal and the
Shardana.[3] Who these are is uncertain. Their later appearances show that they are connected with the Aegean, but
that is all we can safely say. Even at this early date these
peoples caused anxiety to their neighbours, especially on the
frontiers of the Egyptian Empire. In response to an Egyptian
request for information, Abimilki of Tyre reports that 'the
king of the land of Danuna is dead, and his brother has become king after him, and the land is quiet'.[4] The Danuna
here mentioned are probably the Δαναοί of Homer, and in
this, their first appearance in recorded history, they are already straining to get at the East.[5]

The next phase, some forty years later, comes from the
Hittite records and is of a different character.[6] Muršiliš,
king of the Hittites, assists a vassal of his called the king of
Aḫḫiawa to reduce a district in Pamphylia called Millavanda, the later Milyas. This king's name is Antaravas,
and part of his dominion is a district called Lazba or
Lazbaz. E. Forrer has identified Aḫḫiawa with some reason
as 'Αχαίϝα[7] and Antaravas with Andreus, the king of Orchomenus, whose name was preserved in his own city till the
time of Pausanias (ix. 34). If the identification is correct, it
gives us the first mention of an Achaean king, and the role
he plays is important for several reasons. First, he is a prince

---

[1] Cf. H. R. Hall in *Cambridge Ancient History*, vol. ii, p. 281.
[2] Ib., p. 282.   [3] Ib., p. 281.   [4] Ib., p. 322.
[5] The name has also been identified with the biblical Dodanim.
[6] E. Forrer, 'Vorhomerische Griechen in den Keilschrifttexten von Boghaz-
köi,' *Mitt. der deutschen Orientgesellschaft*, No. 63.
[7] Disputed by Mayer and Garstang, 'Index of Hittite Names', *Brit. Sch.
Jerusalem Suppl. Papers*, i. 1923.

in Pamphylia and also in Lesbos. In this there is nothing new or surprising. Pamphylia was certainly a very early Greek colony. Herodotus (vii. 91) ascribed its settlement to Amphilochus and Calchas after the Trojan war, but the period μετὰ τὰ Τρωικά was a favourite device to date any early period in their history, and need not be taken too literally. In historical times, its language, though Greek, resembled no other Greek dialect, and was regarded as a barbarous tongue. It preserved extremely archaic forms, and was isolated from other Greek dialects at an early date. Lesbos plays a large part in the Greek heroic legends, and it is not surprising that the Achaeans should have anticipated the later Greek colonization of it.[1] The presence of Achaeans at Millavanda is significant. It lies near the Solyma Mountains, the traditional scene of the exploits of Bellerophon,[2] in whose story Greek tradition preserved the memory of these early adventures. Secondly, the documents make Antaravas-Andreus a king of some importance. Muršiliš regards him as an equal, and the god of the city of Aḫḫiawa and the city of Lazbas is spoken of by the Hittite king as 'our own god'.[3] Antaravas' position was curious. As the holder of land in Pamphylia he was vassal of the Hittite king, but as the king of the Achaeans he was also a great king in his own right. So, no doubt, the Norman and Angevin kings were vassals of the kings of France as holders of lands in his titular domains, but kings of England in their own right. The seat of this monarchy must have been Orchomenus, which figured in Greek legend as the seat of great wealth and power. It plays little part in the *Iliad*, but Achilles mentions it by the side of Egyptian Thebes as a place of boundless wealth (*I* 381), and to Hesiod it was the home of the great Minyan race.[4] To-day it still shows relics of its great past in its tholos tomb which resembles the Treasury of Atreus.

Some ten years later (*c.* 1325) another king of Aḫḫiawa appears in the south coast of Asia Minor. A chieftain has

---

[1] e. g. its connexion with Orestes, Strabo ix. 401, xiii. 582; cf. Busolt, *Griech. Gesch.*, i, p. 274.   [2] Strabo xiii. 630.
[3] Forrer, op. cit., p. 13; A. H. Sayce, *C.R.* 1924, pp. 164–5.
[4] *Eoiae*, fr. 7, ap. Paus. ix. 36. 7, Ὀρχομενὸν Μιννήιον.

revolted in the Hinterland, and the Lugga[1] peoples call in Tavagalavas to assist them against him. Forrer identifies Tavagalavas with Eteocles, the son of Andreus, known from the same passage in Pausanias. The identification of the names presents no difficulties, as the original form of Eteocles was ʼΕτεϜοκελέϜης and his succession to his father Andreus in the same kingdom and rights is perfectly natural. His position is the same as his father's. He still holds land in Pamphylia, and he is still important, for the Hittite King addresses him as 'brother'.

At this period then the Aegean peoples were the friends and tributaries of the Hittites. So it is no surprise to find a group of them fighting on the Hittite side against Ramses II at the battle of Kadesh in 1288. These allies are enumerated in the Egyptian record as Pidasa, Ariunna or Iliunna, Masa, Dardenui, Luka, and Kalikisha.[2] So far as the names can be identified these peoples come from Asia Minor. The Luka are the Lycians again, the Masa Mysians, the Dardenui Dardanians, and the Kalikisha Cilicians. All these four races are known to Homer as allies or friends of the Trojans. The Iliunna are more obscure. They may be the inhabitants of Oroanda or they may be the men of Ilion.

So long as Egypt and the Hittites were at war, it paid these wandering and predatory peoples to fight on the Hittite side. Egypt held out boundless hopes of booty and settlement. But in 1272 Ramses II made peace with the Hittites, and the whole political situation was altered. Without the Hittites to help them the Sea Peoples acted by themselves. Their action took two forms, an active policy against the Hittite rule in Asia Minor and concerted efforts among themselves to invade Egypt. In Hittite country we find a policy of invasion adopted by the new Achaean king, who is called Attarissiyas. Who he is, we do not know. He has been identified with Atreus,[3] that is, Atresyas,[4] 'the untrembling'. Anyhow,

---

[1] They seem to have occupied the later Lycaonia, Pisidia, Pamphylia, and Lycia. Forrer connects the name with Λυκάονες.

[2] H. R. Hall, C. A. H. ii, p. 281.   [3] By Forrer, l.c., p. 21.

[4] But P. Giles in The Year's Work in Classical Studies, 1924–5, identifies him with Otreus of Γ 186 and Hymn to Aphrodite, 117. Cf. H. R. Hall, The Civilization of Greece in the Bronze Age, p. 250.

he was a thorn in the Hittite side and a man of importance. About 1250 he attacked a Hittite vassal, the king of Zippasla, in South Caria. The vassal appealed for help to Todhalijas, the Hittite king, who ordered the expulsion of Attarissiyas. The sequel is not known, but Attarissiyas was partly successful, as a few years later in 1245 he was still a great king. In a treaty made by Todhalijas with the king of the Amorites, the king of Aḫḫiawa is mentioned by the side of the kings of Egypt, Babylon, and Assyria. The treaty is one of friendship and alliance. So Attarissiyas was worth conciliating. His power is regarded as equal to the other great powers of the time. But this treaty did not hold for long. About 1240 Attarissiyas was up to his old tricks. He made an attack on Caria with what seem to be a hundred chariots.[1] This time, despite the devastation he caused, he was driven 'back to his own land'. About 1225 he makes another appearance. With a mysterious character called 'the man from Biggaya'[2] he devastated Cyprus, and seems to have met with success, as the Hittite king recognized him and his companion as independent princes. Then he disappears from history. The career of Attarissiyas, whoever he was, accords well with Greek tradition. His activities in Pamphylia and Cyprus fall in with Greek saga. Pamphylia, as we have seen, was an early Greek colony. Cyprus, like it, was associated with the same early colonization, and especially with the Achaeans. The priests were called Ἀχαιομάντεις, its northern coast Ἀχαιῶν ἀκτή[3] and the title Ἀχαιϝός[4] existed in the fifth century. Cyprus cherished an association with Achaeans long after they had ceased to count on the Greek mainland, and it may well have dated from the exploits of Attarisijas and his Achaean invaders. From this period, too, may date the Cypriote dialect, with its pre-Dorian characteristics and its close affinities to Arcadian.

At about the same time as these events in Cyprus, Egypt

---

[1] Forrer takes the word to mean 'ships'.

[2] Forrer identifies Biggaya with Cyprus, which had an old name of Σφήκεια. Cf. Step. Byz. Κύπρος.

[3] Hesychius, ἀχαιομάντεις· οἱ τὴν τῶν θεῶν ἔχοντες ἱερωσύνην ἐν Κύπρῳ. For Ἀχαιῶν ἀκτή cf. Strabo xiv. 682.

[4] Hoffmann, Gr. Dial. No. 190, Ζώϝης ὁ Τιμοϝάνακτος Ἀχαιϝός.

was the scene of considerable activities among the Sea Peoples. About 1225, in the reign of Meneptah, the Nile Delta was attacked by a combination between Libyans from the west and 'Northerners from all lands'.[1] The Northern invaders consisted once more of the Luka and with them were the Shardana and Shakalsha, turned enemy instead of tributary, and, for the first time, the Tursha and Akaiwasha. The Tursha may be Tyrsenians, and the Akaiwasha must be Achaeans, though we do not know how this exploit was related to their activities in Asia Minor. The invasion was a desperate bid for settlement, and the invaders, as the Egyptian records say, were 'fighting to fill their bellies daily'. The invasion failed, but not enough to discourage the invaders from trying again. About 1194, at the beginning of the reign of Ramses III, a second, greater attack was made on Egypt. This time it was made both by land and by sea. The familiar Shardana and Shakalsha fought against their brothers in the Egyptian army, and they were assisted by Pulesati—the later Philistines—Washasha, perhaps Oassians of Caria, the Zakaray—perhaps from Zakro in Crete—and the Danaua, who appeared two centuries earlier and must be the Δαναοί. The effects of this great movement may still be dimly seen. It seems to have dealt a death-blow to the Hittite Empire and to have convulsed the near East. In the words of the Egyptian record 'The Isles were restless, disturbed at one and the same time. No land stood before them beginning from Kheta, Kedi, Carchemish, Arvad, and Alashiya. They destroyed them, and assembled in their camp in the midst of Amor.'[2] This double invasion by sea and land was a serious menace to an Egypt whose military strength was weakened by the change of dynasties and the anti-military intrigues of the priestly caste. But Ramses III was prepared. He had reorganized his army, instituted long-distance archery and mobile chariots, and built a navy.[3] The result was that he defeated them both by sea and land. The records of the land victory have perished, though it is

[1] H. R. Hall, op. cit., p. 282.
[2] Cf. J. L. Myres and K. T. Frost, *The Historical Background of the Trojan War* Klio, xiv, pp. 447–67. [3] Ib., pp. 448–9.

clear that Ramses was triumphant. On sea he was equally
successful. His fleet sailed up the Palestinian coast and caught
the fleet of the Raiders anchored in a bay. The Egyptians
penned the enemy in, and the archers opened fire on them.
The Raiders were then, in the words of their conqueror,
'trapped like wild fowl. They were dragged, overturned, and
laid low upon the beach: slain and made heaps from stern to
bow off their galleys.' The fight was depicted on the great
pylon at Medinet Habu which still gives an excellent picture
of the Sea Raiders and their methods of fighting.

The results of this victory were enormous. For Egypt it
was the end of invasions from the sea. The invaders after
their defeat retired into Asia, where the Pulesati settled in
Philistia and the Zakaray at Dor. In Asia Minor new
kingdoms were carved out of the wreck of the old Hittite
Empire, while the Hittites themselves formed a new centre
of power at Carchemish. For the Greeks it was the beginning of those political divisions which they maintained in
the historical period.

Greek tradition placed the Siege of Troy in the year after
this defeat of the Sea Raiders by Ramses. The exactness of
this date may well be questioned.[1] But it is important to
note the historical conditions of the time, and to see that
they were not averse to such unique events as the Siege of
Troy and the Empire of Agamemnon.

Greek tradition, outside Homer, confirms some of the
aspects revealed by these foreign documents, and especially
confirms the existence of a Heroic Age when the Greeks were
on the move and seeking new homes in different parts of the
Eastern Mediterranean basin. The best summary of the
times is given by Hesiod, who speaks of an age of heroes
which fell between the Age of Bronze—the Mycenean Age—
and the Age of Iron in which he himself lived.[2]

The two great events of this time were the Siege of Thebes
and the Siege of Troy. In these two wars the later Greek epic
poets found their subjects, and from them the tragedians

[1] Herodotus (ii. 145) puts it about 1250, the *Marmor Parium* 1218–1209.
The commonest date is that given by Eratosthenes as 1194–1184.
[2] *Works and Days*, 156–69.

drew. The Siege of Thebes seems to have been to mainland
poets what the Siege of Troy was to Ionian, the chief event
of the heroic age. Hesiod mentions the two side by side.
These wars are guaranteed only by poetry, and for sober fact
we must go to two different sources, the traditions of genealogies and families, and the local traditions of colonization in
certain outlying districts of the Greek world.

The Greeks of historic times kept records of genealogies
going back to a distant past. It is easy to disparage their
authority and to claim them as later forgeries. But the
appearance of Andreus and Eteocles in Hittite records has
confirmed the genuineness of the genealogies kept at Orchomenus, and increases the probability that others are genuine.
If they are, they are useful chiefly for the determination of
chronology. They give an approximate date for the close
of the heroic age. The Greeks regarded the heroic age as
ending with the Return of the Heraclids, i.e., with the Dorian
invasion. So any genealogy dating from the Dorian invasion
dates from the close of the heroic age, and of such genealogies
we have several examples.[1] In Sparta the two royal families
of Leonidas and Leotychidas are given by Herodotus (vii.
204, viii. 131) as being descendants of Eurysthenes and
Procles respectively, and being in the fifteenth generation.
If we allow forty years to a generation, this places the Return
of the Heraclids in the eleventh century, where it is placed by
Eratosthenes. In Argos Pheidon is placed variously as in the
sixth and ninth generation from Temenos, the uncle of Eurysthenes and Procles. Unfortunately Pheidon's own date is
disputed, but the earliest reckoning places him in the middle
of the eighth century. So even on the longest reckoning his
family does not reach much farther back than the Spartan
Royal Houses. The Corinthian genealogy places the last
king, who was said to have been killed in 747, in the thirteenth
generation from Heracles, and this takes his family back to
the same date as the Argive Royal House. On the whole,
then, the Dorian traditions agree in dating back their royal
houses to the close of the eleventh century, and this is a
convenient date for the close of the heroic age.

[1] I owe what follows to H. M. Chadwick, *The Heroic Age*, pp. 179–83.

In the heroic age itself naturally the best evidence is Homer, but his accounts of genealogies are well confirmed by other sources, and were no doubt accepted as history. These Achaean genealogies are quite different from the Dorian, and present very interesting features of their own which are important for chronology.[1] In the first place, they come to an end either with the generation of the Trojan War or with the succeeding generation, that is at the time which tradition placed just before the Return of the Heraclids. The House of Pylos ends with Antilochus, the House of Minos with Idomeneus, the House of Sisyphus with Glaucus and Sarpedon, the House of Tantalus with Orestes, and the House of Portheus with Diomedes. Clearly, then, tradition conceived that the heroic families of the Achaeans ended just before the arrival of the Dorians. In other words, the Achaean kingdoms perished before the Dorian invaders, and left no descendants of power or importance. In the second place, none of these genealogies possess more than six generations. If we take the generation connected with the Trojan War as our basis, the longest family tree belongs to Glaucus and Sarpedon, which has in all six generations back to the eponymous Aeolus. The family of Antilochus has in all five generations; so has that of Orestes, while those of Diomedes and Idomeneus have four each. Beyond this we come to a god. On this basis we may deduce that the heroic age was thought to have lasted for five or six generations, that is for about two hundred years, and to have ended soon after the Siege of Troy with the Return of the Heraclids. It is remarkable that this is almost the same length of time which lapsed between the first mention of the Danuna in the Tel-el-Amarna Letters of 1379, and the collapse of the Sea Raiders before Ramses III in 1194.

The local traditions of colonization are less useful for chronology than the genealogies. Their use is rather to indicate the general conditions of life in the heroic age. They show us the Aegean peoples on the move in search of new homes, and adapting themselves to new conditions of life. Greek tradition referred these wanderings and settlements to

[1] Cf. Myres and Frost, op. cit., pp. 459–60.

the period after the Trojan War. But though this may be a convenient label, it must not be taken too literally. In Cyprus, Lesbos, and Pamphylia, Achaeans were busy in the thirteenth century, even if a fuller colonization came later. Perhaps earlier too were the Trojan settlements ascribed to the same date in Sicily at Eryx and Egesta (Thuc. vi. 2), on the north coast of Africa among the Maxyes (Hdt. iv. 191), at Cyrene (Pind. *Pyth.* iv. 84–5), and in Paeonia (Hdt. v. 13). These settlements known to Greek tradition, agree with the activities of Dardenui and Tursha among the Sea Raiders. So, too, Greek tradition knew of what was called Lydian colonization. Ascalon was said to have been colonized by Lydians in the generation of Tantalus,[1] and the *List of Thalassocracies* places a Lydian Sea Power in the second half of the eleventh century.[2] The Lydians may have affinities to any of the unknown raiders from Asia Minor. Not only Greeks, then, but other peoples of Asia Minor are conceived as on the move in the period before and after the Trojan War. The chief event of the kind was the alleged movement of the Etruscans from Lydia to Italy, which Greek tradition dated some time before 1200.[3] Of Greek movements there are many traditions implying a large distribution of settlers at a very early date. The connexion of Lemnos with the Argonauts, of Lesbos with Orestes, are relics of the push across the Aegean which had begun with Andreus. Bellerophon is in Lycia two generations before the Trojan War.

In Palestine the descendants of the Sea Raiders kept memories of their Cretan origin and worshipped Ζεὺς Κρηταῖος.[4] The name of Minos survived in a series of towns from Gaza to Sicily.[5] The best account of these confused movements is in the Cretan legend preserved by Herodotus of the events in Crete that led to the death of Minos. Minos seems to

---

[1] Steph. Byz., s.v. 'Ασκάλων, quoting Xanthus of Lydia.
[2] Cf. J. L. Myres, 'On the List of Thalassocracies in Eusebius,' *J.H.S.* xxvi, pp. 84–130.   [3] Herodotus i. 94.
[4] Steph. Byz. s.v. Γάζα ; cf. S. Casson, 'Cretan and Trojan émigrés', *C.R.* xliv. 1930, pp. 52–5.
[5] In Siphnos, Amorgos, Paros, an island off Megara, Corcyra, in south-west Sicily and twice in Crete. For Gaza, cf. Steph. Byz., s.v. Μινώα. The evidence is collected by A. Fick, *Vorgriechische Ortsnamen*, p. 27.

have invaded first Caria and then Sicily, where he met with
some disasters but eventually effected a settlement. This was
two generations before the Trojan War (Hdt. vii. 171). This
depopulated Crete, and then, after it, we are told that λιμόν τε
καὶ λοιμὸν γενέσθαι until Crete was devastated a second time.
But the real time of dispersion and settlement is the period
after the war. What the poets called the νόστοι, the unsuccessful returns of the Achaean conquerors from Troy were
remembered by legends of foundation in different cities.
Cyprus owed Paphos to Agapenor,[1] and Salamis to Teucer.[2]

These traditions agree with the political conditions described
in foreign records. They show the Mediterranean world in
confusion, rent by intestine wars and the ceaseless effort of
races to find new homes. It is not surprising that Greek his-
torians found no difficulty in believing that the Trojan War
fell in such a time. The evidence of archaeology is less full and
less easy to use. Such a period of movement was not likely to
leave memorials, and sites that can definitely be dated in this
period are rare. But certain broad features emerge which suit
well with what we know of the times from other sources.

The last Minoan period was a time of expansion and
colonization, but the Minoan colonies ended suddenly in a
period of destruction. The Sixth City of Troy was in close
touch with the Mycenean world, and its career ended about
1200. About the same time the Hittite capital at Boghaz
Köi ceased to be inhabited. In Cyprus the large Minoan
settlements end abruptly, and cities like Salamis and Citium
change their sites.[3] On the Greek mainland the Mycenean
settlements at Mycenae, Tiryns, Zygouries, and Korakou all
perished by fire, probably before the Dorians. The Dorian
invasion closes the chapter of disasters, but the destruction of
the other cities must be dated in the period of migrations, and
shows what the Mediterranean peoples suffered after the
collapse of the Minoan Empire. Secondly, archaeology
reveals some gradual changes of customs which indicate the
infiltration of new peoples into the places of Mycenean
culture. The pottery becomes more geometric, new types of

---

[1] Paus. viii. 5. 2.   [2] Strabo xiv. 682.
[3] J. L. Myres in *C.A.H.* iii, p. 636.

swords and safety-pins appear with genuine Mycenean sherds and become increasingly more common. Cremation begins, but is by no means universal. These indications come before the Dorian invasion, and show that a new stream of culture was affecting the life of the Greek mainland. The sparse and scattered nature of the evidence points to the innovations being due to people who had not fully colonized the country nor as yet effected any very lasting occupation. It accords with what we know of these restless and migratory peoples, who were always straining after a new home.

The *Iliad* tells of the power of Agamemnon at war. He is the head of the Achaean confederacy. His power is revealed in his calling of a council to discuss the abandonment of the siege, in his review of the Achaean troops before battle, in taking the oath for a truce with the Trojans, and generally in the dictation of policy and tactics. Others make suggestions, but he issues orders; others may criticize his actions, but in the end his word is final. His power is based on two different considerations, on divine right and on the extent of his sovereignty. His divine right is symbolized by his sceptre. He is the σκηπτοῦχος βασιλεύς to whom Zeus has given glory (*A* 279). On the strength of this Nestor tells Achilles to yield to him. The importance of the sceptre is shown by the poet's account of its descent through the House of Pelops from the original gift of Zeus and Hermes. When Thyestes left it to Agamemnon he left with it the right:

πολλῇσιν νήσοισι καὶ Ἄργεϊ παντὶ ἀνάσσειν. (*B* 108) [1]

Resting on it he addresses the Achaeans. The sceptre brings him honour, and the outspoken Diomedes, who criticizes his chief's courage, has to admit this (*I* 38), and Nestor agrees with him (*I* 99). The sceptre then is the symbol of his power, and it comes from Zeus. It gives him κῦδος and makes him different from other chieftains. The divine quality of the sceptre is shown by its use by other officers who hold their power from the gods. It is carried by Chryses when he comes on his solemn mission to the Achaeans (*A* 15), by heralds

[1] 'to rule over many islands and all Argos'.

when they act as arbiters in the duel between Aias and Hector
(*H* 277), by the judges in the trial scene on the shield (*Σ* 505).
In later days the tradition of this sceptre survived. It was
identified with a wooden staff kept at Chaeronea and honoured as divine. It was kept in the house of the priest, and
at the festival of the god, sacrifices were made to it and a
table was laid before it covered with meat and pastry (Paus.
ix. 40. 11). Kings of later times liked to make the same claim
as Agamemnon had made, and Pindar praises Hieron for
wielding his θεμιστεῖον σκᾶπτον in Sicily.[1] Its use is widespread over the world. The Mexican merchants at the time
of the Spanish conquest took a stout stick with them on their
travels which they worshipped as the god Yiacatecutli. And
Captain Cook found such a staff being worshipped in the
Marquesas Islands.[2] Agamemnon's sceptre may in its farthest
origins have been an incarnation of the god himself. For
Homer it is certainly not this, but it is still holy, confers in-
violability on its holder, and claims universal respect. The
sceptre gives the King his right to rule, but Agamemnon's
claim, as Nestor tells Achilles, is that his power is great:

ἀλλ᾽ ὅ γε φέρτερός ἐστιν, ἐπεὶ πλεόνεσσιν ἀνάσσει.   (*A* 281) [3]

His position is firmly founded on the extent of his kingdom.
What this was we are told in the *Catalogue*, and Homer's
account conforms to this. With Menelaus he holds the Peloponnese except for the Argolid, Pylos, Arcadia, and Elis.
Their joint kingdom is bigger than any other kingdom in
the *Catalogue*, and accounts for Agamemnon's superior position. Even outside his own special realm he seems to have
rights of overlordship. The cities which he offers to Achilles
are in Nestor's kingdom (*I* 153), but Nestor takes no exception
to their being offered by him. No doubt Agamemnon is the
overlord, and Nestor is the vassal. But here a difficulty arises.
Agamemnon's kingdom is regarded in the widest sense as over
the islands and all Argos (*B* 108), but what does the poet mean
by Argos? The actual town is in the realm of Diomedes and
may of course have been under Agamemnon's suzerainty, but
here the name covers a wider area and must be determined.

[1] *Ol.* i, 12.   [2] E. Samter, *Volkskunde im Homer*, p. 43.
[3] 'But he is mightier since he rules over more men.'

The problem would not be serious but for the efforts of
Cauer and others [1] to prove that the epic is essentially Aeolic
and Thessalian. In the interests of their theory they have to
prove that originally Argos meant a district of Thessaly. As
this contention has obscured the issue it must be fully considered. Cauer's first argument is that as the fleet met at
Aulis, the army must have come from northern Greece, and
Agamemnon's kingdom must have been in Thessaly. But
the argument does not hold. Aulis was an admirable centre
for an army gathered from all sides of Greece.[2] For a purely
Thessalian host Pagasae would have been more convenient
and more probable. Often in Greek history Aulis, despite
its tricky tides which so perplexed Leaf,[3] was the scene of
Greek military and naval gatherings, and rightly, because it
provided a large harbour in a notably central position.
Cauer then goes on to say that the Homeric epithet $ἱππόβοτον$
used of Argos can apply to Thessaly, but not, for instance, to
the Peloponnese. It is quite true that the plains of Thessaly
provided wide pasture for horses such as was found nowhere
else in Greece. But the Greeks of the heroic age regarded
themselves as a horse-breeding people and their land as a
land of horses. Diomedes the Peloponnesian is a great horse-
man. Agamemnon offers Achilles twelve horses who have won
prizes (I 265–6), and his mare Aethe, is praised by the side of
his brother's horse Podargus ($Ψ$ 295). Nor is there much more
to be said for Cauer's final contention that the phrase $καθ'$
$Ἑλλάδα καὶ μέσον$ $Ἄργος$[4] refers to Thessaly. Hellas certainly
was a Thessalian name, but of a Thessalian Argos there
is no word in the *Iliad*. Indeed, Cauer's theory seems based
on a misconception. Achilles is certainly a Thessalian hero,
but that is no reason why Agamemnon also should come
from Thessaly. It is easier to believe with Homer that he
came from the Peloponnese.

Even so it is not clear whether Argos means the whole of
Greece or only the Peloponnese. Strabo held the second

[1] *Grundfragen*, pp. 223 ff. Criticized by Drerup, *Homerproblem*, pp. 290 ff.

[2] T. W. Allen, *The Homeric Catalogue*, pp. 49–50.

[3] *Homer and History*, pp. 100–5.

[4] It is worth noting that the words are found in the *Odyssey* but not in the
Iliad.

view (viii. 369), and it has one good point on its side. In the phrase καθ' Ἑλλάδα καὶ μέσον Ἄργος we should have a natural geographical division between Greece north of the Gulf of Corinth and Greece south of it. But the balance of evidence is against this interpretation. It shows with abundant clearness that Homer meant by Argos the whole of Greece. It includes fountains in the Peloponnese and in Thessaly (Z 456), as well as the city of Ephyra (Z 152), which is probably Corinth. It is regarded as the home of all the Achaeans, which they have left (B 287) and to which they will return (B 348). When it is suggested that they will perish nameless far from home, the phrase used is ἀπολέσθαι ἀπ' Ἄργεος (M 70, N 227, Ξ 70). The natural conclusion to be drawn from these phrases is that Argos is the whole of Greece, and that such was the extent of Agamemnon's rule. The word is of course used in two senses, in the narrow sense of the town and district of Argos, which belonged to Diomedes and his overlord Agamemnon (A 30, I 22, Ξ 119, &c.) and in the wide sense of all Greece. The double use of the name need not surprise us. If the overlord of Argos ruled all Greece, the extension of the name would follow the extension of his power, and the two uses would exist side by side and be perfectly intelligible in their contexts. So, too, we find a double use of France in the *Song of Roland*. On the one hand it is used of France proper, that is, the domain of Philip Augustus, and on the other of the whole empire of Charlemagne. Agamemnon then is in some sense the king of all Greece, but in what sense needs unravelling. He is not on the one hand anything like an absolute monarch. When Achilles refuses to fight, Agamemnon can use no compulsion on him. He can offer bribes and apologies, but he cannot use force, and he cannot even claim that he has a right to order Achilles back to the field of battle. He is in no sense an absolute monarch like the kings of Assyria or the Pharaohs of Egypt. But he has some sort of supremacy, and this needs analysis.

The other Achaean princes hold their kingdoms independently of him. That is clear from the story of Phoenix. Peleus has given him the people of the Dolopes, and he rules over them. Here there is no question of holding his land from an overlord. He is made an independent prince (I 483).

Similarly there is no reason to believe that the Achaean princes hold their land from Agamemnon. The *Catalogue* names them as independent princes, and such in their homes they were. In the field it is different. His position is at the head of a confederacy which has come together for a common military purpose. Apart from Achilles the Achaean leaders respect his word and obey him. This respect, as we have seen, is symbolized by his sceptre, and if we look closer it becomes apparent that the sceptre is not so much the symbol of kingship as of leadership in the field. Agamemnon holds it in the council of war. When Odysseus takes it from him and urges the Achaeans not to run away, his prestige is enhanced because for the time he holds this symbol that belongs to the commander-in-chief. This military position is made clearer by Odysseus. For him unity of command is a necessity. There must be one κοίρανος. The word is a military title and nothing else (B 203, M 318).[1] In this scene the princes support their leader against the rabble led by Thersites because they want to win the war and to avoid mutiny. In matters that directly concern fighting Agamemnon is supreme. By virtue of his sceptre he is hereditary commander-in-chief, and he is worthy of honour (I 96). As such he divides the spoil as he thinks fit (I 334), makes sacrifices (B 402), and seems to provide rations for the other leaders (P 248 ff.). He has, too, θέμιστες from Zeus, that is, he is the repository of tradition and precedents, like the law-givers in medieval Ireland and Iceland.[2] In other words, he has the full powers that we expect to belong to a general in the field. But his power is limited by the council of the kings. Though he himself can call this council and does (I 89), it is also called by Achilles (A 54). When it is called, he presides and receives words of respect. But he is also open to free criticism. Not only does he receive the abuse of Achilles: even Diomedes accuses him of lack of courage (I 39). His position in it is that he is βασιλεύ-τερος than the others (I 69, 160), but he is only *primus inter pares*. Even when decisions are made they are regarded more as coming from the council than from him. Achilles speaks

---

[1] Forrer, op. cit., p. 19 claims that Attarissiyas is called 'kuirvanas' by the King of the Hittites and that this is the same as κοίρανος.   [2] B 206.

as if the embassy came not from Agamemnon but from the Achaean chiefs (I 421, 520). The reason for this may be that the embassy to Achilles is not a military but a diplomatic affair, and therefore Agamemnon's word does not carry.

This picture then is of a king who is commander-in-chief of the Greeks drawn from all parts of Greece. To this extent he may be said to rule all over Greece. He even seems to have the right to demand military service of the other Greek kings. For Achilles says that he has not come willingly but for the sake of Agamemnon and his brother (A 152). His rights of military service are like those of the Norman kings, who could demand men and arms from their vassals.

The position of Agamemnon has been thought to be drawn by the poet from the Ionian aristocracy of his own day. This may be true of the conditions described in the *Odyssey*, but the conditions of the *Iliad* smack not of aristocracy but of a confederacy of kings. The council consists only of βασιλῆες (B 98, 188), who are real rulers in their own homes and subordinate to Agamemnon only in military matters. A parallel should rather be found in the position of the Hittite kings.[1] The Hittite monarchy was organized for war. At the head of it was the hereditary leader, the king of Hatti, but under him were many vassal kings who ruled in their own territories while rendering military service to the great king. They formed a council which seems to have given advice on military matters but not to have interfered with internal administration.

The Hittite parallel is important, because it shows that in the age of migrations there existed vast military confederacies whose only bond was a single military leader. That this bond was effective may be deduced from the success which met the Hittite armies and the Sea Raiders. Without a united command adventures like the great raid on Egypt would have been impossible. When the adventure met with a repulse or the command broke down, the whole confederacy disappeared. Some such event accounts for the disappearance of the Hittites from history, and it may equally account for

[1] Cf. W. Weber, *Die Staatenwelt des Mittelmeeres in der Frühzeit des Griechentums*, Stuttgart, 1925, p. 42.

the decay of the Achaeans. The leader of such a united army was a man of great account, and regarded as the peer of the kings of Egypt and Babylon. The important position held by the Achaean leaders in the Hittite documents points to their power being very like that which Homer ascribes to Agamemnon. Only if they were at the head of vast armies like this would they have been able to flout the Hittite king or be treated by him as equals. And their powerful position is the best reason for regarding Homer's account of Agamemnon's power as historical.

Agamemnon's kingdom is by no means an impossibility. Perhaps the poet magnified it, but its structure and extent agrees with the political conditions of the time. The next question is whether the Siege of Troy is equally a possibility. Troy existed, and the poet knew something of its position and natural surroundings, but such knowledge does not prove that the siege took place. Nor do the ruins of the Sixth City provide indubitable evidence of an Achaean conquest. The Hittite records are said to mention towns called Taroisa and Uilusa,[1] and it is tempting to recognize Τροία and Ἴλιος, but nothing of interest is known about them, and their identity is still dubious. Indeed Uilusa, despite its king Alaksandu who recalls Ἀλέξανδρος,[2] seems to be Ἐλαιοῦσα in Cilicia. Of the Trojan War there is not a word, but the library of Boghaz Köi ends in about 1200, a few years before the traditional date of the siege, and need not therefore be expected to mention it. But Greek tradition has been proved correct in other things, and it may be correct in this. Those who do not believe in the siege at all have still to produce good reasons why it cannot have taken place, and those who believe in it have to find some good reasons why it can.

In modern times the siege has been denied or doubted by the unitarian Drerup and the analytical Bethe. Drerup[3] argues that the Achaean movements went south and southeast, and that there was no reason for them to go north or

[1] Cf. Forrer, op. cit., 7; Weber, op. cit., p. 44; A. Götze, *Kleinasien zur Hethiterzeit*, p. 26.   [2] Cf. Kretschmer, 'Alexandros von Vilusa', *Glotta*, 1924, p. 205 ff.
[3] *Homerproblem*, p. 277.

north-east. This is hardly logical or persuasive. It is true that the direction of Achaean expansion was largely to Cyprus and Egypt, but those southern goals may only have been sought because of a failure in the north, or equally failure in the south may have led the Achaeans to try their fortune in the north. It would be as sound to argue that the Normans never invaded England because they invaded Sicily. And indeed our evidence even outside Homer shows the Achaeans active at an early date in Lesbos, which is nearly as far north as Troy.

Bethe develops the same point with rather more show of reason.[1] He denies that any commercial motive could have made the Achaeans attack Troy in the twelfth century. Its position is not well calculated to control the Hellespont, nor was the Hellespont at that date an important trade-route. At a later date the Greeks colonized the eastern shore of the Aegean, but the plain of Troy was not colonized till the seventh century. He himself thinks that the Sixth City of Troy was destroyed in about 1200 by the Thracian peoples who crossed from Europe to Asia and eventually destroyed the Hittite Empire in 1180. His point then is that no reasonable motive can be found for the Achaean siege, and he thinks that the whole story is the invention of later Greeks who saw the ruins of Troy and naturally claimed its destruction for their ancestors. To such a criticism the only answer is to find a reasonable cause for the war, and the causes advanced for it must be considered.

The economic interpretation of history has invaded Homeric study, and Leaf held that Troy was attacked in the interests of trade.[2] Helen was the excuse, but the real objective was the control of the land and sea trade-routes which converged on Troy. He points out that Troy was traditionally a rich city, and that its great walls still bear witness to its wealth. He considers this wealth was due to its position. The tides of the Dardanelles swept traders to the south bank, where they were compelled to unload and sell their goods under the walls of Troy, paying for this doubtful privilege a high tribute to the Trojan King. Some elements

---

[1] *Homer*, iii, pp. 11–18.   [2] *Troy*, passim.

in this view are accepted by M. Sartiaux who, while dismissing the compulsory unloading, thinks that Trojan wealth was based on closing the Hellespont to navigation.[1] Leaf elaborated his view by deducing from the list of Trojan allies that Troy was the centre of four main trade-routes. Homer, of course, does not mention these commercial causes of the war. He was concerned with heroes, and trade was beneath his notice. But the real objection to this theory is that it misunderstands the nature of the heroic age. The Achaeans seem not to have been in the least concerned with trade, and Bethe is certainly right when he dismisses any such notion with contempt. There is no evidence for any commerce with the Euxine in Mycenean days or in the following centuries. It begins with the development of Greek colonization in the seventh century. Mr. T. W. Allen challenged Leaf to produce any evidence of such sea-borne trade, and all that Leaf could find was a Mycenean sherd from Amisos. This, as Mr. Allen has shown, does not require sea-trade at all, as it lies on a land route of great antiquity.[2] And indeed the whole notion of a war for trade is alien to what we know of the Greeks of this time. They were not concerned with wealth, and probably despised it. Their business was fighting, and to make them traders is to anticipate the history of five hundred years later.

More persuasive are the theories of Dr. Eduard Meyer and Mr. Allen, who have no truck with trade and regard the war as fought for purely political purposes. For Mr. Allen 'the reason of the Trojan War was to remove the last power which dominated the Asiatic coast and prevented settlement',[3] and for Dr. Meyer 'the saga of the Trojan War is a reflex of the wars which the Aeolians fought with the indigenous population in their settlement on the Ida peninsula'.[4] He shows how the story of Achilles is closely connected with what was afterwards Aeolis. Achilles is the conqueror of Lesbos (I 129), Tenedos, and the Teuthrantian coast, he has fought a campaign in Lyrnessus, Pedasos, Thebe, and Chryse (Υ 92, A 366, 100), he has taken the 'maid of Brisa'. In essence the two views agree in connecting the Siege of Troy

---

[1] *Troie*, Paris, 1915.   [2] *The Homeric Catalogue*, pp. 175–8.
[3] Ib., p. 177.   [4] *Gesch. der Alt.* ii, p. 400.

with the Aeolic colonization, and differ in the amount of historicity they ascribe to the traditional details. For the moment we are not concerned with the details, and may consider if the siege can safely be referred to the first arrival of the Greeks on the north section of the west coast of Asia Minor. This theory has one main, though not insuperable, difficulty. The Trojan plain is not in itself a very attractive field for colonization, nor is it apparent why a city placed so far north can have seriously interfered with the occupation of Aeolis, unless it was the centre of military and naval power. The main strategic importance of Troy was that it commanded the route from Europe into Asia, and we should expect any attack delivered on it to be aimed at securing this route, not merely at clearing the whole area for colonization. When the Troad reappears in history, it lies on the way of conquerors like Xerxes, Alexander, or Mustapha Kemal. Yet on this theory the great walls were meant for other uses, and the Achaean attack aimed at other ends. Moreover, in Homer's account of the Trojan allies the Thracians, Ciconians, and Paeonians come from Europe. The existence of such an alliance is easily explained if both parties were interested in preserving this easy passage from Europe into Asia. How important it was, the Hittite Empire knew, when the Thracian peoples crossed by it and captured Boghaz Köi. Priam remembered fighting as a boy in the Sangarius valley for the Phrygians, who were of European origin, against the indigenous Amazons of Asia Minor (Γ 189). The connexion between Thracian and Trojan place-names was long ago noticed by Strabo (xiii. 1. 21), and confirms the affinity between the two races. The assumption then seems natural that the importance of Troy, and the base of its wealth and power, lay in its strategic position between Europe and Asia, and it is easy to believe that the Trojan War aimed at seizing this position. A successful siege would place the victors in possession of this invaluable strategic post and make them masters of the main route from Europe into Asia. It seems possible that the Achaean siege aimed at some such end. Its results were only partially successful. Aeolis became Greek, but the Thracian and the Trojan seaboards were still the home of barbarians. But it is tempting to connect the siege with the fall of Boghaz Köi in about 1180, almost the traditional date of the Trojan War. The Achaean siege may have been part of a concerted movement against the Hittite Empire which resulted in its overthrow, or it may have been due to the victors' quarrel over the spoils. In the days of migrations the political scene changed rapidly, and the friends of yesterday were the enemies of to-day. It is unlikely that the Hittite Empire spread as far as Hellespont, but it may well have had friendly relations with Troy which guarded the route so vital to its safety. And it is noteworthy that among the Trojan allies are some who come from the very centre of Hittite power, the Halys valley: [1]

αὐτὰρ Ἁλιζώνων Ὀδίος καὶ Ἐπίστροφος ἦρχον
τηλόθεν ἐξ Ἀλύβης ὅθεν ἀργύρου ἐστὶ γενέθλη. (B 856–7) [2]

It is just possible that another hint of Hittite associations is contained in the passage of the *Odyssey*, where Odysseus speaks of the feats of Neoptolemus in the country of Telephus:

τὸν Τηλεφίδην κατενήρατο χαλκῷ
ἥρω' Εὐρύπυλον· πολλοὶ δ' ἀμφ' αὐτὸν ἑταῖροι
Κήτειοι κτείνοντο γυναίων εἵνεκα δώρων. (λ 519–21) [3]

Perhaps the Κήτειοι are the Hatti or Hittites. Nothing else is known of them, and they were an unsolved puzzle in antiquity. If the identification is correct, and it is no more than a guess, the Hittites were not only friendly to Troy, but assisted actively in operations on the Aegean sea-board. If Troy was in alliance with them, the siege by the Achaeans would be a necessary preliminary to any destruction by European peoples of the city at Boghaz Köi. It may be the case that the Hittites opposed Achaean expansion, and the Trojan War was fought to break that opposition. It may also be the case that the Hittites and kindred peoples were attempting to establish some kind of influence in Greece.

---

[1] Cf. T. W. Allen, *Catalogue*, pp. 159 ff.

[2] 'Odius and Epistrophus led the Halizones from far distant Alybe, where is the birth-place of silver.'

[3] 'He slew the son of Telephus with his bronze, the hero Eurypylus, and many of his Keteian comrades were slain about him because of a woman's gifts'.

About 1270 the Hittite king Hattusil sent his son Orhi-
Tessubas 'behind the sea', and E. Forrer thinks this means to
Greece.[1] But Greek tradition gives better evidence of such
foreign influence in the generations before the Trojan War.
Pelops was thought by Pindar to be a Lydian,[2] and his
charioteer Myrtilus bears a name suspiciously like the Hittite
Myrsil. So, too, Tantalus was said to have lived on Mt. Sipylus
as well as in Corinth, and was unaccountably connected with
Asia Minor.[3] His memory was blackened and he became the
type of the great sinner. Perhaps such men were Hittite
agents or tributaries, whose memory was denounced by the
resurgent nationalism of a later age. These few hints in the
tradition suggest that in the years before the Trojan War
there were rulers in Greece of Asiatic origin. Perhaps the
Trojan War was the last step in the process by which this
Asiatic suzerainty was abolished.

Such hypotheses are only guesses, and the appearance of
any new evidence may overthrow them entirely. The age of
migrations was full of rapid changes, and in the absence of
any sure chronology, the reconstruction of its history is quite
hazardous. For the present, perhaps, we may assume that the
Trojan War was part of the movement by which the Hittite
Empire fell. Such a theory agrees with the geographical
conditions of Troy, and finds some support in Greek tradition. Beyond this it is not safe to go.

Homer normally calls his Greeks Ἀχαιοί, and presents a
problem. Did the Achaeans exist as the single people which he
describes, or has he taken the name of a single tribe and applied
it to a whole people? In his account of Agamemnon's kingdom and the Siege of Troy Homer has not written of anything inherently improbable. So it is natural to ask whether
there ever existed a great Achaean people, dominating the
other races of the Greek mainland and playing a leading part
in the politics of the Aegean.

There seem to be two main alternatives. Either Homer is
right, and Greece of the heroic age was inhabited by a more
or less homogeneous people who called themselves Ἀχαιοί, or

[1] op. cit., p. 15.　　　[2] Ol. i. 24, ix. 9.　　　[3] Ol. i. 39.

he is wrong, and the whole conception of the Achaean world is a poetical invention. This second view, destructive as it is, has prima facie much to recommend it. If we believe that Homer lived at some distance from the events of which he writes, his veracity cannot be pressed too far. He may easily have attributed to a section of the Greek race a power which in fact it never possessed. And this consideration is fortified by the comparative failure of the Achaean name to survive in historical Greece. If the Achaeans were once a great people, why did their name not survive?

Moved by these difficulties Paul Cauer put forward the view that Homer was wrong in regarding the Achaeans as the chief race in Greece. He concluded that they were a Thessalian tribe who afterwards moved to the north of the Peloponnese and the south of Italy under the pressure of invasion.[1] In Homer's day and earlier they lived in Thessaly, but they were given the chief part in the epic because the epic is a glorification of Thessalian saga. This theory has been developed by Mr. J. A. K. Thomson, who goes farther and says that the Achaeans were a people of north-western affinities like the Dorians; they arrived late in Greece, took over the epic and converted it to the praise of Achaean heroism.[2] The essential point in this theory is that it makes the Achaeans late arrivals in Greece. Now neither of these theories quite fits the facts. If the Achaeans were a Thessalian tribe and nothing more, it is impossible to understand why they played the important role in Mediterranean politics of which we hear from the Hittite and Egyptian records. And to place their arrival in Greece with the Dorians is to fly in the face not only of this evidence, but of all Greek tradition, which placed them emphatically before the Trojan War and a fortiori before the Return of the Heraclidae. These theories then are not entirely satisfactory, but they are based on a point which needs explanation: the fact that in historical times most of the tribes still called Achaean seem to have spoken North-west Greek. If true, this is a fact of first importance, and cannot be ignored. The evidence comes from inscriptions, and though late is good evidence of the language

---

[1] *Grundfragen*, pp. 218 ff.   [2] *Studies in the Odyssey*, pp. 117–42.

spoken at the time. But it is not so decisive as Mr. Thomson thinks. In Phthiotis there are not many inscriptions, but such as there are do not necessarily support the view that the Achaeans in this district spoke North-west Greek. Most of the inscriptions are in the κοινή of the Aetolian league, and are not good evidence for the spoken dialect of the country. Of the remainder some are in North-west Greek (*I.G.* ix. 2. 97, 141, 199, 208), while others show traces of old Aeolic forms in the preservation of ρσ (*I.G.* ix. 2, p. xi, Κυρσιλίδα), of ρε (βρέχας), the use of the pronoun ἀμμέ. In Achaea, too, the North-west Greek elements are combined with forms more akin to Aeolic, such as ἐμί and εἶμεν (Lesbian ἔμμι, Thessalian ἔμμεν), the infinitive form ἔχεν, and the preposition ἰν. These are only signs, but they are significant. They come from inscriptions of quite early date, and they are not North-west Greek. On the contrary, they belong to a scattered group of dialects which seem to have been derived from the pre-Dorian language of the Peloponnese. The form ἰν occurs also in Arcadia, Cyprus, Pamphylia, and Crete. The infinitive in -εν occurs also in Arcadia. The dissemination of these forms is strong evidence against the inhabitants of the Peloponnesian Achaea having always spoken North-west Greek. They are survivals of the language which was spoken before the Dorians came. This language survived in Cypriote and Arcadian, perhaps in Pamphylian. It existed, too, in the central parts of Crete, where the language, though predominantly Dorian, had in it other elements drawn from this source. These elements may even be traced in Rhodes and Elis. They are neither Dorian nor Ionic, and there is no reason to connect them closely with either. They are more closely related to Aeolic, though by no means identical with it. The conclusion then is that if the historical Achaeans show traces of an ancient pre-Dorian language in their speech, there is good reason for believing that they were originally not Dorian but related to the Aeolic Thessalians and the pre-Dorian inhabitants of the Peloponnese. That this ancient language disappeared on the coast of the Gulf of Corinth need not surprise us. Erse early disappeared on the east coast of Ireland while it survived in the country districts.

This dialect then, related on the one hand to Aeolic and on the other to Arcado-Cypriote, seems to have been the original speech of the early Achaeans. But of course we must not deduce from this that it was the pre-Dorian language of all Greece. Such a view makes no place for Attic-Ionic which has equally good claim to antiquity. If this language is really Achaean, it was only one of several early Greek dialects. It follows that when Homer calls all the inhabitants of Greece Achaeans, he cannot be basing the title on any fundamental community of language. The language spoken, for instance, by his Athenians can only have been an early form of Attic-Ionic. So when the critics claim that Ἀχαιοί is an artificial title, they have some justice on their side, though they are not justified in claiming that the name was never of more than a local importance. We have then to find a theory which will explain these two facts, the undoubted existence of the Achaean name for a great power in ancient times, and the equally undoubted restriction of the genuine Achaean dialect to certain parts of Greece. The natural conclusion is that the name Achaean belonged to a section of the Greeks in Thessaly and the Peloponnese, but was applied wrongly to the whole race. In the same way the same people are called Δαναοί and Ἀργεῖοι, though to judge by the Egyptian records the Danuna are one tribe among many, and the Ἀργεῖοι are most naturally thought of as the inhabitants of Argos in its narrower sense. In the same way the Angles gave a name to the various tribes who conquered England, and the Franks imposed theirs on France. The existence of the alternative names Ἀργεῖοι and Δαναοί seems to point to all three tribes being in close political connexion, and therefore being able to use any of the three names. And this is what we might expect from the great political combinations which were the leading features of life in the fourteenth and thirteenth centuries before Christ.

Both in Homer and in the Hittite documents the Achaean name is the name which counts. In the *Iliad* Ἀχαιοί occurs 605 times, whereas Ἀργεῖοι occurs 176 and Δαναοί 146 times. Ἀχαιοί is normally used of the whole body of men under Agamemnon, but it also used in a more restricted sense of

Thessalians who followed Achilles (*B* 684). Also some men of Messenia are called Ἀχαιοί (*Λ* 759). It follows that the Achaeans also existed in the Peloponnese, but of this there is no certain evidence, as the word may here be used in its wider sense. The important fact is that Homer calls his heroes Ἀχαιοί more often than anything else, and in so doing he agrees with the Hittite records who knew of an Achaean power. 'Achaean', then, must have been the general name for the Greeks at the time of the great migrations, even if it sunk in later times into a narrower and more local significance. Yet even then it kept something of its early glory. In Rhodes the citadel of Ialysus was called Ἀχαία, and in Cos there was a cult of Ζεὺς Ἀχαιός.¹ Memories of Achaean settlement were treasured in Cyprus, Pamphylia, and the Aleian plain in Cilicia. The name had especially a sentimental appeal, calling up times when Greeks were united. Demeter was called Ἀχαιά,² and when Cleomenes wanted to persuade the priestess of a shrine on the Acropolis that he had a right to enter, though Dorians were forbidden, he said ἀλλ' οὐ Δωριεύς εἰμι ἀλλ' Ἀχαιός.³

Once, then, Achaean was a synonym for Greek, and in this sense Homer uses the word. Any further attempt to analyse the Achaean power is difficult and precarious. The centre of the empire may have been Orchomenus in the fourteenth century. Later it seems to have moved to the Peloponnese. Beyond this, the question becomes: Who were the Greeks? not: Who were the Achaeans? And this lies rather outside out present scope. Homer certainly throws little light on the question, but once or twice he gives hints, and they are worth consideration.

When Achilles prays to the god of his fathers that Patroclus may fight victoriously and safely, he calls him

Ζεῦ ἄνα, Δωδωναῖε, Πελασγικέ, τηλόθι ναίων (*Π* 233) ⁴

and the Achaeans must have lived in Epirus long enough to establish their holy places there. Beyond this we know

---

¹ Athenaeus viii. 360 e, quoting Ergeias of Rhodes, πόλιν ἰσχυροτάτην τὴν Ἀχαίαν καλουμένην.   For Cos, Schwyzer, *Dial. Graec. Ex.* 251 A, 36.
² Hesychius Ἀχαιὰ ἐπίθετον Δήμητρος.   ³ Herodotus v. 72.
⁴ 'Lord Zeus of Dodona, Pelasgian, dwelling afar.'

nothing, and the vexed question whether the Achaeans are the same as the Myceneans is still unsolved. But in this region of guess-work we may hazard one or two ideas. The Achaeans were in some parts of Greece in the fourteenth century. At this date the Mycenean civilization was still in existence. It is improbable that the Achaeans called it into being—it clearly comes from Crete. But they were civilized enough to preserve and even to maintain it. Unlike their Dorian successors they did not destroy what they found; they made use of it and enjoyed it. So, too, the Goth Theodoric maintained the Roman civilization, and employed Roman workmen to build in the old style. No doubt the Achaean rule led to the decay of the mainland culture. The Achaeans were primarily soldiers, and their history seems to have been a continuous series of raids and wars. But they were not such barbarians as the Dorians, and under their rule the Mycenean world continued, even if it decayed.

The physical type of the Achaeans is equally question for dispute. They have been claimed as 'blond beasts' from the north, and as pure Mediterraneans with dark hair and long heads. Homer is at least clear about some of his heroes. Achilles (A 197, Ψ 141), Meleager (B 642), and Menelaus (Γ 284) are all $\xi a\nu\theta o\iota$. So, too, are Demeter and Agamede (E 500, Λ 740). But Zeus is unaccountably dark—he nods $\kappa\upsilon a\nu\epsilon\eta\sigma\iota\nu$ $\epsilon\pi$' $\dot{o}\phi\rho\upsilon\sigma\iota$ (A 528). $\xi a\nu\theta\dot{o}s$ means not so much 'blond' as 'brown',[1] but in any case it is a different colour from that painted on Minoan frescoes, which is blue-black, like the hair of Zeus. On the Mycenean frescoes at Tiryns the hair is of the black Minoan kind, and if Tiryns belonged to fair-haired rulers, either their portraits have not survived, or their artists followed Cretan conventions and gave them black hair.

Homer's Achaeans are $\kappa\dot{a}\rho\eta$ $\kappa o\mu\dot{o}\omega\nu\tau\epsilon s$, that is long-haired. And the details carry this out. In the horse-race the hair of the competitors floats in the air (Ψ 367), and Achilles has dedicated his long hair to the river Spercheius but cuts it off at the funeral of Patroclus (Ψ 141). The use of this epithet has presumably tradition behind it. The Achaeans were somehow distinguished from other races by

[1] Cf. P. Giles in *C.A.H.* ii, p. 22.

wearing their hair long. They also seem to have worn beards (π 176). The Minoans wore long hair but shaved their beards. So did the men of the First Palace at Tiryns. But the Myceneans grew hair on the face. Of the gold burial masks one has a moustache without a beard, and another has both beard and moustache. Later we find an even more flowing way of wearing the hair, and a carved stag-horn from Crete shows long hair and a beard. This evidence cannot be pressed too far. On the one hand it distinguishes Achaean fashions from Minoan and earlier Mycenean, but on the other long hair lasted as the fashion in Greece for centuries and gives little indication of date.

These indications point to the infiltration of some different physical type into the Mediterranean world in later Mycenean days, and this conclusion is confirmed by the examination of skulls belonging to the different periods of Minoan Crete. The statistics drawn from these show that in the greater part of the Minoan periods the inhabitants were of two main types, of the long-headed Mediterranean and the middle-headed Armenoid or Alpine types. In the last Minoan period there is a great intrusion of a short-headed type, which accompanies a decrease in the long heads. Such an intrusion should indicate the immigration of men of quite different physical character, and may well be connected with the arrival of the Achaeans. If so, it shows that in Crete at least the invaders came in sufficiently large numbers to alter the whole character of the population.

From these indications it seems that the Hittite and Egyptian records are not wrong, and that the Achaeans were a power to be reckoned with in the fourteenth and subsequent centuries. What the name means, we have no notion. It is clearly a general name, like the later ῞Ελληνες, covering most tribes of Greeks. As such it survived even into historical times in certain rare and isolated cases. But the Achaean power had so collapsed that politically the name remained only with the men of Phthiotis, the Doricized inhabitants of Achaea. This collapse is not without parallel. The Hittite Empire, which had once held dominion over the greater part of Asia Minor, left no traces of its name to later generations. Men of Hittite stock were ruled by governments who did not claim to be Hittite, and the name was lost even to Herodotus. So, too, the Achaeans were swallowed up by the invading Dorians, to whom they yielded not only in name but in language. That their language disappeared as it did was no doubt due to the extraordinary destruction wrought by the Dorians. But it still survived in isolated regions like Arcadia and Cyprus. What remained was the memory of heroic undertakings, and this survived in Ionia. It must have been taken to Ionia by the first colonists fleeing before the Dorians, and there it was preserved in the epic verse handed down by one generation to another. The Ionians were not Achaeans. Their language is not closely related to Arcado-Cypriote, and their traditions connected them with Attica. But no doubt they had formed part of the Achaean Empire and shared, like other Greek tribes, in the Achaean name. To this past their saga owed its origin, and it was the Ionians who preserved the facts of history in heroic verse. No doubt in the process of years the facts were distorted, and for this reason it is impossible to press too far the account of events which Homer gives. There was indeed a heroic age, and none of the main features which Homer describes, the kingdom of Agamemnon, the Siege of Troy, the Achaean domination, are in themselves impossible or even improbable. But beyond this all is fable. Even Agamemnon himself can only be a poetical figure till his name is found in historical documents of the time. Poetry is not history, and it is absurd to expect an epic poet to write a chronicle or even to take trouble with his names and details. He may telescope centuries and invent as his fancy pleases. But ultimately his story is founded in fact, and claims to tell of what has happened. Homer was too far removed from the heroic age to paint it accurately, but he had inherited the tradition of great things done, and, like Herodotus after him, his subject was ἔργα μεγάλα τε καὶ θωμαστά, τὰ μὲν Ἕλλησι, τὰ δὲ βαρβάροισι ἀποδεχθέντα.[1] His details may be pure invention, but the general political situation which he describes seems to be based on fact.

[1] 'Great and admirable deeds, some done by Greeks, some by foreigners.'

THE CHARACTERS

FROM his predecessors Homer inherited his Tale of Troy. But his task was to tell the tale again in a new form, to remodel it completely. Tradition gave him not only the outlines of the story but the main characters on whom the story turned. To these he had to give new life, while keeping their traditional features. His success was so great that we must believe that he treated his material with the utmost freedom, and re-created when he might only have repeated it. It would be pleasant if we could tell what originally the characters were, and from what different sources they sprung. But here even analogy fails us and we are faced with a complete blank of evidence. His characters have been claimed as genuine figures of history,[1] as gods brought down to the likeness of men,[2] as ancient figures of folk-tale.[3] From any or all of these sources they may ultimately have come. Nor is it impossible that some were even invented by Homer. After all he was a poet, and creation was his privilege. Early epic confounds fiction with fact, and the two elements are hard to unravel unless we have the independent testimony of history. So until the Hittite records confront us with the name of Agamemnon, we cannot tell whether he is a real man like Theodoric in the Germanic epic, or a creature of folk-lore like Beowulf, or a degraded divinity like Satan in *Paradise Lost*. Such questions, however fascinating, cannot yet be solved, but they lie far behind Homer. He must have found his important characters existing in earlier poetry and possessing some of the characteristics which he gives them. His stock epithets bear the marks of ancient tradition, and show his heroes as old story knew them. Agamemnon must always have been ἄναξ ἀνδρῶν, Odysseus πολύμητις, Achilles πόδας ὠκύς. With such simple labels early poetry differentiates its characters, and helps its hearers to remember them. This simple device exists in most early ballad poetry, and no

[1] Leaf, *Homer and History*. [2] E. Bethe, *Homer* iii. passim.
[3] J. A. K. Thomson, *Studies in the Odyssey*.

doubt it existed in the poetry of Homer's predecessors. But Homer goes far beyond this. He presents a set of characters equalled only in the greatest poetry, and our task is to see how he succeeded. In the *Iliad* mere labels have become real men and women. His success was far greater than that of any other early writer of epic, and our present task is to analyse his achievement, to see what he made of the names he learned from his predecessors.

The *Iliad* is the story of the wrath of Achilles. With his quarrel with Agamemnon it begins, and with the close of the disastrous consequences it ends. The character of Achilles is the cause of all that happens to himself, to the other Achaeans, to the Trojans, and particularly to Hector. On his persistence in his anger hangs all that is important in the poem, and Achilles, even when he is off the scene, is the chief person of all. For even then he is still the pattern of martial perfection to which no other can reach—they are always μετ' ἀμύμονα Πηλεΐωνα [1]—and without him his allies become incompetent and disorganized. He may sit far from the battle, but he is always missed, and, just because he is not there, he is most wanted and his greatness is most felt. His personality holds the poem together and gives it a unity where there might be chaos, and though the poet wanders far from him at times, in due course he returns to him, and all through the last books his personality fills the scene and dominates our attention. To keep so many different threads together by the power of a single personality requires great creative and constructive power, and in the characterization of Achilles Homer makes no mistake. He fills exactly the role required of him, and, more than that, in all his speech and actions he is true to himself and to the superhuman majesty which clothes him. He is a heroic warrior on the grand scale, and he possesses in more than ordinary measure all the virtues and all the faults of a hero. If he lacked either the one or the other, he might be a better or a worse man, but he would be less of a hero. His sensitive pride and his brooding over injuries are as heroic as his fleetness of foot or the enchantment of his spoken word. He is not a 'preux

---

[1] *B* 674, *P* 280.

chevalier'. Roland would never have acted, as Achilles acted, from injured pride: that was more the part of Ganelon. But Achilles is still a hero to his bones, and a hero bred for battle. Soldier born and bred, he lacks root in ordinary life and he is alien to domesticity. He went to Troy a mere boy, and he knows that he is to die young and glorious. All his thoughts and all his life are absorbed by battle. Of the ties which bind Hector to home and family he knows little. He has no wife: his father he has not seen for years; his mother, for all her charm and all her care for him, is not a human mother. She can help him, but he can never help her. She is divine and needs no tenderness. In all this he is the opposite of Hector, who is full of thoughts for Andromache and Astyanax, for Priam and Hecuba. Achilles knows little of any home other than the camp, and his only affections are for his old guardian Phoenix, and for his friend Patroclus, who shares with him the adventures and risks of war. His life has been dedicated to battle, and in battle he has found himself. If he were not invaluable in the fight, the Achaeans would have suffered less from his defection, and if he were not cast in so splendid a mould his overmastering passion of resentment would not be so essentially tragic. The resentment of Achilles is deeply rooted in his nature, and without it he would be less of a hero. It is the expression of his thwarted and disregarded self-esteem, and this self-esteem, τὸ θυμοειδές as Plato called it, is the essential quality of a man of action, but, if it is crossed, it turns to bitter resentment and self-pity. His strong self-assertive personality is crossed by Agamemnon, and he is all the more angry because he knows that Agamemnon is acting unjustly. When the quarrel begins over Briseis, Achilles has some justice on his side. In the past, Agamemnon has taken advantage of his position to slight him, giving him only a small share of booty, and on this occasion there is little excuse for Agamemnon taking away Briseis without compensation or courtesy. So there is some case for Achilles when he decides that he will humble Agamemnon by staying away from battle till Agamemnon has to ask him to return. Nestor admits that Agamemnon has no right to Briseis and ought to give her up; he tells

Achilles plainly that for all his strength and divine birth he is still inferior to his feudal lord and has no right to flout him (*A* 277 ff.). But Achilles takes no notice of this. He is indeed stopped by Athene from trying to kill Agamemnon, but he indulges to the full his feelings of injured pride, and leaves his friends to be defeated, wounded, and killed because of his refusal to help them. When he goes to his tent, he is in the wrong, and he does not admit it even to himself. When Thetis comes to comfort him, he has only blame for Agamemnon, and in this frame of mind he endures till it leads him to disaster and deep regret.

The second stage comes with the embassy to Achilles, asking him to abandon his isolation and come to the help of the embarrassed and disheartened Achaeans. Much has happened in the interval. Achilles' hopes have soon been fulfilled, and the Achaean chiefs are beseeching him for help. The situation is changed, and its main result is that Agamemnon has been brought to his senses and is now prepared to make amends for his action (*I* 116 ff.). His change of heart puts the other Achaean leaders in a far better position. At first their only justification was loyalty to him, but he himself was under the shadow of guilt. Now he has decided to make amends and to make them generously. So the embassy goes to Achilles with right on its side and with some expectation of success. The categorical refusal of all their overtures by Achilles is the second step in his tragedy. The offers of Agamemnon are indeed generous and should appease all Achilles' sense of injury and injustice. But Achilles refuses them, and his reasons for refusal are entirely true to himself. In his long reply to the embassy he never falters in his decision to reject all overtures, and he gives the surprising reason that he does not want to fight again, because it is not worth while, because its dangers far outweigh its rewards. In passionate words he claims that no price, however great, is worth more than a man's life (*I* 406 ff.). At first sight this argument may seem inconsistent with his earlier reasons for not fighting, and many have thought that here is a real contradiction due to the hand of another poet. But there is no inconsistency. Rather there is a fine piece of insight into

Achilles' character. He has been sitting in his tent brooding over his wrongs, and what began by being a personal and particular wrong has grown under his brooding to a sense of universal injury, to a strong mistrust of all military glory. Originally his refusal to fight was dictated by Agamemnon's seizure of his lawful booty, Briseis. Now he has thought about it, and he sees that this is only part of a general scheme of things. War is always like this. The profits are small and do not sufficiently compensate for the horror and the risk. So, too, Lear enlarges his particular wrongs into the universal suffering of the universe. Achilles, the man of action, has paused for thought, and his thought has led him to an overpowering disgust with his life. He says that it is not worth while, and he means every word that he says. His anger has lost some of its violence, but it is more deeply and more firmly rooted than before. He is polite to the ambassadors, and for their own sakes he gives them a courteous welcome. But he has thought out his case and justified himself to himself, and for this reason he is hard to persuade. His sense of injury has lost some of its passion, but it has gained in strength. He can afford now to keep his temper, because he feels sure that he is right, and when Phoenix shows that he is wrong, he is not convinced and shows no resentment. He refuses all Agamemnon's offers and says that probably he will go home (*I* 428). He is sure that he is right, and nothing will shake his assurance. But the Achaean leaders know, and Phoenix knows, that he is wrong. In his long speech Phoenix points the moral. But Achilles takes no notice of him. He has hardened his heart in his grievances, and it will take more than words to change his purpose now. When the embassy leaves him, he has almost made up his mind to sail away in the morning, and his decision is quite sincere. To satisfy his pride he is willing to do more than let his friends suffer defeat by his absence: he is now prepared to desert them altogether. The embassy has only strengthened him in his resolution and helped him to formulate his grievances. There is indeed one small ray of hope, which he himself suggests and Diomedes repeats to the Achaeans (*I* 618–19). If the spirit moves him, he will fight. If it does not, he will go back to Greece. He is in fact prepared to follow his emotions and nothing else. So ends the second stage, the refusal of Agamemnon's overtures. Now it is Achilles and not Agamemnon who is in the wrong.

From his tent Achilles watches the battle, and his next appearance is when from his ship he sees Machaon being carried back wounded. As he sees this, he knows that his plan is working, and he tells Patroclus that soon the Achaeans will be at his knees asking for help (Λ 609). There is no contradiction here. He has already had an embassy asking for help. But his plan is progressing so well that he has abandoned all thought of going away and thinks only of how the Achaeans will have to abase themselves more before him. In Book ix their need was not yet final. They could still hope to get on without him, as Diomedes hoped. But now he sees that the situation is worse, and his pride demands even greater humiliation for them. This time they will beseech him in real earnest—χρειὼ γὰρ ἱκάνεται οὐκέτ' ἀνεκτός (Λ 610).[1] So he sends Patroclus to inquire from Nestor, and once again Nestor makes clear the case against Achilles. He has abandoned his friends, and though most of the best Achaeans are wounded and their ships are near to being burned, he still has no thought or pity for them. Nestor makes no mention of the cause of the quarrel with Agamemnon. Clearly he regards that as no longer of importance. Agamemnon has made his overtures and they have been rejected. Everything now lies with Achilles, and Achilles is wrong because he prefers his injured pride to his comrades. He stings Patroclus to regret, and this is increased when Patroclus meets the wounded Eurypylus on his way back from battle and is asked by him for help. Patroclus helps him, and goes back to Achilles with a deep sense of shame.

So the battle goes on, and Patroclus weeps for shame in the tent of Achilles (Π 2 ff.). And this is the beginning of the great change in Achilles. His affection for Patroclus is the only real affection in his life. He loves him on his own admission more than his old father or his young son, whom he has not seen for so long that they are strangers to him (T 321 ff.). So when Patroclus weeps, Achilles cannot and

---

[1] 'For on them comes a need no longer to be endured.'

will not disregard it. It is true that when he asks the reason
of it, he compares Patroclus to a girl crying, and there is some
irony in his words. But under the irony there is nothing but
tenderness. Achilles is deeply moved by Patroclus' unhappiness, consents at once to his going to fight and lends him
his own armour. He helps him in every way that he can,
urging the troops on and seeing that there is no delay. All
this he does for his friend, but his own feelings are still un-
changed. To Patroclus he repeats his grievance against
Agamemnon, and ends his exhortation with a fierce prayer
that neither Trojan nor Achaean may survive, and that he and
Patroclus alone may have the glory of taking Troy (Π 100).
This is not the language of repentance, and yet there is just
a hint that already the sense of grievance is losing its hold on
Achilles. In his solemn invocation to Zeus that Patroclus
may return victorious and unharmed he says nothing of his
own grievances, nothing of his desire to humiliate the
Achaeans. The occasion was indeed too holy for the display
of personal animosity, but that consideration would not deter
Achilles, who sees his wrath as right and justified. His anger
is beginning to die. He has admitted as much to Patroclus.
Though he wishes still for the humbling of the Achaeans,
yet, for the sake of Patroclus, he will let bygones be bygones,
and he admits that no anger can last for ever. But his pride,
and his pleasure in his grievance, prevent him from taking
the one really important step. He does not go himself. And
the result is that Patroclus is killed.

So ends the third act in the story of Achilles. The fourth
begins with the news of the death of Patroclus and ends with
the death of Hector. The horror of the news wipes away at
once all relics of his quarrel with Agamemnon, and in some
ways restores him to sanity. He admits that he has enjoyed
his grievance, that anger can be sweeter than dropping honey,
and with perfect sincerity he regards Agamemnon's gifts as
irrelevant now (T 146 ff.). His anger with Agamemnon has
quite disappeared, but it has left its results. Because of it
Patroclus is dead. Achilles should have been there to protect
him, and because of his self-indulgent wrath, he was not.
And more than this, just as his anger lost him Patroclus, so

the same strain in his nature is inflamed now even more
against Hector, and he goes out to avenge Patroclus with a
mind half-mad with passion, and reckless of all the restraints
which should bind men even in battle. He is now the soldier
at work, and he thinks only of the fight with Hector. If any
other man gets in his way, so much the worse for him. He
kills Lycaon though he is defenceless: he fights the river god,
Scamander, till Hephaestus intervenes: he knows nothing of
mercy or charity. Starving, fierce from shedding blood and
wild with lust for revenge, he kills Hector. But even then he
is not appeased. He allows the Achaeans to stab the dead
body with their spears, he ties it behind his chariot and drags
it to the camp. Just as his anger eventually lost him Patroclus,
so here it has brought him to a pitch of pitiable tragedy. He has
avenged the death of his friend at the price of his own honour
and chivalry. He has indeed had much justification—the
shortness of his life, the hollowness of its glory, the loss of his
friend, have not helped to make him merciful. His fury is
quite intelligible, and therefore the more tragic. And the
tragedy, too, is greater because he is still alive, friendless and
unsatisfied.

In a mood of stunned quietness he conducts the funeral
games, and then slowly he comes back to himself. The last
act of his story, where he gives back the body of Hector to
old Priam is the return to sanity. His wrath has not quite
left him, and for a moment he is afraid that he may want to
kill Priam. But as he speaks to the old man, he thinks of his
own father, and he turns to pity. Soon he is all consideration
and kindness. The body of Hector is given back, and Achilles
is himself again. His passion has run its course and died. He
is no longer avid for battle, and he is willing to let the Trojans
have a truce of twelve days for Hector's burial. So the *Iliad*
ends on this note of peace, almost of purification. Passion
has had its fullest fling, and it is now over. Thus the *Iliad* is
in the fullest sense the story of Achilles, the story of his tragic
temper, which loses him his best friend and makes him break
the rules of heroic chivalry.

No other character is as important as Achilles, and all
centre on him. The other warriors gain by contrast with him,

and particularly is he contrasted with Hector and with Agamemnon. Hector is in many ways all that Achilles is not.
They are both great soldiers, and as such they come into con-
flict. But while Achilles is essentially and always a soldier,
Hector is a soldier almost from compulsion. Achilles fights
for the love of fighting, while Hector fights to save his home.
In Troy his family watch the battle and he is always in their
thoughts and they in his, but Achilles is separated from his
home by 'the shadowy mountains and the echoing sea' (*A* 157).
Achilles has kind words for no one but Phoenix and Patroclus: even for Briseis he has hardly a kind word. Hector is
surrounded by those he loves, and in the intervals of battle he
seeks out his wife, or plays with his child, or speaks words of
comfort to the lonely and tragic Helen. Over his domestic
happiness the poet sheds all his grace and tenderness. Suddenly after a scene of slaughter we see Hector talking to
Andromache, and this is the real Hector. He fights to defend
her and Troy. Prowess in battle is part of his nobility, but it
is only a part. With Achilles it is the whole man. For this
reason Hector is less of a soldier than Achilles. Before
Achilles left the field he never dared to oppose him, and it is
only when Achilles stays sulking in his tent that Hector
dominates the battle. Against lesser men he is a good fighter,
though he is not really a match for Aias, who gets near to
killing him (*H* 270). But he is a better general than fighter,
and he has gifts for leadership rather than for individual
feats of valour. Here, too, he is different from Achilles, who is
too deeply absorbed in his own fighting to give thought to
leadership. Time and again Hector rallies the drooping
Trojans and spurs them on to another effort. His is the leading
spirit in the attack on the Achaean ships, and when he is
wounded, the Trojan army loses heart. He rallies cowards and
sluggards with a timely rebuke, and men like Paris admit that
they deserve his words, and go gladly to battle (*Γ* 59, *Z* 333).
He is willing, like the good captain that he is, to take advice
and act on it. Again unlike Achilles, who cares little for
religion except on occasions of high solemnity, Hector is
scrupulously religious. He welcomes Helenus' suggestion
that the Trojan women should try to placate Athene by

putting a robe on her image's knees (Z 102), and he is careful
not to make a wine-offering to Zeus when he has blood on his
hands (Z 266). Even when he makes his famous cry:

εἷς οἰωνὸς ἄριστος ἀμύνεσθαι περὶ πάτρης   (M 243) [1]

he is not blaspheming. His contempt for omens is based on
his trust in Zeus. Zeus has promised him that he may attack
the Achaean ships, and no mere omen is enough to shake his
confidence in that promise. But where perhaps he differs
most from Achilles is in a fundamental lack of confidence.
Achilles is all too conscious of the brief span of his life and of
the inevitable doom which awaits him, but he is still entirely
sure of himself and his heroic destiny. He knows that in
battle no one can resist him, and he is not ashamed of saying
so. But Hector lacks confidence at heart. Even for his wife
he has few words of consolation, and tells her that some day
Troy will be taken, and she will be sold into slavery (Z 448 ff.).
It is true that while he fights his courage is unimpeachable.
He can be brave not only in attack but in endurance. In the
mêlée he can forget himself and fight like the hero that he is,
but when it comes to a single fight with Achilles, his courage
is of a different and more human order. He is determined to
risk the fight with him because Achilles must die if Troy is
to be saved, and though Apollo warns him off, nothing in
the end can keep him from facing his adversary. But he
has no illusions about the issue. He knows that he must
die, and yet he steels himself for the struggle and tells his
companions that he will fight:

τοῦ δ' ἐγὼ ἀντίος εἶμι, καὶ εἰ πυρὶ χεῖρας ἔοικε,
εἰ πυρὶ χεῖρας ἔοικε, μένος δ' αἴθωνι σιδήρῳ.   (Υ 371-2) [2]

Here is moral courage as well as physical. He braces himself
for the event and follows a forlorn hope, knowing that there
is no chance of victory. When at last it is clear that Achilles
is ready for him, he has thoughts at first of compromise, but
he realizes at once that it is out of the question. Despite his
resolution the first appearance of Achilles is too much for

---

[1] 'One omen is best, to defend our country.'
[2] 'I will go to meet him, even if his hands are like fire—if his hands are like
fire and his might like bright iron.'

him and he runs away, but then his courage recovers, and he faces his enemy and dies. He is a brave man and he dies a hero's death, courteous and chivalrous to the last, thinking of his own people, and asking that his body may be given to them. For were he victorious he would do the same for Achilles. His courage is less instinctive than deliberate. He has to be brave, and he is. But behind it there lies the melancholy of those to whom the gods have given so much that they have to take it away. At times he is carried away by the fierce ecstasy of battle, but in his heart he thinks of home, and it is most characteristic of him that when he is making up his mind to face Achilles, his thought wanders instinctively to the most remote of all things from this meeting with death, and he thinks of a young man and a young woman talking to one another:

οὐ μέν πως νῦν ἔστιν ἀπὸ δρυὸς οὐδ' ἀπὸ πέτρης
τῷ ὀαριζέμεναι, ἅ τε παρθένος ἠΐθεός τε,
παρθένος ἠΐθεός τε ὀαρίζετον ἀλλήλοιιν. (X 126–8) [1]

Even at that last hour of danger and decision his thoughts are suddenly wafted to the ordinary things of life.

Agamemnon, too, is contrasted with Achilles, but differently from Hector. He competes with Achilles on his own ground, and loses by the comparison. He too has an imperious temper, and dislikes having his will crossed; he too makes no attempt to control his passions. But their parts in life are different. Achilles can afford to indulge in whims, because he is in a way his own master, but Agamemnon is in command of a great army, and tied and fettered with responsibilities. He is first and foremost a general. For his post nature has fitted him well. The aged Priam notes his height and kingly bearing (Γ 165 ff.), he holds his power from Zeus, and he is as good a fighter as any one but Achilles. The Achaeans regard him as a suitable antagonist for Hector (H 180), and when he takes the field he is irresistible till he is wounded. So good a fighter is he that Zeus sends a message to Hector warning him to keep out of the way (Λ 202–5).

---

[1] 'It is not now possible to converse with him from oak-tree or from rock, as a maiden and a young man, a maiden and a young man converse with one another.'

Such courage is essential in the general of a great army, but
Agamemnon's personal prowess is subordinated to his position as general of the Achaean confederacy. He has to be
more than a fighter, he has to be a leader of men, and here
the poet contrasts him skilfully with Hector. He is less of a
general than Hector, and his task is more difficult. The
Trojans are united in their defence of home against the
enemy, and they are fighting for an end which they all desire
and think important. The Achaeans are invaders who fight
'Ελένης ἕνεκ' ἠϋκόμοιο, and sometimes they feel that the war is
not worth while. The confederate princes are a difficult team
to manage, and in his attempt to control them Agamemnon
is not helped by his own nature. He is liable to be swayed by
sudden and violent emotions. He can be ungovernably
arrogant and tyrannical in his treatment of Chryses or his
insistence upon taking Briseis from Achilles. But when the
passion passes and he decides to make amends, he is as generous as before he was unreasonable. So, too, in his public
duties he passes from one extreme to the other. When he
tours the Achaeans and urges them to battle, he is full of
confidence and ready to chide any one who is at all slow to
get ready (Δ 250 ff.), but at the first approaches of disaster
he loses heart and is ready to throw up everything. Twice he
has half a mind to leave Troy and sail home (I 27, Ε 74), and
when he is wounded, he feels sure that Hector will kill the
Achaeans and burn their ships (Ε 44 ff.). His character is
real and consistent, though it suffers from comparison both
with Achilles and with Hector. He has not the heroic
grandeur and the burning confidence of the one, nor the
perfect blend of qualities in the other. It would have been
easy to make him a more attractive man, but Homer has
made him more dramatic by giving him violent emotions and
hampering him with heavy responsibilities.

Achilles, Hector, and Agamemnon are the protagonists of
the *Iliad*, and they dictate its plot. From their passions and
conflicts the story grows, and they rightly play the main parts
in it. Hence they are characterized in detail and even with
subtlety. In all their utterances and actions they are their
own heroic selves. But the creative imagination which formed

them did not stop its work there, and they are surrounded with other figures who are less dramatically important but always vivid and passionate. In its way this too is a remarkable piece of creation. No doubt tradition provided traits and characteristics for the Achaean heroes, giving Aias his shield like a tower and Odysseus a reputation for strategem. But the other heroes in the *Iliad* have such marked personalities that they can be nothing but real creations of the poet. A variety of poets would not create a group of men so differing from each other and from the principal characters. Each stands out separate and individual, though they all are soldiers engaged on the same task and compelled *ex hypothesi* to be brave and eloquent. To create different living beings within such narrow limits is a hazardous task. The peerless heroes of the Middle Ages or the Renaissance are very like each other, and though not all are as lifeless as the gentle knights of *The Faerie Queene*, they are seldom more vivid or more differentiated than the minor characters of the *Song of Roland* or the *Morte d'Arthur*. Where many poets have failed, Homer has succeeded. His minor Achaean heroes are entirely real, and they are all different. They fall roughly into two classes, the soldiers and the statesmen. In the first class are Aias, Diomedes, and Menelaus, and in the second are Nestor and Odysseus. Both Aias and Diomedes are men of action, and not much else. Aias is no good at the council and he gives no serious opinion, while Diomedes is sceptical of the value of statesmanship, and deplores the embassy to Achilles (*I* 698 ff.). So far they are of a type, but beyond this point they differ. Aias is frankly a soldier and no more. He is below the heroic standard of intelligence, and his chief assets are his physical strength and physical courage. The poet gives us his view of him in two similes in close juxtaposition. In the first his reluctant retreat before the Trojans is compared to a lion who is kept out of a byre of oxen by dogs and herdsmen (*Λ* 548). This is the soldier of great endurance and courageous pertinacity. But immediately afterwards he is compared to an ass who breaks into a field and cannot be got out of it (*Λ* 557). The two similes give the whole of Aias' nature. He is brave as a lion, but he lacks brains, and his persistent courage is of an animal quality. But he has the grandeur which goes with great physical strength, and he is at his best when he defends the Achaean ships with a boarding-pike twenty-two cubits long (*O* 678), or throws a stone as big as a millstone at Hector (*H* 268). He even achieves moral sublimity in defeat, where his refusal to retire has a real heroism and inspires him to eloquence in his call to the Achaeans to hold their ground because there is nothing behind to save them from death in a foreign land (*O* 733 ff.). Diomedes is far less ponderous than Aias. He is the young man *par excellence* among the Achaean captains and has the qualities of youth. He is impetuous and careless of restraint or compromise. When Achilles leaves the field, he is the first to lead the attack against the Trojans with any success, and even in defeat his courage does not leave him. He believes firmly in a fight to a finish, and he has as little use for Nestor's plan for conciliating Achilles as he has for Agamemnon's plan for flight. He has, too, the chivalry of youth. The delightful scene with Glaucus, where the two enemies discuss their ancestry and end by exchanging armour, is in the best traditions of heroic good manners, and he always gives advice with a happy optimism, which is often infectious. He is pre-eminently a soldier, and his performances on the battle-field are in the best heroic tradition. He advances like a river in full flood, and nothing can withstand him (*E* 87). When Pandarus and Aeneas combine against him, he refuses to think of safety while his strength is still unimpaired (*E* 252). In particular he shows how real heroes can treat the gods. Athene is his friend and he shrinks from attacking Apollo (*E* 444), but he thinks nothing of attacking the two least reputable inhabitants of Olympus, Aphrodite and Ares. His action is not impiety, because Athene advises him to it, but it is the most that a man is allowed this side of impiety. The poet saves his character by making Aphrodite ridiculous and Ares revolting. In all his actions Diomedes is serenely brave and confident, the young hero in the prime of his powers, who steps into the breach left by the defection of Achilles.

Menelaus, though he is important to the story, is not so

important a character as either Diomedes or Aias. He suffers
under two grave disadvantages: he is the younger brother of
Agamemnon and he is the husband of Helen. Because of the
first he has to follow Agamemnon's lead, and he tends to
agree with what the elder brother says. Because of the
second he is irretrievably committed to the war, and he finds
it hard to maintain his dignity as a betrayed husband. He
is essentially unfortunate. Even when he seems to have Paris
in his grasp, the helmet strap breaks and Paris is carried off
from him by Aphrodite. This misfortune dogs him and dis-
heartens him. So he lacks enterprise, and acquiesces in the
lead of others. This makes him rather a mock to his enemies,
who call him μαλθακὸς αἰχμητής (P 588). This is unfair, but
he is not a great warrior. He is a useful confidant for
Agamemnon, conscientious and responsible. But he lacks
glamour, and perhaps the poet thought him rather a bore.
At least it is clear why Helen left him for Paris.

The two men of counsel, Nestor and Odysseus, are painted
in great detail, and their personalities have the sharpness and
the breadth of great portraiture. Nestor is the Polonius of
the *Iliad*. In Coleridge's words he is a 'statesman past his
prime'. He lives in the past, which means far more to him
than the present, and its great names are always on his lips.
But from his ripe experience he is full of advice, and it is
usually good. When Agamemnon and Achilles quarrel he
attempts a perfectly sensible reconciliation, asking Agamemnon not to take Briseis, and Achilles to yield to his
superior officer. If they had listened to him, things would
have turned out very differently. When Agamemnon is
ready to make amends to Achilles, it is largely because of
Nestor, who tells him that he is to blame and must apologize.
And it is Nestor who eventually brings Achilles into the fight,
by showing the state of affairs to Patroclus and appealing to
his sense of honour. But Homer is not content to leave him
as an experienced and sage dispenser of good advice. He has
made him more human by making him rather ridiculous.
He has a habit of recounting interminable reminiscences on
the slightest provocation, and though in moments of crisis
like the quarrel of the chiefs or the council before the embassy

he controls his garrulity, on more favourable occasions he inflicts his stories on whatever hearers he can find. When Patroclus comes to inquire about the wounded Machaon and claims to be in too much of a hurry to come into his tent, Nestor keeps him waiting outside while he recounts a long tale of an old war between the Pylians and the Epeans. In battle, where considering his years he cuts a remarkably good figure, he is made to appear slightly laughable, when his horse gets wounded in flight from Hector and he has to be saved by the kind offices of Diomedes, who smiles at his weakness and the slowness of his horses and takes him into his own chariot (Θ 102 ff.). His last appearance is at the Funeral Games of Patroclus, and is quite typical of him. There he gives long, elaborate, and none too honourable advice to his son Antilochus how to win the chariot race with inferior horses. Antilochus does not win but he gets near to winning, and gets a fine consolation prize from Achilles. So Nestor is delighted.

Odysseus is the nearest approach to 'l'homme moyen sensuel' in the *Iliad*. Of all the heroes he has the widest range of talents and the keenest appetites. He is a man of exceptionally powerful intelligence, and he uses his brains for every sort of purpose. He can fight like a hero in times of emergency, but his importance comes from his gift for advice and stratagem. If any difficult duty has to be done, Odysseus does it. He undertakes to return Chryseis to her father, and accomplishes the task with perfect tact and correctness, performing duly all the religious ceremonies which the occasion demands. He, too, goes on the important embassy to Achilles. There he makes a careful statement of Agamemnon's offers, and when they are rejected, he makes no attempt to dispute his decision with Achilles. His tact is part of his enormous self-control. He never gets flustered or frightened. In the difficult situation created by Agamemnon's speech urging the Achaeans to give up the struggle in *B*, he stops the panic which follows by timely and vigorous action. In his night-reconnoitre with Diomedes he removes the corpses from near the horses of Rhesus in case the horses should be terrified at the strange sight and betray him (*K* 490 ff.).

His intelligence is at times not more than cunning, and when
he wrestles with the dull-witted Aias, he whispers to his opponent that they must make it a sham contest, and Aias must
let him throw him. Aias does, but when it comes to his turn
to be thrown, Odysseus does not keep the bargain. He has
no illusions about the heroism of ascetic practices, and he
thoroughly enjoys his food and drink. On the night of the
Dolon adventure he eats three meals, and when Achilles
refuses to eat before fighting, Odysseus insists that at least
he should allow his soldiers to eat (*T* 225 ff.). His good
sense makes him popular, and he is everybody's friend.
Achilles likes him, Diomedes chooses him as the right companion for night work, and in the foot-race he is the popular
favourite. He is even trusted with measuring the ground
for the duel between Paris and Menelaus. Altogether he is
a complete man. Because of his common sense and unfailing
success he lacks the romance of the great heroes, but of all he
is the best man of action, and he is drawn with such scrupulous
care that he must have been near to Homer's heart.

Compared with the Achaeans the Trojan warriors, other
than Hector, are lightly sketched. They are adequate, but
Homer does not seem to have allowed his imagination to play
round them. There may be good reasons for this. He had
created in the circle of Achaean warriors a complete set of
military types of great richness and variety. It would have been
inartistic to create a corresponding set of Trojans, and would
have necessitated much reduplication. Moreover, to his Greek
audience Achaeans were more interesting than Trojans, and
there was no need to multiply Trojans *praeter necessitatem*. Most
of his Trojans are shadowy enough. But art demanded that
the Achaeans should have foemen worthy of themselves, and
Homer gives us not only Hector but Sarpedon, Glaucus, and
Aeneas. None of these three is drawn in much detail, but they
are all true men and fit opponents for the Achaeans. Aeneas
is so overshadowed by his later literary life that he seems to
lack vitality, but he is quite real, and indeed he is quite a
suitable forerunner of his later self, 'pietate insignis et armis'.
The Aeneas of Homer is quite a considerable warrior, who
dares to confront Achilles at the height of rage, and he is a

ùevout worshipper of the gods, to whom he makes countless
sacrifices (Υ 299). He is, however, less attractive than Glaucus
and Sarpedon, who, perhaps because of their Lycian ancestry
and Hellenic affinities, are the poet's heroes among the
Trojans. Both are young and reckless, but while Glaucus is
touched with comedy, Sarpedon is a tragic figure. They work
together, and their role in the story is one of friendship and
mutual confidence. They are Hector's main support; when
he is wounded, their shields protect him (Ξ 426), and both on
different occasions upbraid him (E 473 ff., P 141 ff.) for not
conducting the battle to their liking. Of the two, Glaucus
is in the full flush of generous youth. It is he who loses by
the exchange of his golden armour for the bronze armour of
Diomedes—ἑκατόμβοι' ἐννεαβοίων—but it is to him that Homer
gives some of his finest words, the words on the shortness of
human life which he says to Diomedes:

οἵη περ φύλλων γενεή, τοίη δὲ καὶ ἀνδρῶν   (Z 146) [1]

and the deeply religious prayer to Apollo in his hour of
danger (Π 514 ff.).

He and Sarpedon do their work together, and stand side
by side to the last with a perfect mutual understanding.
Together they attack the Achaean ships, and Glaucus obeys
Sarpedon in silence when all his efforts are called for (M 329).
When Glaucus is wounded, it is Sarpedon who is sorry for his
loss (M 387 ff.). So, too, in Sarpedon's last fight it is Glaucus to
whom Sarpedon says his last words, and Glaucus who tries to
save his body. Glaucus well remembers his last encourage-
ment to keep the fight going. The alliance is broken by the
death of Sarpedon. With Hector and Patroclus he is one of
the few soldiers in the *Iliad* whose death is a real tragedy. His
youth and gallant bearing are lost irreparably, and the poet
wisely gives us some consolation by sending him in the arms
of Sleep and Death to burial in his own Lycian home.

Apart from these the Trojan warriors are not very interesting or important. Homer's real creative successes with
Troy are of quite a different character. In the Achaean
camp he created his galaxy of warriors. In Troy he creates

---

[1] 'Like a generation of leaves, so is a generation of men'.

women the old man Priam, and the cause of all the trouble, Paris. Clearly he is right. In this assembly we get the life of the beleaguered city, the life which Hector is fighting to defend. Paris is the connecting link between the Trojan soldiers and the civilians. His character is drawn with such mastery that it is surprising that it has been so often mis-understood. He is not, as has been said, a coward. He is captain of a great host of Trojans (*M* 93), Aeneas believes in him (*N* 490), and Hector believes in him (*N* 766). On the third day of fighting his skill saves the Trojans from disaster (*Λ* 504 ff.). It is true that he is an archer and open to some charge of being unsporting, but he is quite willing to put on armour when he is called to do so and to fight a duel with the redoubtable Menelaus. Nor would the Trojans respect him if he were a coward, and that they certainly do. For in the council where Antenor suggests that Helen should be re-turned to Menelaus, the refusal of Paris is enough to get the proposal rejected at once (*H* 357 ff.). But he is vain and rather frivolous. Hector treats him for what he is worth, and sends him to battle with a few harsh words. Paris bears him no resentment for this and goes to battle gladly (*Γ* 59, *Z* 333). His emptiness comes out most in the moving scene with Helen, where he does not understand that she is tired of him, and insists on his rights over her. He is frivolous and sensual, and therefore Hector rather despises him. But he has super-ficial grace and charm, and some animal qualities of gaiety and courage. He is not good enough for Helen, and part of her tragedy is that she knows it.

Priam is the old man who has learned not to expect too much out of life but to take things as they come. His facul-ties are still alert, and he inquires with insight into the personalities of the Achaean heroes, and thinks how far greater their army is than any he saw as a boy. He is the antithesis of Nestor, for whom nothing is as good as it once was. He has lost his illusions, and the loss has left him gentle. He has only words of kindness and comfort for Helen, and he bears with resignation the loss of most of his sons. But he nurses one dear hope in Hector, and his tragedy is that he loses even this. He watches Hector with eager eyes, and he is the first to mark the approach of Achilles which presages his death. Then he tries to dissuade Hector from fighting him, for he knows well what will happen if Hector is killed, the fall of Troy with all its horrors to young and old. Of course he is unsuccessful: Hector is killed, and the old man's life is shattered. But then in scenes of immortal beauty his heroic blood urges him to ransom his son's dead body, and though he knows the murderous temper of Achilles he faces the adventure like the old fighter that he is. His gentleness shrinks before the renowned slayer of men and his blood-stained hands (Ω 479), but his courage keeps him to his duty, and in the end he gets what he wants. In dignity and peace he goes home and gives orders for the funeral of Hector.

In Priam we have the pathos of old age in man. He is utterly reliant on Hector, but he still has courage and determination. Hecuba is an old woman, and her pathos is more helpless and more pitiful. She is full of unquestioning simple piety, and makes an offering to Athene (Z 286 ff.) or pours a libation to Zeus when Priam goes on his errand to Achilles (Ω 284 ff.). But most of her life has been absorbed in her children, and especially in Hector. His loss is to her less national than personal. To Priam it means the sack of Troy, but to Hecuba it means the end of her life. Without him there is nothing left worth living for. In a few hysterical words she begs him not to fight Achilles (X 82 ff.), and when she hears of his death, she knows that all is over for her —νῦν αὖ θάνατος καὶ μοῖρα κιχάνει (X 436).[1] Her confidence is so broken that she has no hopes of the success of Priam's visit to Achilles, and she tries hard to dissuade him from going. In her great grief she has cruel thoughts, and longs for revenge on Achilles (Ω 211). But she accepts the mission when it comes, and when the body of Hector is brought back to her, she is glad because of it and pleased to have her son's body for burial.

If Hecuba is foremost a mother, Andromache is both a mother and a wife. Her whole life is in the home. Her father and brothers are dead, and she finds everything in Hector and her little son, called Astyanax because of his father. She

---

[1] 'Now comes death and doom'.

is enormously proud of Hector, but she is even more anxious for him, and tries to persuade him not to go again at once to battle (Z 431). When he refuses to listen, she says no more and applies herself to her child and her household tasks. In these she spends most of her time, giving wheat and wine to Hector's horses (Θ 187–9), or embroidering flowers with her loom (X 441). Just before the news of Hector's death comes to her she is busy heating the bath-water for him on his return (X 444). Her life is given to these things, but its peaceful tenor is ruined by the insistent terror of his death. When the worst happens, her woman's instinct suspects the news before it reaches her. She hears the sound of lamentation and she rushes out like a mad woman to see if her fears have come true. When she knows that Hector is dead, half her life is gone. She has indeed her child still, but she knows that a fatherless child can expect little honour. Even her domestic duties are ended, and she knows that she must burn the fine clothes which her women have made for Hector. When at last the body is brought back to her, she alone finds no comfort in it. For her it is a second death, and starts again her terrors for her child. Now she knows that there is no hope for his safety. He will follow her into captivity or be thrown from the battlements by the Achaeans. She has not even the memory of her husband's last words to comfort her. He was killed out of her sight and hearing.

Andromache is absorbed in her husband and home. When they are gone, she is lost and heart-broken. But Helen's tragedy is that nothing absorbs her. She has the indefinable sadness which often goes with great beauty. She is the victim of destiny, and Aphrodite plays with her. She yields, but it gives her no happiness. Her end in life is to be beautiful, and as the old men say on the wall:

αἰνῶς ἀθανάτῃσι θεῇς εἰς ὦπα ἔοικεν. (Γ 158) [1]

Because of her beauty she is accepted, and it is understood that it is right that men should fight because of it. But to her it is an endless weariness. She longs for death and deliverance, and curses her fate and its author, Aphrodite (Γ 399 ff.).

[1] 'She is terribly like the immortal goddesses to look upon'.

But she is in the grip of a goddess too strong for her, and she yields when she is sent to Paris in his chamber. Her only friend is Hector, and to him she unburdens her unhappiness and her guilt. And when he dies, he is as great a loss to her as he is to Andromache or Hecuba. Among the Trojans she is always afraid of some harsh word because of the sorrow that she has brought with her, but Hector has never said a harsh word to her and has always restrained others. And now he has gone, and she is left to her loneliness. For twenty years she has been in Troy (Ω 765), away from her brothers and her child. She loves Paris no more, and she has made no new friends in Troy apart from the old Priam and the dead Hector. She is always a stranger and the cause of suffering. She has kept her undaunted beauty, but it is little to her, and she faces the future without hope and without resistance.

The list of these important characters does not exhaust the wonders of Homer's creation. Even quite unimportant persons are brought by some magic touch to a sudden and short-lived vitality. Thersites, with his physical deformities and his flow of rancorous speech, Dolon, the only son with five sisters (K 317), Briseis, who loses her only friend in Patroclus (T 287 ff.)—all these come to life in their small parts, and there are others who come at once to mind for some passionate moment or heroic gesture, Asius driving recklessly across the Achaean trench (M 110 ff.), or old Chryses calling on Apollo in his despair (A 37 ff.). The *Iliad* is full of real beings, and Homer's creation never fails. There are many characters, but they never lack reality, and no character is the pale shadow of another. Homer's task was a hard one. The circumstances of war are not the easiest for the creation of a wide range of different characters, but he met the difficulty by setting his picture of war against a background of home life in Troy, and creating a world of women and old men to contrast with the heroism and cruelty of war. He was tied, too, by the convention of his time that his characters must be heroic, and though he keeps the convention, they are still alive. He is largely helped in this by the unexampled richness of his language, but they might easily have sunk sometimes from the heroic level. Only those whom he despises, Thersites and poor Dolon, are below standard, and they are so created intentionally. The heroes are always heroic in their language, their bravery, their amazing vitality. But unlike many heroes, they never lose their humanity. By selecting the essential characteristics and stressing them, Homer makes his personalities real. They may lack the complication or the subtlety possible in drama or the novel, but they have always outline and clarity, and their actions come from themselves. In the strict limits of the epic story there is no place for irrelevance. The character must hit the mark at once, or it is a failure. The outline must be clear, the poet cannot afford to blur the edges. Otherwise the characters would be too like each other and there would be no essential difference between Achilles and Diomedes.

X

HOMERIC THEOLOGY

THE position of Homer's gods in the evolution of Greek religion is remarkable. On the one side they differ greatly from what we know of Minoan-Mycenean deities, and on the other side they differ from the gods worshipped in historical Greece. Minoan religion seems to have had fetishes and totems, to have been deeply concerned with life after death, to have had deities in animal as well as in human form.[1] Of all these there is hardly any trace in Homer. Greek religion of historical times was deeply tinged with the salvationist rites attributed to Orpheus and Dionysus, and greatly concerned with all manner of burial and other rites. Of these, too, there is little mention in Homer. We find instead of these heterogeneous and often inconsistent beliefs a theology remarkably simple in its main outlines. A well-organized theology is usually the work of thinkers who try to systematize a mass of different, even conflicting, beliefs. In its early days the Christian Church tolerated many differences of opinion among its members and hardly noticed them. The systematization and simplification came with the deliberate intellectual effort of Church councils in the fourth century. The unity of the Homeric religion implies some equally strenuous effort.

The gods are all members of one family, they live together on Olympus, they submit, not always easily, to the rule of Zeus, they are all in the likeness of men. Such a system is different from primitive religious belief, which locates its gods in special places, gives them different and peculiar appearances, and never troubles to settle their precedence or relative powers. In historic Greece there was no such hierarchy of gods, and Olympus was their home only for the poets who derived from Homer. There were local and there were official cults, but a general acceptance of a systematic theology did not come till Greek religion was practically dead,

[1] Cf. G. Glotz, *La Civilisation Égéenne*, pp. 263–346.

and existed chiefly in literature and allegory. Yet in Homer we find a simple theology which can only be the result of some special and peculiar conditions. It may of course be due in part to the poet's own feelings, but the poet composed for an audience and had to present them with gods whose ways and functions they knew. His own feelings could only appear in the details of his treatment. He had to choose the familiar gods and give them their familiar attributes. So the actual features of Homeric theology must be found not in the peculiarities of Homer's temperament but in the social conditions under which he lived. These conditions can be found in Ionia after the migrations. Minoan religion seems to have been concerned with cults held at holy places, in caves and woods, at the tombs of the great dead. Every race has its holy places, and no doubt the Greeks who came to Greece in the second millennium had theirs. But when the Ionian colonists moved to Asia, they left their sacred places behind them, and this uprooting of tradition materially altered their beliefs. They preserved the names and memory of their shrines, but rites could no longer be conducted at them, and theology was naturally altered. Achilles still remembers the shrine of Apollo at rocky Pytho (*I* 405) or the oracular oak of the Pelasgic Zeus at Dodona (*Π* 233), and to such the emigrants might turn in moments of stress. But for ordinary purposes the mainland was too far. So they uprooted the gods from their seats and collected them together on Olympus. On the mainland gods and goddesses had each their own town to protect, and with it they were specially connected. A close connexion survived till a late date between Athene and Athens, between Hera and Argos. But the Ionian wanderers coming from more than one home brought different gods with them. The ties with special places were broken, and the different patrons were combined into a pantheon. The result of this uprooting was a great simplification of theology. Special rites could no longer be paid, and special functions were forgotten in the creation of new loyalties and new political conditions.

Such must have been the fundamental causes of the peculiar character of Homeric theology, but in Homer another

feature appears which can only be called rationalism.[1] This
is in itself the fruit of the changed conditions, or rather
without them it would have been impossible. But this
rationalist spirit owes much to causes other than a change of
home. It is essentially aristocratic and careless. So long as
life is difficult, the gods must be placated, but when it becomes easier, theology is a fit subject for intellectual inquiry.
Homer sang for an audience who were prosperous and open-
minded, and he could afford to treat the gods in a critical
spirit. On the mainland, where conditions were harder,
Hesiod could only repeat the old stories without trying to
alter or to simplify them.

Homer's rationalism is of a type not uncommon in the
history of religion. He observes all the formalities and gives
them due respect, but he tempers his respect with curiosity
and with humour. Such an attitude is more common in an
age of faith than in an age of unbelief, and is indeed only
possible when faith is still vigorous. The sculptors of the
Middle Ages could play prettily round some sacred theme
without any suspicion of impiety, and St. Theresa could joke
with God. Homer's attitude is more akin to this than it is to
the rationalism of Voltaire or Anatole France.[2] At least he
accepts the gods and makes them part of his scheme of things.
But he lived in an inquiring age, and the theology which
he accepted and represented is not the theology of an unquestioning tradition. It is highly rationalized and simplified,
and for the understanding of the Homeric poems it is essential
to see how far criticism has destroyed the old scheme, and how
far it has replaced it by something new.

So far as the formalities of religion are concerned, Homer is
thoroughly conservative. His heroes go through the correct
ritual to the gods on any important occasion. When sacrifice is possible, it is made. The poet tells of bulls sacrificed
to Poseidon (Y 403–5), of horses sacrificed to Scamander

---

[1] Cf. M. P. Nilsson, *A History of Greek Religion*, pp. 134–79.

[2] His attitude is best paralleled by the Icelandic *Lokasenna*. Cf. W. P. Ker,
Epic and Romance, p. 41. 'It is not a satire on the gods; it is pure comedy; that is,
it belongs to a type of literature which has risen above prejudices, and which
has an air of levity because it is pure sport—or pure art—and therefore is freed
from bondage to the matter which it handles.'

(Φ 131–2). Oeneus is considered wrong for not giving the θαλύσια to Artemis (I 534). On occasions of rejoicing the gods are remembered, and Chryses sacrifices a hecatomb to Apollo when his daughter is restored to him (A 447). So, too, on any great occasion the formalities are fulfilled. Before the duel between Paris and Menelaus a solemn oath is taken, and lambs are sacrificed (Γ 292). When Achilles sends Patroclus to fight he cleanses his cup with sulphur and pours a libation to Zeus (Π 228 ff.) and, when he himself goes to battle, he swears an oath with the sacrifice of a boar that he has never defiled Briseis (T 258 ff.). The solemnity of any libation is shown by Hector's refusal to pour wine to Zeus while there is still blood on his hands (Z 266–8). These examples, and others like them, show how deeply the ceremonies of religion affect the life of the *Iliad*. But all these ceremonies are such as might have been preserved by a wandering people. They require no holy place for their performance and they concern common acts of every day in a fighter's life. But there are other cases where changed conditions did not allow old rites to be properly observed, and Homer presents us with a curious anomaly in which the form of the rite is preserved though its meaning is lost. At the funeral of Patroclus Achilles slays twelve prisoners and sacrifices four horses, two dogs, and a large number of oxen and sheep at the pyre (Ψ 171 ff.). Yet such an offering only had meaning if Patroclus was going to be buried, when the animals would be of use to him after death. Cremation involves quite a different set of ideas, and excludes the notion of the dead man using sacrificed animals after death. Yet Homer makes Achilles keep up the formality after it has lost its meaning. In this he adheres to tradition at the expense of consistency, but it is characteristic of him that it is the ritual that matters.

So far then Homer follows an ancient tradition, even if it has lost some of its meaning for the world in which he lived. But ritual is the only part of his religion which has not been subjected to the simplifying processes of criticism. It forms a background to a theology which has been simplified by considerable rationalism, and is very far from the primitive

beliefs which existed before and after him. The most noticeable feature of this rationalism is its consistently anthropomorphic view of the gods. The origins of such a view are
not hard to find. They occur in most religions which are
passing from the worship of animals. To the growing consciousness it becomes apparent that an animal is less worthy
of worship and less easy to entreat than a being with human
characteristics. The transition is gradual, and sometimes the
animal characteristics are combined with human; the animal
head stays on a human body and possesses at least human
intelligence. In other places the transformation is complete,
and the animal only continues its importance as the sacred
beast of the anthropomorphic god who has supplanted it.
But in the *Iliad* not even this consideration is paid to the
original worship of animals, and Homer must be far distant
from such a practice. In Ionia the change to anthropomorphism was accelerated by the break with traditional
rites and by that incalculable factor, the Greek intelligence.
In this Homer again lies between two worlds. Minoan
worship certainly involved the worship of animals. The
genii on the ring of Nestor[1] or on the Mochlos seals may not
be full divinities, but they are at least genii, and of such
there is no trace in Homer. Other Minoan divinities are closely
associated with animals, such as lions, bulls, snakes, goats,
sphinxes, and griffins.[2] But of these, too, Homer says nothing.
In post-Homeric Greece such animal cults existed. Demeter
was worshipped with a horse's head in Arcadia,[3] but this is
as alien to the *Iliad* as the Minoan deities. Homer's anthropomorphism is remarkable in that it has no known roots and
left few results on the popular worship of Greece. It grew
up in the unique conditions of Ionia, and it only survived
where the epic survived and affected the literature and life
of the Greek world.

Homer's gods are made in the likeness of men, but he
seems to have heard of some earlier stage, even if he failed to
understand it. In some cases he uses adjectives which are
only intelligible when used of gods who looked like animals.

---

[1] Cf. Arthur Evans, *The Ring of Nestor*, pp. 68–70.
[2] Nilsson, l.c., pp. 18–21.   [3] Paus. viii. 42.

Hera is βοῶπις, Athene γλαυκῶπις, Apollo Σμινθεύς and
λυκηγενής. Originally Hera may have been a cow-goddess and
Athene an owl-goddess. At Mycenae Schliemann thought
he had found cow-headed female idols, and though this has
been questioned, it remains true that the cow plays an important part in Argive legends relating to Hera. The natural
assumption is that Hera was originally a cow-goddess, then a
goddess with a cow's head or a goddess whose sacred animal
was a cow. Of all this Homer says nothing, but he calls her
βοῶπις though she is in human form. Athene in the same way
must have been an owl-goddess, and the owl is still her
emblem and sacred bird on the coins of fifth-century Athens.
Homer calls her γλαυκῶπις, and in some places recalls ancient
saga by making her take the form of a bird. In a well-known
passage she appears as a vulture,[1] and in the *Odyssey* she
makes her disappearances in the form of a bird.[2] This is a
relic of Minoan belief which held that the gods appeared in
the shape of birds. On the Hagia Triada sarcophagus a bird
sits on each of the double axes under which the sacrifice is
conducted. A terra-cotta from Cnossos shows three columns
with a bird on each. Two gold plates from the IIIrd shaft
grave at Mycenae represent a woman accompanied by
birds. The idol from the Sanctuary of the Double Axes at
Cnossos has a bird on its head. So, too, Homer makes use
of old tradition and makes Athene turn into a bird. His
epithet γλαυκῶπις must come from the same source, even if
for him it meant no more than 'bright-eyed'. The two titles
of Apollo must have a similar origin. λυκηγενής can only
mean that he was a wolf-god; such gods survived in Greece
and may be the descendants of some animal-headed divinities of Minoan times. But for Homer Apollo is in human
form, and in this same line is called κλυτότοξος, a purely
anthropomorphic conception. Homer must have used
λυκηγενής without any sense of its meaning, taking it over from
some predecessor who had used it of Apollo. But in the case of
Σμινθεύς Homer is on better ground. Σμινθεύς is the mouse-
god, and he is called by Chryses to stop the plague because
mice were the traditional purveyors of plague. It was mice

---

[1] H 59.   [2] α 320, γ 372, χ 240.

which ate the bow-strings of Sennacherib's army, and mice of which the Philistines made images. So the appeal by Chryses is important and significant. The word comes from the pre-Hellenic word σμίνθα which, as we have seen, survived in the vernacular parlance of Cyprus. How Homer knew the title is quite uncertain. In this case he uses with perfect correctness a title which certainly dates from when Apollo was a mouse-god and had to be placated as the sender of plague.

These are the only cases where Homer's gods and goddesses seem to owe something to Minoan ancestry, and even in these they do not lose their anthropomorphic status. In place of animals and birds Homer presents us with a divine society very like that of his own heroes. Zeus and the other gods sit on their acropolis of Olympus, whose gates are guarded by the Hours. His palace is higher than that of the others and its floor is of gold plates (Δ 2). Against its walls rest the chariots of the gods (Θ 435), and in it Zeus and Hera have their own chamber (A 606 ff.). Round it are the palaces of the other gods. The life in Olympus is one of politics and feasting varied with love. Zeus controls his vassals with no more ease than Agamemnon controls his. Once they revolted against him and he subdued them with difficulty (A 399). Even now they dispute his decisions and at times disobey him, so that he has to chide and threaten them with punishments. The whole episode of the Διὸς ἀπάτη is contrived to draw his eyes from the battle that the gods may take a part in it. His efforts to keep them out of the war are unsuccessful, and in the end they fight each other. The life on Olympus is human in its politics, and in other ways too. The gods pay visits to the Ethiopians (A 423), and, while they are away, much can be done without their seeing. Their blindness is indeed remarkable. Ares does not know when his son Ascalaphus is killed (N 521) because he is clad in a golden cloud on Olympus, and only hears the news later from Hera (O 110 ff.). Hera indeed is more intelligent, and her female intuition tells her that Thetis' visit to Olympus bodes no good to her (A 536 ff.), and Athene knows that the defeat of the Achaeans is Thetis' work (Θ 370). All this is delightfully human, and no doubt Homer's audience appreciated it as

such. But the poet seems to have felt that he was making it
rather too human and to have used the resources of tradition
to differentiate his gods from men without destroying their
human characteristics. He did this by the simple devices of
making them capable of miraculous actions. When Zeus
nods, he shakes Olympus (*A* 530). When Poseidon comes
from Samothrace to Aegae the mountains and woods shake
under him and he does the journey in three steps (N 20).
When Ares or Poseidon cry aloud, their cry is like that of nine
or ten thousand men (*E* 860, *Ξ* 148). The gods live on nectar
and ambrosia, and their blood in consequence is not ordinary
blood but ἰχώρ (*E* 340)—a word which seems to be borrowed
from Hittite.

This complete anthropomorphic system has of course no
relation to real religion or to morality. These gods are a
delightful, gay invention of poets who were prepared to use
their material freely in an age which enjoyed its gods. But
having his gods so like men and such excellent figures for
drama, Homer was confronted with two difficulties. In the
first place, though they were raised above the beasts, they
were only like human beings and therefore often laughable,
and in the second place such a system almost excluded any
notion of the gods being concerned with human morality.
These two sides of the question had naturally to be considered,
and the result was that Homer followed both lines and paradoxically made the gods both ridiculous and impressive.

It is but a small step from humanizing the gods to making
them ridiculous, and Homer easily takes it. But his special
method of getting a laugh out of them is to adapt some old
story to their present anthropomorphic circumstances. The
gods had their traditional attributes, and though perhaps
these might have been ignored, Homer preferred to keep
them and work them into the plot. The lame metal-worker,
Hephaestus, is still kept lame. That was part of his character,
for he hurt his leg when he was thrown out of Olympus by
Zeus. But Homer makes his lameness rather absurd. He
busies himself with the gods' feast and the gods laugh at him
διὰ δώματα ποιπνύοντα (*A* 600).[1] Ares, the war-god, was in

[1] 'bustling through the halls'.

ancient story a monster of great size with a tremendous voice. So when he is wounded by Diomedes, the poet ignores his otherwise anthropomorphic character and makes him cry like nine or ten thousand men and cover seven roods with his body (*E* 860). Folk-lore gave even odder stories than these, and Homer makes use of them. When Zeus wants to frighten the other gods and goddesses he threatens to hang a golden rope from heaven and fasten them all to it (*Θ* 19). This hides some ancient myth which is lost to us. Here it is pure comedy. So, too, in tradition Zeus had numerous wives. The large number was due to the conquering sky-god annexing local sanctuaries, and therefore being connected with local goddesses by the simple expedient of marriage. But Homer finds humour in his polygamous Zeus. His best treatment is when Zeus, overcome by his revived love for Hera, tells her that her charms far surpass any of his great loves (*Ξ* 315–28). The long list of erotic triumphs is of the most sophisticated character and well compared to Leporello's Catalogue in *Don Giovanni*. So, too, tradition made Zeus and Hera brother and sister. This was awkward, but Homer laughs at it. He recalls the early days of love-making between Zeus and Hera, and adds the immortal touch φίλους λήθοντε τοκῆας[1] (*Ξ* 296). Perhaps some other tradition lies at the back of the remarkable scene in which Hera beats Artemis with her bow (*Φ* 491 ff.). But by far the most remarkable is the astonishing Διὸς ἀπάτη. In the *Iliad* this is a delightful, if slightly lubricious, comedy. There is great humour in the way in which Hera sets to work in cold blood to attract Zeus, and some irony both in her success and in Zeus' later reactions. The story is relieved from coarseness both by wit and beauty, and sustains a high level of elegant and delightful blasphemy. But it is based on a very old religious notion of the ἱερὸς γάμος, the wedding of the god and his bride, which is at the back of much ancient religion, and certainly seems to have been part of Minoan religion.[2] This belief was no doubt celebrated with ritual such as we find in the celebration of the marriage of Zeus at Gortyn under a green plane-tree. Homer takes the familiar myth

---

[1] 'escaping the notice of their dear parents'.   [2] Nilsson, op. cit., pp. 33–4.

and ritual, and turns it into a story, quite devoid of religious significance and interesting almost entirely as a story. But the story was based on religion, and this gave his treatment a little additional piquancy for those who knew the rite and the belief which it celebrated.

This gay treatment of the gods was no doubt excellent so far as poetry was concerned. It made the gods interesting and amusing, and it helped by contrast to display the excellence of men, at least of men in the heroic age. But of course to the moralist and the theologian it presented grave difficulties. To ascribe the universe to divine governance and then to rob that governance of any moral responsibility or significance, this struck a deep blow at the moral consciousness, which demands that a man's actions shall be sanctified by some power above himself. And herein lies the fundamental paradox and contradiction of Homeric theology. For the poet it was excellent that the gods should be as he described them, irresponsible, amusing, unimportant. But conscience demanded that the gods should control human actions and be the guardians of justice. So Homer paradoxically makes the gods the arbiters of human behaviour and makes no attempt to solve the contradiction. He developed his views of divinity and its importance for morality and religion on quite different lines, and left it at that. Fundamentally this contradiction is a fault. We expect a poet to give us his views of life, and though Homer does so, he wraps them up in a disguise of comedy which is at variance with what he really seems to think. Modern literature presents hardly any parallels to such a treatment of religion. And yet there is something of the same contradiction in Milton. The puritan in him condemned Satan and all his ways, but the artist wanted a redoubtable antagonist to God and endowed Satan with heroic qualities of courage and endurance. It is true that in the later books of *Paradise Lost* Satan becomes less heroic, but the first impression of sublime grandeur is ineffaceable and quite alien to the theology preached elsewhere. Milton's discord is less obvious than Homer's, but it shows that a single poet may combine such discordant elements and applaud as a poet what he deplores as a moral-

ist. Some such explanation may account for Homer's varying
treatment of the gods, but an explanation might equally be
found in the circumstances of his time. In Ionia thought had
moved rapidly and left some traditional elements far behind.
The religion of the Ionian nobility was no longer based on
fear of the Unknown and a desire to placate it. It had reached
a point where belief in the gods was associated with a moral
consciousness and genuine religious feeling. But its art and
folk-lore knew of gods who hardly fitted into this scheme and
were yet perfectly familiar from story and ritual. The old
stories were too deeply interwoven into its life to be abandoned, but they failed to satisfy its spiritual needs. Ionian
society had reached a transitional point. It clung to the old
beliefs, in which it had been educated, but its conscience
rejected them. Homer represents this change, and gives us
the old world of theology and the new world of religion and
ethics. Both elements are worked into his poem, and if he
fails to co-ordinate them, we must blame his circumstances
as much as himself.

It is a fundamental postulate of religion that the gods have
power to answer prayers. But this power may be limited in
place or in character. A god may be efficacious here and not
there, he may be able to answer this prayer and not that.
Normally Homer's gods are attached to special places, but
their power extends beyond them. Apollo is the lord of
Chryse (A 37), and even Zeus rules on Ida or at Dodona
($\varGamma$ 276, $\varPi$ 233). But on the whole the gods move and have no
special shrine. Nor have they strictly limited fields of action.
So far as the war is concerned, one god can do as much as
another. In the story, moving as they do in human form, the
gods are conditioned by time and place. Zeus and his fellows
visit the Ethiopians, and it is assumed that nothing can be
done with them till their return. But this is mere story. The
religious consciousness knows better, and though the gods
are in Ethiopia, Athene comes down from Olympus to stop
the wrath of Achilles from ending in murder. So, too, the
story demands that certain things should be kept secret from
them. Zeus sleeps while the gods fight, but religion demands
that the gods should know what happens, and the poet tells

us that in the fight between Menelaus and Paris the gods know which one is to die (*Γ* 308–9). The *Iliad* nowhere says so explicitly as the *Odyssey* that the gods know everything— θεοὶ δέ τε πάντα ἴσασιν (δ 379)—but it credits them with more knowledge than much of the plot allows. Ignorance is attributed to Zeus as he lies in Hera's arms (*Ξ* 346 ff.) surrounded by a mist which the sun cannot pierce, but he knows how the battles will end and that there is no hope for Hector. The poet takes the story and tells it, but he allows new religious convictions to be mixed with old, and transforms mere myth by the infusion of genuine belief in the omnipresence and omniscience of the gods. This religious conviction can be put to great imaginative uses. When Sarpedon is fatally wounded, his friend Glaucus calls on Apollo wherever he may be, for he can hear anywhere if a man in trouble calls on him:

" κλῦθι, ἄναξ, ὅς που Λυκίης ἐν πίονι δήμῳ
εἰς ἢ ἐνὶ Τροίῃ· δύνασαι δὲ σὺ πάντοσ' ἀκούειν
ἀνέρι κηδομένῳ, ὡς νῦν ἐμὲ κῆδος ἱκάνει." (*Π* 513–15)[1]

This is the real experience of religion in time of trouble.

Alongside of this genuinely religious view of the gods, Homer has views of their place in the moral guidance of the world. These develop naturally from the belief that the gods control men's existence, and in Homer the two views are combined. The gods exert an effective control over men by taking part in their lives. They are benefactors and teachers. Apollo gives their bows to Pandarus and Teucer, and his helmet to Hector (*B* 827, *O* 441, *Λ* 353). Artemis teaches Scamandrius to hunt, Athene Phereclus to make ships, and Apollo Calchas to prophesy (*E* 51, 60, *A* 72). The gods give beauty to Bellerophon (*Z* 156), wealth and power to Peleus (*Ω* 534–6). They are then the benefactors of man, and they control his life with their gifts. This control is extended to his actions, and especially to his death. It is considered that they have it in their power to destroy Troy and send the Achaeans home (*A* 18, *I* 135), to decide the issue of a battle (*H* 102).

[1] 'Hear, lord, who art in the rich land of Lycia or in Troy. Thou canst hearken anywhere to a man in trouble, as now trouble comes to me.'

When death comes it is they who send it, whether to Achilles
(Σ 115–6), or to Patroclus (Π 692), or to Hector (X 297).
Exerting as they do this control they are naturally the arbiters
of conduct. Greek tradition based much on the gods' anger
with men for rites left undone and of their envy at any human
attempt to rival them. Both these themes are used by Homer,
and as they survived till the fifth century, there is no need to
doubt his sincerity in using them. Apollo sends a pest to the
Achaeans because Agamemnon has wronged his servant
Chryses (A 9, 64); Aeneas thinks the gods must be angry
with the Trojans for neglecting sacrifices (E 177); Artemis
punishes Oeneus for not giving her her due θαλύσια (I 533);
the Achaean wall is destroyed because its builders have not
made the usual sacrifices (M 6). Any attempt to rival the
gods is equally punished. Thamyris is blinded for competing
with the Muses (B 594 ff.), Lycurgus is blinded for flouting
Dionysus (Z 139), and Niobe for comparing her children to
Leto's is made to lose them (Ω 602 ff.).

This is traditional theology and based on the notion of
gods being jealous gods and punishing all rivalry or boastfulness. But Greek morality had extended the sphere of the
gods' punishment to acts which were not direct challenges of
the gods' power and privileges but affected the mutual intercourse of men. Certain activities were under their direct
protection, and violators of these sacred rights were punished.
In particular the gods are the overseers of oaths and treaties.
They are called on to witness the truce for the burial of the
slain (H 411), and Hector calls Zeus to witness that Dolon
shall have Achilles' horses for himself if he succeeds in cap-
turing them (K 329). When Hector at last faces Achilles, he
tells him on his word of honour that he will not maltreat his
body and he calls on the gods to witness:

" τοὶ γὰρ ἄριστοι
μάρτυροι ἔσσονται καὶ ἐπίσκοποι ἁρμονιάων." (X 254–5)[1]

But Achilles in his frenzy defies all agreements, and was
thought the worse for it by Homer's hearers. But the most
significant scene for this purpose is the duel between Paris

[1] 'They will be the best witnesses and overseers of covenants.'

and Menelaus. The proceedings begin with a solemn pray‹
to Zeus that the man may die who is to blame for all tl
trouble and that their oaths may be kept (*Γ* 320). The oal
has already been taken in the most solemn terms by Ag‹
memnon (ib. 276 ff.), and all the men of both armies ha‹
assented to it. It is understood that Paris is the guilty ma‹
and so Menelaus expressly says (ib. 351). The expecte
result is that Menelaus will kill Paris, and hence his gre‹
surprise when his sword is broken in his hand. No wond‹
that he cries out:

" *Ζεῦ πάτερ, οὔ τις σεῖο θεῶν ὀλοώτερος ἄλλος.*" (ib. 365)[1]

The fight closes owing to the treachery of Pandarus, b‹
Agamemnon knows that the Trojans will pay for this. H
tells the Achaeans that even if Zeus does not punish them ‹
once, yet he will punish them with their wives and childre‹
and Ilion will be destroyed. This shows a belief that the go‹
are just in that they punish the oath-breaker, and such
belief has nothing to do with jealousy or injured vanity.

What holds good for oaths, holds good for certain oth‹
activities. Morality demanded reverent treatment of th
old, and neglect of such treatment was punished. To illustrat
this point Phoenix tells the story of his own guilt. To pleas
his mother he lay with his father's concubine, and for th‹
his father cursed him and the gods carried out his curs
(*I* 448 ff.). The gods watched such cases and punished the evil
doers. But there is one trace of an even more careful super
vision of human morality, and as it comes in a simile it ma‹
well represent the poet's own view. It tells of Zeus sendin‹
storms because he is angry with men who give crooked judge
ments in the market-place and drive out justice, paying n‹
attention to the wrath of heaven (*Π* 384 ff.). This ange
covers a wider field than the other cases of divine anger, bu
the principle is the same. The gods watch over men's rela
tions with each other, and if they are unjust, the guilty ar‹
punished. So far then Homer's conception of the divin‹
governance of the world is simple and straightforward. Th‹
gods punish certain recognized evil actions by their direc

[1] 'Father Zeus, no other of the gods is more baneful than you.'

action and interference in human affairs. So, too, the people
of Israel were punished when they did evil in the sight of
the Lord.

Homer, however, is not quite satisfied with this solution.
Like Aeschylus, he seems to have been puzzled why men did
evil at all, and his difficulty has been shared by most thinkers
on religion and morals. It was well for Agamemnon to be
punished—he had done wrong. But why did he do wrong?
Homer has his solution; Agamemnon is the victim of ἄτη.
Zeus has robbed him of his wits, and later he realizes it and is
ready to make amends. ἄτη is the arrogant infatuation which
made him take Briseis from Achilles, but Agamemnon is sure
that it comes from Zeus. When he sends his embassy to
Achilles with offers of amends he says that he is not to blame,
for Zeus has robbed him of his wits (*I* 377), and when the real
reconciliation comes, Achilles accepts the excuse that Agamemnon is the victim of

$$Z\epsilon\grave{v}s \; \kappa a\grave{\iota} \; Mo\hat{\iota}\rho a \; \kappa a\grave{\iota} \; \mathring{\eta}\epsilon\rho o\phi o\hat{\iota}\tau\iota s \; \text{'}E\rho\iota\nu\acute{v}s \quad (T \; 87)^1$$

and has been suffering from ἄτη (ib. 136). But farther than
this Homer does not go. He leaves the problem, as others
have left it, unsolved.

Homer then, while accepting the stories and forms of
traditional religion, both deepens its religious import and
widens its ethical basis. Such a process is the work of
rationalism in the best sense, which accepts religious experience and tries to found it on a more solid base than
superstition. But having made these discoveries he was faced
with certain difficulties. A unified morality demands a
unified and single pantheon. Morality has turned many
religions from polytheism into monotheism simply because
monotheism eliminates the conflicting claims of different
deities. Homer never comes near to the conception of a
single god, and indeed his traditional material made such
a view impossible. But in some ways he co-ordinates his
gods into a single system. Of greatest importance is the part
played by Zeus in it. On Olympus he is only a constitutional
monarch. His power is limited by the other gods, and though

---

¹ 'Zeus and Fate and the Fury who walks in darkness.'

in the last resort he can threaten and control them, he has to put up with disputes and even with disobedience. In all this his position does not differ much from that of Agamemnon on earth. But for men his position is different. He is pre-eminently the god who controls their lives. The others are mentioned *honoris causa* with him, but he is the chief controller of their fortunes. Diomedes knows that it was Zeus καὶ θεοὶ ἄλλοι who sent Tydeus wandering (Ξ 120): Achilles knows that the capture of Troy lies with Zeus (Α 128): Aeneas knows that it is Zeus who gives men strength and diminishes it as he wills (Υ 242). It is Zeus who lays heavy sorrow on men at their birth (Κ 70) and has given the burden of Paris to Troy (Ζ 282). For men at least there is one god who overshadows the rest. The others take their part in the battle and have their own favourites, but on the whole it is Zeus who directs mortal affairs and decides what is to take place.

Zeus is the chief god, but at times it looks as if he were himself the victim of another and less defined power, Μοῖρα or Fate. Normally this fate is the instrument of Zeus. The doom laid on Helen comes from him (Ζ 357), like the doom laid on Achilles (Ι 608) or on Troy (Χ 60). But at times Zeus seems to obey it. Three times he weighs his balances, twice for the general issue of the battle (Θ 69, Π 658) and once to see whether Hector or Achilles shall die (Χ 209 ff.). In this weighing he is clearly not his own master but the servant of something more powerful than himself, however dimly apprehended. So, too, some heroes recognize that there is another power besides Zeus which controls their destiny. Achilles is told by his horses that the day of his death is near, and that Zeus and mighty Fate are the cause of it (Τ 410), and when Patroclus dies, he knows that his death is due not only to Zeus but to μοῖρ᾽ ὀλοή also (Π 849). This notion of a fate independent of Zeus is concerned mainly with death, and that explains its peculiar position. It is due to the belief that for every man the day of his death is fixed in advance and appointed for him, and nothing he does can postpone it. The gods can alter most things, but this they cannot alter, and therefore it stands apart from their activities and seems to be above them. It is true that this notion contradicts the belief that death comes from Zeus, for clearly in these cases it is outside his control. The contradiction is there, but it is quite intelligible. That Zeus sends death was the natural conclusion of a theology which was struggling to ascribe everything to divine management, but such a conclusion could not quite defeat the deeply established notion that a man's days were numbered and nothing could add to them. It was only natural that in a time of changing opinions Homer should accept both views and use them differently for his dramatic purposes. The artistic gain is obvious. The pity of Hector's death is the more pitiful because not even Zeus himself can avert it. He is the victim of powers which even the gods themselves cannot control.

Fate is an abstraction, not a personality, and yet it plays its part in the Homeric scheme of things. As an abstraction, realized, however feebly, and named, it shows that Homer and his age were reaching beyond their anthropomorphic deities to other powers. And this tendency to go beyond the gods is shown by Homer's habit of using other abstractions who have no part in the Olympian theocracy. To this company belong Ἄτη, Blind Folly, Φόβος and Δεῖμος, Terror, Ἔρις, Strife, Κυδοιμός, Turmoil, Ὄσσα, Rumour, Λιταί, Prayers, and perhaps we might add Θάνατος, Death, who at times usurps the functions of Hades. Homer does much to give reality to these abstractions. At least two of them are described in some detail. Ἄτη has delicate feet from not walking on the earth: she walks over men's heads and harms them (T 91 ff.). The Λιταί are lame, wrinkled, and cross-eyed, and are easily passed by the swift Ἄτη (I 502). To make them more real the poet puts them in the company of the gods. Δεῖμος, Φόβος, and Ἔρις urge on the opposing armies in the company of Ares and Athene, and we are told that Ἔρις is the sister and companion of Ares and lifts her head into the sky (Δ 440 ff.). On the Shield of Achilles Ἔρις and Κυδοιμός are depicted on the battle scene in human form dealing death and dripping with blood (Σ 535 ff.). But such efforts do not make these abstractions gods. They remain mere abstractions, because they have functions and not personalities. Their existence is due to a desire for simplification. They lack the complication and idiosyncrasies of personal gods, and in consequence they remain lifeless and rather uninteresting. Once indeed they achieve great poetical beauty. Sleep and Death may be mere abstractions, but when they carry off the dead body of Sarpedon they make one of the finest scenes in the *Iliad* (*Π* 681). And the reason for this is clear. Sleep and Death are real things in our experience, and by their intervention what might be merely horrible, the death of a noble young man in his prime, is softened and made tolerable. If he must die, it is best that he should die thus, and find sleep after his labours. In this scene Homer has no need to resort to allegorical description. Sleep and Death are real things, and they do not need pictorial details to bring them home to us.

The Homeric religion is then a combination of different ideas, or rather it is a religion struggling out of traditional forms into a rationalized system. The traditional forms are themselves of a quite sophisticated nature, but the poet uses them for poetry, and reserves his rationalization to get beyond them to an even more simplified arrangement. To the religious consciousness his results are not perhaps always successful, and for purely aesthetic appreciation perhaps he is best when he keeps to simple material and allows his fancy to play with it. The nod of Zeus which shakes Olympus is better poetry than the personified terrors of his battle-fields. These new creations seem to have appealed more to his head than to his heart. His imagination never really got loose on them, and they remain abstractions. But once he made poetry out of his doubts, and the result is deeply moving. Before his cremation the ghost of Patroclus appears to Achilles in a dream. Achilles tries to clasp him, but the ghost evades him and goes away. Such a scene would anyhow be pathetic and terrible. For the last time Achilles sees his friend, and he cannot embrace him. But Homer makes it the more moving by leaving us uncertain whether it is a real ghost or only a dream. It appears to Achilles in sleep, and Achilles himself does not know whether it is real or not. If it is real, it is but an incorporeal phantom:

" ὦ πόποι, ἦ ῥά τίς ἐστι καὶ εἰν Ἀΐδαο δόμοισι
ψυχὴ καὶ εἴδωλον, ἀτὰρ φρένες οὐκ ἔνι πάμπαν."

$$(\Psi \ 103\text{-}4).^1$$

This is a cry from the heart of a man who is not sure of life
beyond the grave, even if he has some slight experience which
confirms it. Achilles wishes to speak to Patroclus, but what if
the ghost is a mere illusion, a phantom which can be seen in
dreams but slips away like smoke from his embraces?

---

[1] 'Alas, there is in the house of Death a soul and a phantom, but there is
no life in it at all.'

HOMER AND THE HEROIC AGE

HOMER found the subject of the *Iliad* in the doings of an age of heroes. For him the world had changed since those spacious days, and the race of the heaven-born had perished. The world of his similes is different from the world of his story, and he is fully conscious that his contemporaries are weaker than the great men of old. He knows that men, οἷοι νῦν βροτοί εἰσι,[1] cannot do what his heroes did. Between him and them everything has grown more commonplace, and the golden past is dead with Agamemnon in the grave. This gulf between Homer and his subject has often been overlooked, but it is of great importance for a proper appreciation of his poetry. It is, especially, one of the many differences between him and most early poetry. Neither the author of *Beowulf* nor the author of the *Song of Roland* shows any such feeling that his own days were vastly inferior to those of which he writes. Perhaps they thought so, but both are silent on any such sense of inferiority. Even the marvels and miracles which they describe seem to belong to a world which still existed for them. The comet which appeared to the Conqueror would have seemed to Turoldus no less a wonder than the darkening of the earth at Roland's death. And the author of *Beowulf*, full of a newly-discovered Christianity, must have believed that the world was full of things passing his understanding. But Homer, whose story makes horses speak and the gods walk on the earth, avoids all traces of miracle in his similes and seems to have lived in a world not unlike our own. He does not, like Shakespeare, create the heroes of his fancy to match the great men around him. For these he seems to have felt more affection than reverence, and he made his ideal world out of the stuff of story and song.

Homer lived in a generation later than the heroic age, but his creative imagination is so powerful that in his company we are normally among the thoughts and actions which belong to such periods in human history. Nor can we properly understand the *Iliad* unless we know something of the thoughts and ideals underlying an age of great, heroic activity.[1] At the back of the *Iliad* lies that peculiar notion of honour which is developed in the camp and on the battle-field. This notion has many sides, and in later literature it has been enormously complicated by the notions of medieval chivalry. But in Homer it is comparatively simple in its outlines. The sense of personal honour means that the special reputation of every soldier is of enormous importance to him. He may not and cannot endure slight or insult. His reputation is of the utmost moment, and he will die rather than lose it. This partly explains why Achilles is unable to endure the slights inflicted on him by Agamemnon. His personal reputation is of more account than his loyalty to his colleagues. What holds good of Achilles is true in a lesser degree of several others. Sthenelus cannot endure to be chidden by Agamemnon (*Δ* 404 ff.). Paris refuses to give up Helen, when the Trojans request him (*H* 357 ff.). Hector refuses to listen to Priam when he begs him to take shelter in Troy from Achilles (*X* 78 ff.). This is the same spirit as that in which Roland refuses to blow his horn, and prefers death with honour to safety and even to victory. So far Homer is in the best traditions of heroic story. The pride of his princes yields in nothing to the pride of Beowulf or Sigurd. But lying as he does outside the actual age of heroes, he has modified the heroic point of view in some directions, and here he is sharply distinguished from the writers of early Teutonic or French epic. In other early epics honour is all that matters, and defeat is nothing compared with it. The result is a magnificent sense of ultimate failure, which is of no importance provided death be found gloriously against overwhelming odds. The *Fight at Maldon* is a glorification of defeat, and the *Song of Roland* ends on a note of unwearying struggle against unconquerable forces. The *Edda* poems are full of the same proud spirit. Sigurd, Gudrun, Brynhild are in turn beaten and brought to disaster. But the *Iliad* is not like these. Even in the death of Hector, a theme worthy of

[1] Cf. H. M. Chadwick, *The Heroic Age*; W. P. Ker, *Epic and Romance*, pp. 3–15.

early Germanic poetry, we do not feel a savage exultation in death just because it is glorious. Homer feels differently, and he makes defeat more tragic than glorious. Hector's death is an irreparable loss. It means the fall of Troy, the enslavement of Andromache, the misery of Astyanax. The pitiful side of it is what concerns Homer even more than the heroic. Hector dies magnificently, but his glory is no comfort to his defenceless family and friends. Still less has the fate of Achilles the grandeur we find in the death of Roland or the unabating toils of Charlemagne. His heroic prowess is important, but it is not the most important thing about him. Instead of pride in his death we are presented with pity for the shortness of his days and the waste into which his anger leads him. The other old epics are tragic enough in their themes, but they combine their sense of tragedy with a feeling that glory triumphs over death. Homer has no such feeling. His heroes die as heroes should, but their death is an irreparable and uncompensated disaster. We do not even get the comfort, which Shakespeare gives us, that death is peace after the torments of this life. Homer might indeed have felt that 'the rest is silence', but to him the words would have meant lamentation and not comfort.

This acute sense of the tragedy of death distinguishes Homer from the age of which he wrote. When battle is an everyday affair and death is always present to their thoughts, men lose their sense of its wastefulness and horror. It is magnified into great glory or reduced to the dull level of common things. But for Homer death was a thing of horror, not 'a good end to the long, cloudy day', but the lament of souls leaving their manhood and their youth.[1] This melancholy view was common to most Greeks. Even the most mystical of them found little lasting comfort in the thought of islands beyond the Western Sea or an everlasting spring below the earth.[2] But it is certainly surprising that Homer, writing of an age of heroes, never felt the glamour of defeat and death. The reason for this failure, if it can be called a failure, seems to be twofold. In the first place he is severed from the heroic age, and he views it in retrospect with the eyes of a

---

[1] *Il* 857, *X* 363.   [2] Contrast Pindar, *Nem.* ix. 15–16 with *Ol.* ii. 67–88.

man used to other things. The heroic view is possible only for men who know the fierce joy of battle and the splendour of looking death in the face. Homer must have lived in quieter times. The great outburst of the Greek peoples over the Mediterranean had spent its force, and the Ionian colonists were settling down to the long task of creating civilization again. Under such conditions much of the heroic outlook would be lost, and its place taken by an outlook more humane and more full of pity. But there is also a second reason. The medieval epics are full of the great struggle between Christians and Pagans. Inspired by the Crusades their writers are full of the overpowering justice of the Christian cause. For it men willingly lay down their lives, because it is of more importance than they are, and to die for it is to go to Paradise. When Roland dies, angels carry him to heaven, but Hector's body is maltreated by Achilles and thrown to the dogs. Christianity provided a consolation such as Homer never knew, abating the tragedy of death, and giving consolation in the worst disaster. Nor can Homer's heroes find a stern Stoic pleasure in dying for a cause of paramount importance. When Patroclus dies, it is for fair-haired Helen's sake. Even Hector, though he dies for Troy, is so great a loss that for the moment Troy seems little beside him. And what is more significant, Homer's fatalism forecasts the fall of Troy, whatever happens, and we know that Hector's death is only part of the foreordained scheme of destruction. Even in the Icelandic poems, which know little of the consolations of Christianity, the view of death is different from this. There is nothing more terrible than the speechless grief of Gudrun over Sigurd's body, but the Icelandic poets do not elaborate the horrors of death as Homer does, and we are confronted only with the bare fact. Homer belongs to a more sophisticated stage of thought, when horror can be abated by lyrical emotion, and a splendour of poetry cast round what is otherwise stark and almost unendurable.

It might be expected that the *Iliad*, being cast in a tragic mould, would have no place for comedy, and it is commonly assumed that the high seriousness of a heroic age leaves no room for laughter. But the *Iliad* has its moments of comedy,

and these have often been thought to represent a later period
than most of the poem, when themes once respected are
turned to mockery. If this were true, these comic elements
would be another of Homer's departures from the true
character of the heroic age. But such a judgement certainly
needs considerable modification. Though there is no trace
of comedy in *Beowulf* or the *Song of Roland*, there are definite
traces of it in other heroic poems. The *Song of William*, a
French epic as old and in some ways as noble as the *Song of
Roland*, has as one of its heroes Rainouart, who is a forerunner of Porthos in his size, simplicity, and engaging
naturalness.[1] Nor is heroic humour confined to men. In
the *Edda* poems it is applied to the gods. In the *Lokasenna*
Loki taxes the gods of Asgard with their weaknesses, and
scores good debating points at their expense.

So Homer's humour is not essentially unheroic. He reserves it chiefly for his gods, as we have seen, but he is not
above making gentle fun of his heroes. He can only mean us
to laugh when Glaucus gets the worst of his exchange of
armour with Diomedes. He may even aim at a much grimmer
humour in some of his battle scenes, when Mydon, wounded
by Antilochus, falls from his chariot and stays standing on his
head in the deep sands (E 585 ff.), or when Cebriones drops
and Patroclus compares him to a diver looking for oysters
(Π 745 ff.). Such bitter jesting is natural enough in the
mouth of a hero. There are, too, the semi-humorous characters, Nestor, with his inopportune garrulity and embarrassment in battle, his sly advice to his son in the chariot race and
fuss over the result, or Aias with his obstinate courage and
slowness, like the grand fools of the French epic. The humour
with which Homer sometimes views his heroes is different
both in quantity and in quality from that in which he treats
his gods. It is never more than a benevolent tolerance of
some amiable human weaknesses, but when he makes fun of
the gods he gets very near to farce. The Διὸς ἀπάτη or the
Θεομαχία are completely gay and light-hearted without any
sense of the dignity due to the Olympians. They approximate
to the spirit in which Loki mocks the Norse gods and belong

[1] Dante puts him in Paradise, *Par.* xviii. 46.

to the best traditions of a heroic age, which has so high a sense of the dignity of man that it can afford to make fun of the gods. This may seem a paradox, and indeed it is one. But it is none the less true. The heroic standards of honour were so high that they revealed the weaknesses of theologies older than themselves, and the natural result was that the gods were made figures of fun. Such an attitude could only come at the end of a heroic age. The *Edda* poems, despite their simplicity and strength, cannot be earlier than the ninth and tenth centuries. They belong to a time when Icelandic society had standardized its values and was maintaining its stories in the face of a changing world. Such a standardization meant that the intellect was fully and freely at work on old material, and primitive conceptions of the gods were bound to come in for some criticism. In the ages of chivalry and romance, laughter plays little part in poetry. It tends to spoil the elegance of a gesture or to cast doubt on a nice point of honour. But the men of a heroic age are so natural and so sure of themselves that they can afford to laugh, even at what they hold solemn and sacred.

This intellectual honesty and clarity is common both to Homer and to the Icelandic poets, and it is fundamentally a quality of the heroic age. In Greek literature, because of Homer's example, it persists until it is overlaid by rhetoric and sentimentality, but even in the late evening of Greek poetry it is still noticeable and characteristic. It is indeed a heroic quality, and it has its roots in that conception of human dignity which thinks a man too great to need the embellishments of adventitious posturing. It saves Homer from the romantic notions which turned the French epic into the artificial romance of the thirteenth century, and which even in Chaucer sometimes lend unreality to the story. The honesty of the great early epics falls between the childish simplicity of the folk-tale and the artificiality of the chivalrous romances. Homer's intellectual honesty is fundamental to him. He never strains his points or seeks to achieve a melodramatic effect. In the *Iliad*, where his theme is tragic, it makes his whole poem entirely serious in tone. The comic intervals are only intervals. They do not affect the funda-

mental character of the poem. Homer knows nothing of
either irony or fustian. His seriousness differs from that of
later Greek poetry because it is the seriousness of an age and
not of an individual. Sappho and Alcaeus, Aeschylus and
Sophocles, have the same candour and sincerity, but they
set the impress of their personalities on everything they write,
and they achieve their effects because of their remarkable
individualities rather than from any qualities held in common
with their contemporaries. Even Pindar, who took so much
for granted, was more conscious than Homer that his views
were the only views that mattered. And Euripides, who lived
in doubt, was quite uncertain what he really felt. In particular
Homer accepts without any reservations the heroic code of
honour, and his view of it is hardly different from that held
by other heroic poets. A man's duty is:

αἰὲν ἀριστεύειν καὶ ὑπείροχον ἔμμεναι ἄλλων. (Ζ 208, Λ 784)[1]

His life is in battle, and for the risks of battle his whole life
must be prepared. Hence all Homer's heroes are brave.
Even Paris, idler though he is, is stung into courage by Hector's words. The gods may cry from pain, but men take their
wounds without flinching. But courage is not enough.
Battle demands that men must stand together, and the
central tenet of Homeric morality is based on this need. In
his notion of αἰδώς Homer gives the clue. αἰδώς, as Professor
Murray has said, 'is what you feel about an act of your own',[2]
but it only has a meaning in relation to what you do to others.
It is respect for your fellow men. It applies first and foremost
to the men you commonly meet, to superiors and inferiors,
to strangers and beggars, to the gods and to the old. The
martial qualities needed some admixture of tenderness and
decency to preserve them, and this was found in the notion
of αἰδώς. Because of it men refrain from excessive cruelty, and
help each other in their needs. This quality which Homer
gives to his heroes is particularly noticeable in the *Iliad*
itself. He does not spare us horrors—they are part of his
tragic scheme—but he is careful never to condone acts of
injustice or of cruelty. The *Iliad* is profoundly moral, just

[1] 'ever to be the best and to surpass others'.   [2] *Rise of the Greek Epic*, p. 83.

because Homer has absorbed the morality of the heroic age. To claim that this singleness of moral outlook is the work of continual expurgation[1] is to misunderstand the temper of an age of heroes. Such an age has its own high standards based on a man's sense of his own dignity. They differ, as might be expected, from other systems of morality, but they are not less exalted. Homer's ethics, though taught by Athenian educators, are not the ethics of Periclean Athens. For him the standard is the individual, but for Pericles it is the city. Of national or racial boundaries he takes little heed. It does not matter that Hector is a barbarian, provided he behaves as a true soldier. Nor has Homer the Athenian view of women, based on their position in an all-absorbing state. His individualism is perfectly logical, and he treats Helen and Andromache with the seriousness and understanding which he gives to Achilles. They have their part in life, and that is enough for him, just as the Icelandic poets were content to portray with complete candour and dignity their tragic heroines, Gudrun and Brynhild. The heroic age honoured its women and gave them power. So Homer was saved from making them too womanly, as Euripides sometimes did, or from raising them to that sublime selflessness to which Sophocles raised Antigone. Still less has Homer any sympathy with those waves of self-denial and puritanism which occasionally swept over later Greece. Such eccentricities are alien to the spirit of an heroic age. The Trojan War was fought for a woman's sake, and over a woman Achilles quarrelled with Agamemnon. The facts of sex are frankly stated, and there is no glorification of purity or self-abnegation. The sword that lay between Tristram and Iseult is unheard of in Homer. But love plays a small part in the story, and though this may be due partly to the exigencies of camp life, it is due much more to heroic standards of conduct. In the *Song of Roland* there is hardly a mention of *la belle Aude*, though she is Oliver's sister and Roland's betrothed, and Beowulf's wife rests on a conjecture made in a single line. Before love became a romantic ideal for which men were ready to undergo any privation and undertake any adventure, it was held

[1] Murray, *Rise of the Greek Epic.*, pp. 120–45.

below the true dignity of a fighting man. The French
romances combined the amatory ideals of Provence with
the martial ideals of Normandy by creating the conception
of chivalry, which made the beautiful woman the judge of
honour and prowess. But in true heroic poetry this combination does not exist, and love is kept out. This is not easy in
the story of a war fought about a woman, but Homer's skill
is nowhere more apparent than where in a few lines he shows
how men can fight about Helen. In the scene on the wall
there is no trace of erotic sentimentality such as we might
find in the French romances. There is the single wonderful
touch of the old men finding it no matter for indignation
that men should fight about her (Γ 156–7).

The dignity which excluded any detailed treatment of
love excluded other less interesting themes. Some critics
complain that Homer is lacking in those scenes of brutality
and bestiality such as we might hope to find in a primitive
epic. They are to be found in Hesiod, why not in Homer?
We might answer, for the same reason that they are found in
the Old Testament but not in the old Germanic or French
epics. The audience which likes horrors for their own sake
is out of touch with the ideals of martial heroism. Soldiers
normally see enough of horrors in their work not to want to
hear more about them. But the explanation lies deeper than
that. The love of horrors and obscenities lies outside the
code of manners common in a heroic age. The great emphasis
on personal dignity forbids any lowering of human stature by
such concessions to human weakness. This does not mean that
poets who write of heroic themes must entirely eschew anything horrible or disgusting. The wide scope of their stories
makes such themes sooner or later inevitable. But when they
come, they are either treated hastily or made the subject of
tragic emotions. The saga no doubt had its crudities, and
they were essential to the story, but decency forbade that the
audience should be titillated by a detailed exposition of
them. When Phoenix tells how he obeyed his mother and
slept with his father's concubine, he says simply τῇ πιθόμην
καὶ ἔρεξα (Ι 453)[1] and leaves it at that. Only an age sure of

---

[1] 'I obeyed her and did it.'

its standards could achieve such a simplicity with no attempt
at palliation or lubricious detail.   In the heat of battle it is
natural that soldiers should want to strip the dead and even
to mutilate corpses.   The first of these, however, was not
well thought of.   Achilles thought it wrong to strip Eetion
(Z 417), and when stripping takes place, the poet hurries over
it (N 439).   Mutilation of the dead was a worse offence.   We
have seen that his desire to maltreat Hector's body was part
of the moral degradation of Achilles, and how the poet saves
him from putting his threats into effect.   But in one place in
the saga it seems to have been too difficult for the poet to
subdue the horror.   When Hector dies, the Achaeans plunge
their spears into his body (X 370 ff.).   The scene is full of
tragic power and pity.   The poet makes no attempt to justify
the wanton exultation over the dead.   He just describes the
scene briefly and passes on to the worse things in store.   On the
other hand, when such themes were absolutely essential to
the main plot, Homer is not ashamed of mentioning them, but
he treats them in a moral and even tragic way.   In particular
this comes out in the account of Achilles, whose every lapse
from heroic virtue is a new chapter in his tragedy, and whose
failures, though perfectly understood, are never condoned.
Apart from him hardly any hero fails in the heroic standards
of behaviour.   It is true that in the battle scenes there are
many incidents which shock the sensitive conscience.   But
the heroic age felt no disgust at them.   To kill your man
quickly and well was a warrior's business, and there is no
reason to think that Homer did not share the heroic view.
Like the great poet that he was, he lamented the loss of life
and youth, but he hardly seems to have felt it wrong to
kill or be killed in battle.   Even the killing of Dolon after he
has asked for mercy does not receive his condemnation.
Dolon was a spy, and there is no reason to believe that the
Homeric age was kinder to spies than the twentieth century.
Such an execution might be unpleasant, but Dolon was not
entitled to the respect due to an enemy who fought in open
battle.   His action excluded him from the society of honourable men, and he was killed at once for it.   In the same way
the traitor Ganelon is torn to pieces by horses for his treachery,

and that is the end of him. The heroic code was severe to those who did not accept its standards, and they could expect no mercy. This code of behaviour seems to have been accepted by Homer without limitations, and it is the common code of all heroic ages. It lauds the virtues of loyalty, generosity, and courage, and it deplores meanness, cowardice, and treachery. In its own way it knows mercy, and Homer's characters are more merciful than those of the Athenian tragedians. Or rather he shrinks from themes which they treated, such as the suicide of Aias or the death of Pentheus. His standards are not theirs, because his audience was stricter in its taste and delicacy than the Athenian democracy, and he shared the taste of his time. This moral responsibility, so often absent from the Old Testament and even at times from Shakespeare, is an aristocratic virtue, derived from a high sense of dignity and decency. It had to cater for men used to privilege and responsibility, not for a Semitic populace trained to suffering, nor for the jaded or primitive tastes of the groundlings whom Shakespeare despised and placated. Hesiod's poor farmers may have liked crude tales, but Homer's audience was bred to better things and had no use for them. If the *Iliad* had really been expurgated, as is claimed, we should not have this surprising consistency of moral outlook. We might have in some ways more noble actions, but the morality of the heroic age would have suffered in the process, and it is precisely this which Homer gives us. He himself may well have rejected earlier versions of his story, which revolted his conscience or were unsuited to the ethical taste of his age. It is more than likely that in the old saga Achilles really mutilated Hector's body. But the credit for the far nobler story in the *Iliad* must be given not to some anonymous expurgator, but to the creative genius and moral sensibility of Homer.

We have assumed that Homer wrote for an aristocratic class. Such a view needs development and moderation, and is liable to serious misconception. Homer's heroes indeed are all princes. The only member of the populace is Thersites, who is a figure of contempt and scorn. Dolon perhaps may be classed with him, and he too meets a spy's death after a short career of undignified ambition. Of the multitudes who die in battle for their leaders we hear little. Their deaths are as unrecorded as the deaths of the twenty thousand men who died with Roland at Roncesvalles. On the other hand Homer knew and loved humble men and women. In his similes there are many mentions of simple people—shepherds and cowherds, poor women and children. He excluded them from the main current of his poem, not because he was not interested in them but because a heroic age finds its heroes in men who have power and the opportunities of using it. On such men attention is focused, because they alone can fully realize the heroic ideal in adventure and the struggle against great odds. For the poet there is, too, another reason. He has to select his characters, and naturally he selects those whose condition makes them take part in great undertakings. It must not be deduced from this that he only cares for the great. His similes prove the contrary, and, as W. P. Ker well pointed out, in an age like that in the poems there was no essential difference between the activities of a prince and those of his followers.[1] The Homeric king is the type of all his subjects. Like him they pass a large part of their life in the camp or on the sea. Their only pleasures are of the simplest, like his. They share his risks and discomforts, and they share too his ideas and outlook. In Thersites we get the beginning of a new order of things. He is conscious of a gap between the ruler and the ruled, and he has a sense of injury and injustice (B 225 ff.). He strikes the same note as Hesiod strikes when he speaks of βασιλῆας δωροφάγους (Op. 39). Homer, in this as in other ways, comes at the end of the heroic age. He knew that the conventions which sustained it were beginning to be broken, and, though he himself sympathized with the older order, he was honest enough to record the first advent of the new.

Although Homer lived at the end of the heroic age, and perhaps outside it, it was for him perfectly real. Even if he created it out of saga and story, he must have believed that every word they told him was true. He gives us the impression

---

[1] Epic and Romance, p. 7. 'There is a community of prosaic interests. The great man is a good judge of cattle; he sails his own ship.'

that though things have changed for the worse, the world of his poem is perfectly natural and real. This sense of reality is rare in all poetry, and it is particularly rare in epic poetry. For some reason or other epic poets are seldom wholly persuaded that things are or were just as they describe them. Milton's imagination fails when he creates a cosmogony out of Homer and Virgil, or when he struggles to expound the mysteries of godhead. Virgil, who is so true and intimate in all that concerns the emotions, lacks conviction when he deals with his minor characters or with the heroic prowess of Aeneas in war. The Italian poets of the Renaissance, who understood chivalry and elegance, are frankly cynical in their imitations of antiquity.[1] Nor do even earlier poets always achieve a true and convincing vision of their subjects. The author of *Beowulf* is not quite certain whether Grendel's parent is male or female, and his imagination totters before the description of a waterfall. Only perhaps in Dante and Icelandic poetry do we get that circumstantial reality which carries conviction in every part of the poem. To this select company Homer belongs. He knows his characters and the world they live in. His landscape of Troy may perhaps be less detailed than Dante's vision of Malebolge, but it is perfectly natural and vivid. Even his minor characters have their family connexions and personal histories. He makes us believe in Axylus who lived by the road-side at Arisbe and entertained the passers-by (*Z* 13 ff.), or Euphorbus, with his peculiar method of doing his hair (*P* 51 ff.), or Simoeisius, who was bred on Ida to look after flocks but did not repay his parents for his upbringing (*Δ* 473 ff.). How much more real and convincing these characters are than Virgil's 'fortemque Gyan fortemque Cloanthum'. They have that personal touch which endears them to us and stirs the curiosity, just as we are interested in the delicate white hands of the Archbishop Turpin,[2] or those friends of Dante whom inflexible Justice put in Hell. This sense of reality comes out particularly when Homer treats of marvels. Here his method differs from Dante's, whose pictorial imagination

---

[1] Cf. W. P. Ker, *Collected Essays*, i, p. 317.
[2] *Song of Roland*, l. 2250, ' ses blanches mains, les beles '.

is so vivid that he creates scenes as if he were really a spec-
tator of them, the man whom his contemporaries thought
had been in Hell. Homer, however, states them with such
simplicity that it is impossible not to accept them as facts.
When Achilles drives out to war, he speaks to his horses and
tells them to save the body of Patroclus. Quite naturally
the horse Xanthus shakes his head and his mane falls to the
ground—then suddenly without more ado the poet says:

αὐδήεντα δ' ἔθηκε θεὰ λευκώλενος "Ηρη   (T 407)[1]

and the horse prophesies the death of his master. Or again,
how natural is the scene where Achilles appears at the trench
and frightens the Trojans. It begins quite plainly with
almost a formula:

αὐτὰρ 'Αχιλλεὺς ὦρτο Διὶ φίλος   (Σ 203)[2]

and it ends with the sudden death of twelve Trojans from the
shock of the sight:

ἔνθα δὲ καὶ τοτ' ὄλοντο δυώδεκα φῶτες ἄριστοι
ἀμφὶ σφοῖς ὀχέεσσι καὶ ἔγχεσιν.   (Σ 230–1)[3]

The scene is really supernatural. Achilles rises at divine
orders from Iris, round his head Athene sets a miraculous
flame like the flame of a burning city, and the mere sight of
him is enough to put the Trojans in terror and to kill twelve
of their best warriors. But the miraculous scene is perfectly
imagined and kept within the bounds of verisimilitude. The
similes which bring it home are chosen from real life, and the
marvellous elements are stated in language so simple that it
is impossible not to believe in them. In the same way we
have to believe in the flight of Paolo and Francesca in the
fiery wind, because of the exquisitely apt simile which compares them to doves flying on steady wings to their nest.
Homer and Dante resemble one another in their perfect
sincerity in dealing with the objects of their imagination.
This sincerity saves them from exaggeration and from vagueness. It is when a poet wants to say something fine and does

---

[1] 'White-armed Hera made the horse speak.'
[2] 'Then rose Achilles dear to Zeus.'
[3] 'There and then died twelve of the noblest warriors among their chariots
and spears.'

not quite know what it is, that he lapses into one or the other of these traps. The great Elizabethans, despite their manifold and splendid virtues, sometimes aimed beyond experience and found only chaos. Homer, sure of his traditional material, set down what his clear vision saw and made his marvels credible.

Homer's vivid intelligence found interest in many different things, and this wide curiosity accounts for one of his notable characteristics, his freedom from melancholy. In much early verse there is a brooding sense of futility and despair. The note of *Vanitas vanitatum* echoes through *Beowulf* and even through the *Edda* poems. Nor is such melancholy hard to understand. Heroic life is short and perilous. Its greatest prizes can only be won at the price of death, and for the undistinguished life is full of dangers for which there is not even the consolation of glory. This fundamental melancholy is different from the true tragic temper. For Shakespeare or for Sophocles tragedy helped to enhance the magnificence of the fleeting and defeated present. But the real pessimist feels that even this, too, is futile and purposeless. Such an attitude is not a modern creation. It is as old as *Ecclesiastes* or Theognis, but it owes nothing to Homer. His conception of life is simple and tragic, but not pessimistic. He hardly believes in life beyond the grave, and for this very reason he attaches more importance to life in this world. Generation succeeds generation like the leaves in spring, but the real importance of human life is not affected by this at all. The famous words of Glaucus are only a prelude to a tale of Bellerophon's heroism, and this is the key to Homer's attitude. It is the heroism that matters, and man being mortal has more chance of glory than the immortal gods. The only real pessimist in the *Iliad* is Achilles, who doubts the value of heroism, and complains that in the end the brave man and the idler find the same fate (*I* 319 ff.). But Achilles is the victim of passion, even of obsession, and his despair is part of his lapse from true nobility. Hector provides the right corrective to him. In the beautiful scene with Andromache he is not deluded by any false hopes of the future. But he never falters in his conviction that what he does is the right thing to do. Even when Achilles pursues him with certain death, in his moment of doubt and indecision he knows that it is best to face his adversary and kill him or be killed. This is not the decision of a desperate man, but of one who knows what his task is and does not shrink from it. What holds for Hector holds for the other heroes. From none of them goes up the cry that their efforts are to no purpose and not worth making. The absence of this note of despair is remarkable. In their different ways both Sophocles and Euripides at times give way to it. It is the burden of some of the finest words written by Shakespeare and by Pindar. It is the cry of Cassandra as she goes to her doom in the *Agamemnon*, and of Macbeth when he hears that his wife is dead. But in the *Iliad* for all its sorrow and suffering this despair hardly exists. The heroes themselves do not feel it and the poet himself with his usual self-abnegation passes no comment of this type. The explanation of this lies in Homer's view of life. He knew and loved the heroic world, and he knew quite well that such high deeds meant loss of life and destruction, but he valued them too highly to think that the loss quite outbalanced the gain, and that death made everything meaningless.

From these scattered and diverse indications it may be seen that Homer is well in sympathy with the ideals of the heroic age. At times he reveals that for him the heroic age is already lost, but he still continues to believe that its ideals are the right ideals and that the world is the worse for their loss. The present has its beauties for him, but it is to the heroic past that he looks for all that he holds best in human nature. And the past is not for him entirely beyond recall. He lives in it so intimately and is so absorbed by it that he must have been in some sort of touch with it. Whether his connexion with it is due to its continued survival in his day or to his absorption in the stories of heroic legend is a hard question. Chaucer, coming at the end of medieval romance, understands it perfectly, but inspired by the early Renaissance he sometimes makes gentle fun of it. But Homer hardly makes fun of his heroes, and has hardly any point of view that is not theirs. His perfect sincerity has no sentimental love of the past in it, and the world of the *Iliad* is a real world. Such clarity and consistency of outlook could not easily have been based only on legends; they must have been fed on the thoughts of the living men about him. No great poet can live entirely in the past, certainly no poet with Homer's width of understanding and great creative energy. The poet who draws on other poets may create a dream world like that of *The Faerie Queene* or *The Earthly Paradise*, but he cannot create Helen or Achilles. Homer must have lived in a world which still held the ideals of the heroic age, even if on his own admission men were no longer what they once had been.

HOMER'S TIME AND PLACE

THE date of the *Iliad*, as of most Greek poetry before Aeschylus, is matter for conjecture. The Homeric controversy has of course affected views about it, but the problem is really outside the limits of the proper Homeric question. For the problem is simple: when did the *Iliad*, excluding small and obvious interpolations, reach its final form? And this question is as important for the unitarian as for the advocate of multiple authorship.

In antiquity, despite great divergences of detail, there were three main views of Homer's date. The first, held apparently by Hecataeus and repeated by Eratosthenes and other late writers, made him either a contemporary of the events which he described or within a century of them, thus placing him in the twelfth or eleventh century before Christ.[1] The second view was that held by Herodotus, that Homer lived not more than four hundred years before himself, that is, in the latter half of the ninth century.[2] A third view held by Theopompus placed him even later, making him a contemporary of Gyges and of Archilochus.[3] Allowing for some divagations these three views still hold the field. Andrew Lang[4] and the stricter unitarians hold that Homer lived at the end of the Mycenean Age, and that he records the world he knew. Mr. Allen[5] and Mr. Scott[6] place him about 900. The third view seems to be held in an advanced form by Professor Murray, who regards the final form of the *Iliad* as the work of the rhapsode Cynaethus who lived in the sixth century.[7] Roughly, the question of date is the question of choosing between these three alternatives.

That Homer lived in the Mycenean world seems on the face of things improbable. The details of the life which he describes are not Mycenean except in a few points which he may well have learned from the saga. On the other hand

---

[1] Proclus, *Vit. Hom.*, p. 25. 17; Diodorus vii. 2; Ps. Plut. *Vit. Hom.* 5.

[2] ii. 53. 2.   [3] Ed. Grenfell and Hunt, fr. 194; cf. Tatian *ad Graec.* 31.

[4] *The World of Homer*, p. 33.   [5] *The Homeric Catalogue*, p. 21.

[6] *The Unity of Homer*, p. 3.   [7] *The Rise of the Greek Epic*, p. 308.

these details suit almost any century between the tenth and the fifth, and cannot be trusted as a certain clue. Nor does his language seem to be the language of the Mycenean world. If it is, there must be a gap of four hundred years or more between it and the language of Archilochus. Homer's language has its archaic characteristics, but it is certainly not so far removed from Archilochus as that. Four hundred years is the interval between the *Song of Maldon* and Chaucer, between Chaucer and Wordsworth. The passage of so long a time can only mean great changes even in the most traditional and formal language, let alone in the living speech of youthful Greece. Despite their manifest differences the language of Homer is recognizably like the language of Archilochus, and in many of its Ionic characteristics not different at all. Such similarities would not exist if the intervening gap was four hundred years or more. Nor is it probable that the hexameter, after being brought to perfection so early, should have been altered not at all in the space of some centuries but have kept its essential characteristics in the *Homeric Hymns* and the hexameter lines of the elegiac poets of the sixth century. An ancient form may survive, as certain Anglo-Saxon forms of verse survived till the thirteenth century and even later, but it must become archaic and ossified.[1] Repeating the language of a lost age and taking no account of the present, it can only be stiff and formal. And formality is the last charge that can be laid to Mimnermus or Tyrtaeus or the authors of the *Homeric Hymns*.

The real foundation of this view that Homer lived in the Mycenean Age seems to be the belief that he describes the life of the period. It is claimed that the armour of his heroes, their houses, their domestic utensils, their jewellery, and even their clothing belong to this period and to no other period in Greek history. If this were so, the case would be well founded, but actually Homer presents far more points of dissimilarity than of similarity to the life of the Mycenean Age as we know it from its monuments. It is true that the shield of Aias 'like a tower' has only been understood since

---

[1] William Dunbar wrote his *Scottish Field* on the battle of Flodden in the alliterative metre of *Piers Plowman*.

Schliemann found such shields depicted on the dagger-blades from Mycenae, that the shield of Achilles recalls Mycenean inlaid metal-work, that the cup of Nestor is like the gold cup found in the Fourth Shaft Grave. But such similarities prove nothing in the matter of date. The shield of Aias is a traditional feature of the saga, as inseparable from its owner as his telescope from Nelson or his hat from Napoleon. The shield of Achilles is the poet's invention, based perhaps on some heirloom he had seen or some ancient description he had heard. But its details evade elucidation, and it must largely be invention like the shield of Aeneas in the *Aeneid*. The cup of Nestor, too, may have survived for generations in some Ionian home, but it, too, has been transformed by poetry. The cup from the Shaft Grave is of no remarkable weight, but Nestor's cup was so heavy that he alone could lift it easily (Λ 636). Against these similarities we may place a large number of differences. Homeric armour is not in the main that of the Mycenean Age. It employs the breast-plate and greaves, shields of different sizes and shapes, and its nearest parallel seems to be that used in the age of migrations when the horned helmet and body-armour came into full use. His women do not show their breasts or wear crinolines like the Minoan women. His gods are like men and not like animals. His men wear not Mycenean clothes but a cloak kept on by a brooch (K 133). The metal work he describes can usually best be paralleled in the period of Phoenician influence—the breast-plate and shield of Agamemnon (Λ 19 ff.), the ivory bridle (Δ 141), the silver bowl which Achilles gives as a prize (Ψ 741). On the whole the picture is not of the Mycenean Age but of the age which followed it, beginning with the great migrations and ending with the growth of Ionian civilization. Of the Minoan and Mycenean Ages Homer has memories. The dancing-floor of Ariadne, the great walls of Troy, were still visible in his day, and he knew enough of them to connect them with the great past. But in the mass of his details he describes a later age, and all he knows of the Myceneans can be reduced to a few scraps of saga or to the survival of visible monuments.

Nor on the other hand is there much to be said for

Theopompus' estimate. In the seventh and sixth centuries a new type of poetry grew up in Ionia and Aeolis. The impersonal poetry of the heroic age gave way to the personal poetry of the aristocratic cliques. We are confronted with the new phenomenon of poets who were concerned with their own emotions and made them the subject of their verse. Alcaeus and Sappho, Archilochus and Alcman give those intimate, personal details which Homer so rigorously denies to us. Nor is this distinction merely the result of a difference of temperament. Homer's self-effacement is part of his epic and heroic temper, and belongs to his age. The self-expression of the lyric and elegiac poets belongs to another world. Heroic standards excluded the conviction that nothing mattered to a man so much as his emotions, and of such a view of life, so common in Sappho and Archilochus, there is no trace whatsoever in Homer. He is, as we have seen, spiritually of the heroic age, and the age of the great poetry of Lesbos is not his. But if this argument seems too subjective, we may remember that the change from impersonal epic to personal lyric is a natural development in the history of poetry. In France the *Chansons de Geste* disappeared when men learned how to write love-songs on the Provençal model, and the result was the great lyric movement which ended in François Villon. In Germany the medieval epic was superseded by the new poetry of Walther von der Vogelweide and Dietmar von Aist. The change is natural and indeed inevitable. The epic in its early form takes too little account of the personal emotions, and in its love of the great past it neglects the fascinations of the present. No wonder that in leisured and aristocratic societies its anonymous splendours gave way to the personal lyric.

Perhaps the best argument put forward for this late date is that advanced by E. Bethe.[1] He takes the passage in Z 302–3 where the Trojan Women take a garment and the priestess lays it as an offering on the knees of Athene's statue:

ἣ δ᾽ ἄρα πέπλον ἑλοῦσα Θεανὼ καλλιπάρῃος
θῆκεν Ἀθηναίης ἐπὶ γούνασιν ἠϋκόμοιο[2]

[1] *Homer*, ii, pp. 310–14.
[2] 'Fair-cheeked Theano took the robe and set it on the knees of lovely-haired Athene.'

and points out that the statue must be both seated and life-size. He then claims that such statues cannot have existed much before the end of the seventh century. The earliest stone statues which survive cannot be dated before 650 and they are not fully life-size. Homer then, he argues, cannot be earlier than 620. This point is persuasive, but fortunately not fatal to an earlier scheme of dating. The statue need not be fully life-size to have a garment placed on its knees. Nor is it impossible that statues, particularly wooden statues, existed before this date. The working of wood naturally precedes that of stone, and wood perishes and leaves no traces for archaeology. So without difficulty we can take the *Iliad* back rather farther than Bethe allows, though we must bear this consideration in mind if we try to place it a long time before the earliest known statue.

It remains to halve the difference between these two extreme dates and to see whether there is anything to be said for Herodotus. His words are explicit and pregnant: Ἡσίο-δον γὰρ καὶ Ὅμηρον ἡλικίην τετρακοσίοισι ἔτεσι δοκέω μευ πρεσβυτέρους γενέσθαι καὶ οὐ πλέοσι (ii. 53).[1] This statement is our earliest and most reputable date for Homer, and would, if it could be proved trustworthy, place the *Iliad* in the second half of the ninth century. But Herodotus unfortunately is not impeccable in matters of chronology, and, unless we know his sources, his word must not be treated as final. In this case his sources are unknown, and the significant word δοκέω shows that he is quoting not established authority but his own opinion. If he is working on tradition or on genealogies, he may well be right, but if he is giving us the results of his own calculations, he may too easily be wrong. In one respect, however, his date claims our regard. Thucydides in his discussion of the Trojan War agrees with him on one important point. He evidently knows Herodotus' view and not only refrains from contradicting it but implicitly supports it when he says that Homer existed long after the Trojan War (i. 3. 3). He agrees with Herodotus in principle, and though he gives no reasons, his support may

---

[1] 'I think that Hesiod and Homer flourished four hundred years and no more before myself.'

help to make us believe that Herodotus is right. There are, however, certain external considerations which tend to support this view in placing Homer long after the Trojan War, but before Archilochus and the earliest extant fragments of lyric poetry.

In the lyric and elegiac poems we have indications that the *Iliad* was well known when they were written. Its subject and characters are perfectly familiar. Sappho writes of Helen;[1] Alcaeus of the Atridae, Aias, and Achilles, of the fall of Troy and the wedding of Peleus and Thetis.[2] In the scanty fragments of Alcman we find the names of Paris, Helen, Aias, Menelaus, and Odysseus.[3] The quotations are few and fragmentary, but they agree with what we know from Homer. For Alcaeus and Sappho Helen is the cause of Troy's destruction, and for Alcman both Odysseus and Paris seem to be what they were for Homer. By the time of Ibycus the story of the *Iliad* had become so well worn a theme that in his poem to Polycrates he takes pains to say that he will not tell the tale of Troy, and his opening words are full of Homeric reminiscences.[4] The heroes take the great city of Dardanid Priam by Ζηνὸς μεγάλοιο βουλαῖς—an echo of Homer's Διὸς δ' ἐτελείετο βουλή—and he runs through the names and achievements of Homer's heroes, including πόδας ὠκὺς Ἀχιλλεύς and Τελαμώνιος ἄλκιμος Αἴας. The story then is well known even in the few fragments of seventh- or sixth-century lyric which have escaped the ravages of time. But of course the mere existence of Homer's story does not prove the existence of a completed *Iliad*. It might be claimed that the lyric poets used not the *Iliad* but its forerunners which told the same story. This view might carry weight if the lyric poets confined themselves to mention of the characters and plot. But they do not. They use phrases which can only be copied from Homer. Alcman writes of Δύσπαρις, Αἰνόπαρις, κακὸν Ἑλλάδι βωτιανείρᾳ,[5] an elaborated echo of Homer's Δύσπαρι, εἶδος ἄριστε (Γ 39, Ν 769), and his mention of a

---

[1] Ed. Lobel, ā 5, 7.   [2] Ed. Lobel, Nos. 26, 48, 116, 150.
[3] Bergk, *P.L.G.* iii, Nos. 40, 56b, 68, 41. E. Diehl, *Anth. Lyr. Graeca* ii, Nos. 75, 86.
[4] *Ox. Pap.*, 1790, vol. xv, 1922.   [5] Bergk, fr. 40.

ἵππον παγὸν ἀεθλοφόρον¹ recalls those horses which Agamemnon offers to Achilles, the twelve ἵππους πηγοὺς ἀθλοφόρους of I 124. When Sappho writes of βροδόπαχυν Αὔων² she is transposing into her own dialect Homer's ῥοδοδάκτυλος Ἠώς, and Alcaeus' ἐκ δ' ἔλετο φρένας³ is modelled in defiance of Aeolic grammar on Homer's φρένας ἐξέλετο Ζεύς (Z 234). But there are earlier echoes than these. When Mimnermus writes:

ἡμεῖς δ' οἷά τε φύλλα φύει πολυάνθεμος ὥρη
ἔαρος, ὅτ' αἶψ' αὐγῆς αὔξεται ἠελίου,
τοῖς ἴκελοι πήχυιον ἐπὶ χρόνον ἄνθεσιν ἥβης
τερπόμεθα⁴

he is developing the Homeric sentiment put in the mouth of Glaucus:

οἵη περ φύλλων γενεή, τοίη δὲ καὶ ἀνδρῶν (Z 146),

and the greater elaboration of the same theme shows that it is later than the line from the *Iliad*.

Another seventh-century poet who seems to develop a passage from the *Iliad* is Tyrtaeus. The passage developed is the famous scene in X 71 ff. where Priam describes the horrors of dying in battle:

νέῳ δέ τε πάντ' ἐπέοικεν
ἀρηϊκταμένῳ, δεδαϊγμένῳ ὀξέϊ χαλκῷ,
κεῖσθαι· πάντα δὲ καλὰ θανόντι περ, ὅττι φανήῃ·
ἀλλ' ὅτε δὴ πολιόν τε κάρη πολιόν τε γένειον
αἰδῶ τ' αἰσχύνωσι κύνες κταμένοιο γέροντος,
τοῦτο δὴ οἴκτιστον πέλεται δειλοῖσι βροτοῖσιν.

There are clearly echoes of this in Tyrtaeus' poem urging young men to fight:

αἰσχρὸν γὰρ δὴ τοῦτο μετὰ προμάχοισι πεσόντα
κεῖσθαι πρόσθε νέων ἄνδρα παλαιότερον,
ἤδη λευκὸν ἔχοντα κάρη πολιόν τε γένειον,
θυμὸν ἀποπνείοντ' ἄλκιμον ἐν κονίῃ,
αἱματόεντ' αἰδοῖα φίλαις ἐν χερσὶν ἔχοντα—
αἰσχρὰ τά γ' ὀφθαλμοῖς καὶ νεμεσητὸν ἰδεῖν,—
καὶ χρόα γυμνωθέντα· νέοισι δὲ πάντ' ἐπέοικεν,
ὄφρ' ἐρατῆς ἥβης ἀγλαὸν ἄνθος ἔχῃ.⁵

---

¹ Bergk, *P.L.G.* iii, fr. 23, l. 48.   ² δ. 1. l. 19.   ³ Ed. Lobel, No. 97.
⁴ Bergk, *P.L.G.* ii, fr. 2.   ⁵ Bergk, *P.L.G.* ii, fr. 1, ll. 21–28.

The circumstances and contexts of the two passages may differ, but the verbal similarities are remarkable, and some considerations point to Tyrtaeus copying Homer. In the first place, Tyrtaeus is here revealed as a not very skilled poet and therefore likely to borrow from a poet who knew his business. He uses the same word ἔχοντα in two senses in three lines. And his φίλαις ἐν χερσίν looks like a loan from Homer. Secondly, αἱματόεντ᾽ αἰδοῖα . . . ἔχοντα is considerably less appropriate than the Homeric line. It can at best describe a not very common wound, while the Homeric line is perfectly natural for a body devoured by the dogs. Thirdly, in Tyrtaeus the use of the plural noun in the phrase νέοισι δὲ πάντ᾽ ἐπέοικεν consorts ill with the singular ἔχῃ in the next line, while the Homeric use of the singular νέῳ is perfectly natural and correct. Lastly Homer repeats the word πολιόν while Tyrtaeus alters the first πολιόν to λευκόν for the simple reason that πολιόν would not scan. If Homer were imitating Tyrtaeus and not vice versâ, the chances are that he would have given us λευκόν τε κάρη, but as the manuscripts agree on the repeated πολιόν, it is more likely that Tyrtaeus imitated the *Iliad*.

There is still another passage in an elegiac poem which may be older than any of these. A fragment attributed by Stobaeus to Simonides quotes as the work of 'the man of Chios' the line which, as we have seen, Mimnermus paraphrases.

ἐν δὲ τὸ κάλλιστον Χῖος ἔειπεν ἀνήρ·
οἵη περ φύλλων γενεή, τοίη δὲ καὶ ἀνδρῶν.[1]

The usual view is that this poem is the work of Simonides of Ceos, and if so, it cannot be much earlier than 500. But Wilamowitz has argued that the form and style are unworthy of Simonides, and that the real author is the much earlier poet, Semonides of Amorgos,[2] who flourished in the middle of the seventh century. The linguistic argument for this ascription is certainly persuasive, and Semonides is a likelier candidate for the poem than Simonides. So there is some probability that the famous line of Glaucus was quoted so early as 650 as being spoken by the 'man of Chios'.

---

[1] Bergk, *P.L.G.* iii, fr. 85. 'One thing most beautiful was said by the man of Chios: "Like a generation of leaves, so is that of man." '

[2] *Sappho und Simonides*, pp. 273-4.

The quotations do not extend much beyond these cases, but both the lyric and elegiac poets employ certain linguistic forms which look like a direct imitation of the epic style. When Sappho writes hexameters, she sometimes divagates from her usual style, especially in some metrical licences which Homer employs, such as the shortening of a long open final syllable before a word beginning with a vowel, or the scanning of a short vowel as short before the combination of a mute and a liquid.[1] Alcaeus is more deeply penetrated by epic usage. In defiance of Aeolic grammar he sometimes omits the augment in phrases such as παῖδα γέννατο[2] and ἐπεὶ δὴ κάτθανε;[3] he scans the first syllable of ὕδωρ long,[4] he uses the forms πολιάταν[5] and ᾿Αΐδαο,[6] and non-Aeolic words like παρθένικαι[7] or the Homeric genitive ἐρχόμενοιο.[8] The elegiac poets write in Ionic and therefore their language might be expected to resemble Homer's. So it does, but they use certain combinations of words which look like direct borrowing. Callinus speaks of κουριδίης ἀλόχου,[9] Tyrtaeus of τανηλεγέος θανάτοιο,[10] and Mimnermus of ἠὼς ἠριγένεια and ἤματα πάντα.[11]

It follows from this that the language and story of parts of the *Iliad* were well known in the seventh century, in fact so well known that they play quite a large part in a literature of which only small fragments survive. The Homeric echoes in this poetry are not confined to one or two books, but come from different parts of the *Iliad*, including *A*, *Γ*, *Z*, *N*, *E*, *I*, and *Ω*. The natural assumption is that when these poems were composed the *Iliad* was well known and existed substantially as it now exists both in its language and its story. And this conclusion is supported by the scanty cases where scenes of the *Iliad* are depicted in early Greek art. The remains of seventh- and sixth-century sculpture are few, and so limited to certain types that we can hardly expect much treatment of Homeric story. But a bronze mirror in Berlin of Argive origin has on its handle a scene in relief

---

[1] Lobel, ᾿Αλκαίου Μέλη, p. xi.   [2] ed. Lobel, No. 26, l. 13.
[3] Ib., No. 93, l. 2.   [4] Ib., No. 29, l. 8.   [5] Ib. No. 23, l. 6.
[6] Ib., No. 32, l. 15.   [7] Ib., No. 29, l. 5   [8] Ib., No. 130, l. 1.
[9] Bergk, *P.L.G.* ii, fr. 1, l. 7.   [10] Ib., fr. 12, l. 35.   [11] Ib., fr. 12, l. 10, 12, l. 1.

where Priam visits Achilles to ransom the body of Hector. This episode, as we have seen, is probably a late element in the story, and its portrayal on the mirror practically means that it was taken from the *Iliad*. The chest of Cypselus, described by Pausanias as belonging to a still earlier date, had a series of scenes drawn from all quarters of Greek saga. Among them are two which come from the *Iliad*, the fight of Aias and Hector in *H* [1] and the fight of Agamemnon and Coön over the body of Iphidamas in *Λ*.[2] Early vases are more disappointing but they contribute their share of evidence. Two Sicyonian vases depict the fight of Bellerophon and the chimaera just as Homer describes it.[3] A seventh-century patera from Rhodes, now in the British Museum, depicts the fight between Menelaus and Hector over the body of Euphorbus.[4] The scene is not clearly set out in the *Iliad*, but that such an event is meant by the poet seems to follow from that part of the story between *P* 50 where Menelaus kills Euphorbus and *P* 108 where Hector is in the forefront of the battle. In the sixth century the portrayal of Homeric scenes becomes commoner. The funeral games of Patroclus were painted on the François Vase by Clitias and Ergotimus, and other black-figured vases portray the dragging of Hector's body, its ransoming, and the return of Briseis to Achilles. Even in the fifth century Homeric scenes are rare compared with the story of Theseus or of Heracles. But the fact remains that early Greek art of the seventh and sixth centuries is acquainted with parts of the story of the *Iliad*, even if such themes are not popular. And to this extent they support the evidence of the literary fragments.

The conclusion then is that the *Iliad*, apparently much in its present form, was well known in Ionia and less well known on the mainland by the beginning of the seventh century. In other words it existed long enough before 650 for it to be frequently quoted and to have an important influence on the earliest elegiac and lyric poets. How long such a process would take is extremely hard, and perhaps impossible, to

---

[1] Paus. v. 19. 12.   [2] Ib., v. 19. 4.
[3] K. F. Johansen, *Les Vases Sicyoniens*, p. 148.
[4] E. Buschor, *Griechische Vasenmalerei*, p. 79, fig. 59.

estimate. When writing is common and communications easy, the appearance of a great poet may exert a sudden and remarkable influence. The publication of the *Divine Comedy* immediately affected the whole character of Italian verse, and the publication of the *Canterbury Tales* at once began to affect not so much English poetry as the English language itself. But where poetry is still recited and intercourse restricted, the growth of such an influence must necessarily be slower, and the chances are that the *Iliad* must have existed before 700 if it was to have such an influence on the poetry of the succeeding century.

From other considerations it seems that we must put a gap between Homer and the poets of the seventh century. As we have seen, Homer is still one with the heroic age, and they are not. Even Tyrtaeus has more individuality than Homer, and Semonides is full of himself and his feelings. Callinus, it is true, has much of the Homeric spirit, but Archilochus belongs to an age not of heroes but of aristocrats. We do not know when the heroic age of Greece ended. No doubt the princes of Ionia maintained its traditions and standards long after its political conditions had disappeared, just as the Pilgrim Fathers of Iceland maintained the manners and stories of that Norway which they had left because of its modern cult of monarchy. Homer does not belong to the age of the lyric poets in any way. Even in military matters Callinus and Tyrtaeus differ from him. Their idea of fighting is the pitched battle where men stand together and take the onslaught of the enemy. Homer's idea of a series of single combats belongs to a different idea of tactics.

There still remains one more source of evidence, though its use is beset with difficulties—the poems ascribed to Hesiod. These poems are clearly of different dates, and must be taken to be the work of a school of poetry which lasted almost for centuries. The obviously later poems show so many reminiscences of the *Iliad* that they hardly call for comment. The *Shield of Heracles* is perhaps modelled on the *Shield of Achilles*, and the *Eoiae* are full of Homeric language. In either case these poems are of so uncertain a date that their evidence cannot be pressed. But it is different with the *Theogony* and the *Works and Days*. The *Theogony* is later than the *Works and Days*, to which it refers as to a poem already well known (*Theog.* 22), mentioning Hesiod as a man who is clearly not the author of the *Theogony*—αἵ νύ ποθ᾽ Ἡσίοδον καλὴν ἐδίδαξαν ἀοιδήν.[1] The most probable date of the *Theogony* is some time late in the eighth century; it is at any rate too confined in its geography and outlook to belong to a time much later than the first part of the seventh century with its wide colonizing activities and rapid growth of geographical information. The *Works and Days* must be at least a generation older, as it belongs to a time when rulers are called βασιλῆες and iron is a metal only recently turned to general use. The chances are then that these two poems belong to the eighth or early seventh centuries, that is to at least a generation earlier than Semonides of Amorgos. Accepting this hypothetical date, we may now compare the relations between Homer and Hesiod. The resemblances, such as they are, belong more to the *Theogony* than to the *Works and Days*. First we must notice the similarity between the account of the rivers in *M* 20 ff.:

'Ρῆσός θ᾽ Ἑπτάπορός τε Κάρησός τε 'Ροδίος τε
Γρήνικός τε καὶ Αἴσηπος δῖός τε Σκάμανδρος
καὶ Σιμόεις, ὅθι πολλὰ βοάγρια καὶ τρυφάλειαι
κάππεσον ἐν κονίῃσι καὶ ἡμιθέων γένος ἀνδρῶν

and the similar account given by Hesiod, *Theog.* 340 ff.:

Φᾶσίν τε 'Ρῆσόν τ᾽ Ἀχελώϊόν τ᾽ ἀργυροδίνην
Νέσσον τε 'Ροδίον θ᾽ Ἁλιάκμονά θ᾽ Ἑπτάπορόν τε
Γρήνικόν τε καὶ Αἴσηπον, θεῖόν τε Σιμοῦντα . . .
Εὔηνόν τε καὶ Ἄρδησκον, θεῖόν τε Σκάμανδρον.

The two passages are very like. Both are simply lists of names, and of the eight rivers given by Homer seven are in the list of Hesiod. Such a similarity should imply borrowing on one side or the other, and it should be possible to decide which has borrowed from which. The case for the priority of Hesiod has been urged with much skill by E. Bethe.[2] He bases his case on two main considerations. First he argues that four of Homer's rivers, the Rhesus, Heptaporus, Caresus, and

---

[1] 'Who (the Muses) taught Hesiod his lovely song.'
[2] *Homer*, pp. 303–10.

Rhodius, are probably not genuine rivers of Asia Minor at
all. Homer himself does not mention them anywhere else
and gives no clue as to their position. But in Hesiod's list
the Rhesus is put between the great rivers Phasis and
Acheloüs, while the Rhodius is put between the great rivers
Nessus and Haliacmon. It looks from this as if at least the
Rhesus and the Rhodius were big rivers, which had no place
so far as we know in Asia Minor. Bethe's second argument is
also forcible. He points out that in the Homeric passage we
have a reference to the ἡμιθέων γένος ἀνδρῶν, and he claims
that the whole idea of ἡμίθεοι is, except in this place, alien to
Homer, who never regards his heroes as more than men.
Hesiod, however, is quite explicit on the point in the *Works
and Days*, where he says (ll. 159–60):

> ἀνδρῶν ἡρώων θεῖον γένος, οἳ καλέονται
> ἡμίθεοι, προτέρῃ γενεῇ κατ' ἀπείρονα γαῖαν.

Bethe claims that the use of ἡμιθέων in *M* 23 shows that the
passage is derived from Hesiod. These two claims are important and deserve serious consideration. The attempts to
destroy their validity have so far proved unsuccessful, but it
is quite possible that both Homer and Hesiod are deriving
from a common source. Certainly this seems probable
in the case of the rivers, where both writers give
merely a catalogue, and catalogues are one of the oldest
forms of poetry. In the case of the ἡμίθεοι, it is noticeable that
while Hesiod thinks it necessary to explain what he means,
Homer does not. So possibly Homer may be writing for an
audience better informed than Hesiod's, and employing a
word to which a long epic tradition had accustomed them.
This possibility of a common source is confirmed by a passage
in which the *Iliad* speaks of Tartarus as being:

> τόσσον ἔνερθ' Ἀΐδεω ὅσον οὐρανός ἐστ' ἀπὸ γαίης   (Θ 16)

which recalls the Hesiodic:

> τόσσον ἔνερθ' ὑπὸ γῆς ὅσον οὐρανός ἐστ' ἀπὸ γαίης.
>
> (*Theog.* 720)

The two lines are clearly related. Homer's is inconsistent
with much of his cosmogony, notably with the passage in

which Hera speaks of the Giants living at the end of the world (Θ 480). So it is claimed as an imitation of Hesiod, whose line is in harmony with the rest of his descriptions. But this point cannot be pressed too far, as in his cosmogony Homer incorporates many different views of the world, just as he has different views of the life after death. He was not concerned with exactitude in such matters, while Hesiod, who was reducing theology to order, had to create a unified and self-consistent system. However, both poets had to get their cosmogony from somewhere; so perhaps here too they are borrowing from the same traditional source. A last parallel is to be found between Homer's account of Zeus sitting on his throne:

$$\tau\hat{\omega} \; \delta' \; \hat{\upsilon}\pi\grave{o} \; \pi o\sigma\sigma\grave{\iota} \; \mu\acute{e}\gamma\alpha\varsigma \; \pi\epsilon\lambda\epsilon\mu\acute{\iota}\zeta\epsilon\tau' \; "O\lambda\upsilon\mu\pi o\varsigma \quad (\Theta \; 443)$$

and Hesiod's account of his thundering:

$$\pi o\sigma\sigma\grave{\iota} \; \delta' \; \hat{\upsilon}\pi' \; \hat{\alpha}\theta\alpha\nu\acute{\alpha}\tau o\iota\sigma\iota \; \mu\acute{e}\gamma\alpha\varsigma \; \pi\epsilon\lambda\epsilon\mu\acute{\iota}\zeta\epsilon\tau' \; "O\lambda\upsilon\mu\pi o\varsigma$$
$$\hat{o}\rho\nu\upsilon\mu\acute{e}\nu o\iota o \; \hat{\alpha}\nu\alpha\kappa\tau o\varsigma \cdot \; \hat{\epsilon}\pi\epsilon\sigma\tau\epsilon\nu\acute{\alpha}\chi\iota\zeta\epsilon \; \delta\grave{\epsilon} \; \gamma\alpha\hat{\iota}\alpha. \quad (\textit{Theog.} \; 842\text{--}3)$$

Here the Hesiodic version is more elaborate than the Homeric and might well be suspected of being taken from it. But here, too, the unlikeness of the two passages may equally well be explained as two variations on a common theme. So then, so far as the evidence from Hesiod goes, there is no final proof that either is earlier than the other. Both are equally well explained as derived from the same common source.

So far, then, as the literary evidence may be pressed, it seems to prove that some parts of the *Iliad* had reached their present form by the early part of the seventh century. But, even so, is there any proof that the whole of our *Iliad* existed in anything like its present form at that date? Is it not possible that the quotations and adaptations were made, not from our *Iliad*, but from different poems which were afterwards incorporated into the greater whole of the existing *Iliad*? The answer to this can only be got from our notions of how the *Iliad* arose, and if we are convinced that it is the work of one hand, it can satisfactorily be put back at least to the seventh century. But if it embodies work of different centuries, the answer is less secure. There is, however, one piece of literary evidence which shows that early in the seventh century there was a large body of literature belonging in name at least to Homer. Not only does Semonides speak of the Χῖος ἀνήρ as if every one knew who he was, but Callinus, who lived a generation earlier, attributes to Homer the epic of the *Thebaid*.[1] This at least proves that the name of Homer was connected with epics of considerable length in the early part of the seventh century. If it was connected with the *Thebais*, it may well have been connected with the *Iliad*.

The conclusion to be drawn from this somewhat chaotic and nebulous evidence is that, though we have no certain evidence for the date of Homer, the statement of Herodotus that he lived in the latter part of the ninth century and was a contemporary of Hesiod may not be far from the truth. If we place him some time late in the eighth century, it suits what we know of his language and his influence on later Greek poetry. It suits, too, what we know of the world which he admired. The heroic age can hardly have survived into the age of the aristocracies, but it was their natural predecessor, and prepared the way for their new scheme of life. So, too, the French epic conventions of the tenth and eleventh centuries prepared the way for the romantic and personal poetry of the twelfth century with its emphasis on love and personal relationships. The Homeric epic stands in much the same relationship to Greek poetry. On Homer the elegists and lyric poets drew for their language and their imagery. From him they borrowed their themes, and they assumed a knowledge of his story and characters in their verse. So, too, Villon expected his readers to know of Charlemagne and Berthe aux grands pieds. But between the lyric poets and their epic predecessors there lay a great gulf, the gulf between an age of heroism and an age of romance, which valued passion and pleasure more than courage and the qualities which find their best expression in war. On the farther side of this gulf lies Homer. He is too far from Solon for Theopompus to be right in thinking them contemporaries, but he is near enough for his poetry to be vivid and powerful in forming the verse of the seventh and sixth centuries.

If this is all that can be guessed of Homer's date, not much

---

[1] Quoted by Paus. ix. 9. 5.

more can be guessed of his place. But most poets sooner or
later disclose their places of origin, and perhaps Homer is no
exception to the rule. His language, as we have seen, gives
no certain indication of his race, but it implies a knowledge
of the Ionic and Aeolic dialects such as might most easily be
found on the coast of Asia Minor. Of the many towns which
disputed his birth in antiquity, only two have really reputable
claims, Chios and Smyrna. The first was the home of the
Homeridae and has the support of Semonides or Simonides.
The second has the support of so good an antiquarian as
Pindar.[1] To decide between the two is impossible. They lie
in the same region, and such indications as Homer gives of
his homeland might apply to either. But the important
point is that these two ancient traditions support what small
evidence Homer gives of his home. To decide between them
is impossible and indeed unimportant. What emerges and
really matters is that Homer was an inhabitant of Asia Minor
and discloses his origin in certain portions of the *Iliad*. In
the first place his ignorance of the remoter parts of Greece is
balanced by his knowledge of the eastern Aegean regions.
He knows little of the Peloponnese, but he knows something
of the Troad and something of familiar Asiatic sights such as
the weeping Niobe on Sipylus (Ω 614 ff.), the volcano εἰν Ἀρί-
μοις (*B* 783), the small towns on the south of the Aeolic peninsula, Thebe, Pedasus, Lyrnessus (*A* 366, *B* 690, *Υ* 191, 235), the
Leleges and Caucones (*K* 429, *Φ* 86). But the best evidence
comes from the similes, which more than the narrative are
drawn from the poet's own experience and reveal his own
feelings. In these we see the poet living on the coast of Asia
Minor and noticing the landscape of the country round
Ephesus and Smyrna. He knows the flocks of birds in the
Asian Meadow round the streams of Cayster (*B* 459 ff.), and
the Icarian Sea when the east and south winds blow over it
(*B* 144–6). He has seen some woman from up country, a
Maeonian or a Carian, staining ivory for a horse's bridle
(Δ 141–2). In his descriptions of sea and storm, he often
mentions the north and the north-west winds as driving
waves on to the shore. He speaks of them as blowing from

[1] fr. 204.

Thrace (I 4–5), and his words must refer to Asia Minor. So, too, he implies a coast facing west when he speaks of Notos, the south-west wind, driving waves on to a promontory (B 394–5) or covering the mountains with mist (Γ 10), or bringing up clouds and a rough sea and covering the shore with seaweed (Δ 305–8). The same coast is implied in his use of Zephyros, the north-west wind, which the goatherd sees bringing up storm (Δ 275–9), which drives waves on to a rocky shore (Δ 422–6), and sends a shudder over the water (H 63–4). In two places, however, he seems to indicate a different geography. Achilles sees the sun rise over the sea, and later he watches the dawn ὑπεὶρ ἅλα τ᾽ ἠϊόνας τε (Ψ 226–30, Ω 12–13). The language of these passages might be derived from living in an island like Chios or Lesbos, but it might also mean simply that the early morning light is diffused everywhere without laying stress on the actual sunrise. In all these places he writes naturally of the coast of Asia Minor or of the adjacent islands. Of Thessaly or the Peloponnese there is no hint, and to this extent the internal evidence agrees with the traditions which made Homer an inhabitant of Chios or Smyrna. Further than this it is impossible to go. He may well, as Wilamowitz points out, have been connected both with Chios and Smyrna.[1] Alcidamas, quoted by Aristotle (*Rhet.* 2. 23. 1398 b) says τετιμήκασι Χῖοι Ὅμηρον οὐκ ὄντα πολίτην, and it may be the truth that Homer was born in Smyrna and lived later in Chios. That he was a travelled man his knowledge of the Troad and of some of the inland regions of Asia Minor shows. Antiquity connected him with both, and it may well have been right. If he lived and travelled in these parts, we can the more easily understand how his great vocabulary was formed. From his travels he learned new words in other dialects and annexed them to his own artificial language. Travel, too, helps to explain his lack of provincial or local outlook. He, like Odysseus, had seen the cities of men and learned their minds, and therefore he saw wider than some of the elegiac poets with their intense local patriotism. If he travelled, he cannot have been attached permanently to a court like Demodocus. He seems rather

[1] *Die Ilias und Homer*, pp. 368–71.

to resemble the later type of wandering bard, like Cynaethus, who found his living from city to city.

If Homer lived in Asia Minor in the eighth century, it remains to decide how he knew and wrote of events which took place in the twelfth. In this question as in so many others analogy gives the best help. The *Nibelungenlied* was written in the twelfth century, but it treats of events dating back to Attila and Theodoric. The *Song of Roland* may have been written in the reign of William the Conqueror, but it tells of Charlemagne who lived nearly three hundred years earlier. These two poems got their facts not from contemporary chronicles, but from local traditions and earlier poems on the same subject. The fight at Roncesvalles was a tradition of the Pyrenees,[1] and the story of the Niblungs was an old story told often before in short epic lays like the *Song of Hildebrand*.[2] Homer's material must have been much the same as these. Perhaps the site of Troy was connected with the story of a great siege; it must anyhow have been celebrated often before in poetry. Perhaps, too, he used other short poems, like the later *Shield of Heracles* or even much simpler and more rugged ballads, which the Greeks allowed to die once their stories had been told by Homer.[3] But in this shadow-land it is impossible to move with certainty. Of poetry before Homer no trace at all survives. But it certainly existed, and there we must leave the problem, invoking, as the Greeks themselves invoked, the names of Orpheus and Musaeus and the other half-divine minstrels whose names survived as the progenitors of Greek song.

The fact remains that all we know of Homer comes from the poems he wrote, and we are not likely to know more. He lived before written history, and he belonged to a class whose business was to tell of the doings of others, not to blazon himself to posterity. His name survived, and in this he was luckier than the great poets who wrote the *Edda* poems or the Border Ballads. His memory, too, was revered, even if com-

[1] J. Bédier, *Les Légendes épiques*, vol. iii.
[2] Cf. W. P. Ker, *Epic and Romance*, p. 91.
[3] Ib., p. viii. on the *Chançun de Willame*: 'It is the sort of thing that the Greeks willingly let die; a rough draught of an epic poem.'

petition for his origin obscured his history. And in this he was luckier than the author of *Beowulf*, whose fame rests on a single anonymous and charred manuscript. Even the Elizabethan dramatists, who lived in an age which valued individual personality more than any other thing, failed singularly to acquaint posterity with their lives. We know very little of Shakespeare, and almost nothing of Webster or Beaumont. So it is hardly surprising that we know nothing of Homer.

And yet we know something. His name survived, and for the Greeks it was a name which so outshone other early names that writers of other epics were confused with him and their works attached to his. That the author of the *Iliad* wrote the poems of the Epic cycle is most improbable. These poems differed from it in scale, temper, and construction. Aristotle censures in the *Cypria* the absence of that unity which he finds in the *Odyssey*,[1] and no doubt these other poets lacked Homer's sense of construction. But antiquity was so impressed by the existence of the *Iliad* that it was fain to credit its author with other epic poems on the same cycle of events. In turn he is claimed as the author of the *Thebais*,[2] the *Epigoni*,[3] the *Cypria*,[4] the *Nosti*.[5] The well-informed naturally did not accept these ascriptions, and in some cases rival claimants were put forward. But the names of the real authors were disputed and forgotten, while the authorship of the *Iliad* was invariably ascribed to Homer. To him, too, were ascribed other heroic verses written in his style and attributed to no certain poet.[6] Of Homer little may have been known, but his name survived as the name of the heroic poet *par excellence*, the author of the *Iliad*. So pre-eminent was his position that towns like Phocis[7] thought it worth their while to claim him as the author of their local epic, and his imitators were careful to ascribe their works to him. He is claimed even for such frivolities as the *Margites*[8] and the *Battle of the Frogs and Mice*,[9] as if a great poet would stoop to

[1] *Poetics*, 1459 a 30. [2] *Cert. Hom. et Hes.*, l. 255, Paus. ix. 9. 5.
[3] Hdt. iv. 32. [4] Ael. *V.H.* ix. 15.
[5] Paus. x. 28. 7. [6] Collected by T. W. Allen, *Homeri Opera*, v, pp. 147–51.
[7] Ps.-Hdt. *Vit. Hom.* c. 16. [8] Arist. *Poetics*, 1448 b 30.
[9] Suidas. s.v. Πίγρης.

such poor parodies of himself. The varied efforts to claim Homer as an author are the best evidence for his existence and for his early fame. If Callinus thought he wrote the *Thebais*, then it follows that in the seventh century Homer's fame was so great that it was felt that any good epic must have come from him. And if his authorship was worth claiming, he can only have been a real man and a great poet. When the Jews attributed their psalms to David or their moral maxims to Solomon, they may or may not have been right in their attributions, but they certainly took it for granted that David and Solomon were real men worthy of such work, not embodiments of the Hebrew genius or late editors compiling earlier work and claiming it as their own. It is not the way of humanity to attribute great poetry to those who had little to do with it. So far from attributing good poetry to a bad poet, the general tendency is to attribute all sorts of poetry to a good poet. But before he can be endowed with spurious attributions, a poet must have made his name by his own excellent performances. Shakespeare may have the doubtful honour of having written *Titus Andronicus*, but it would never have been added to his folio if he had not already written *Hamlet*. So bad a play had only one chance of survival—if it was attached to a poet whose other works might compel men to read it out of curiosity. But it is against nature to take *Hamlet* and advertise it as the work of some unknown hack.

Homer's name, remembered and honoured, is perhaps the best evidence for his early fame and influence, and the best answer to those who think that the *Iliad* is the work of several great poets and several bunglers. Even the *Odyssey* in antiquity was sometimes taken from him, but the *Iliad* remained his till scientific criticism strained at the gnat of some difficulties in composition, and swallowed the camel of multiple authorship. The credit for the *Iliad* rests primarily with Homer who gave the poem its shape, its unity of character and style, its dramatic impetus and high, imaginative life. Such gifts come only from genius, and genius does not belong to compilers or guilds. But Homer owed a vast debt to his predecessors. From them he took his stories, his metre, many of his mannerisms, and much of his vocabulary. There are poets who suddenly create a new thing, and the world wonders at them. A man like Rimbaud does something which is new in nearly all its aspects and owes little to his predecessors. But he pays a price for his achievement. Being an experimenter in new forms of expression he can hope only to be a pioneer; it is extremely difficult for him to create masterpieces. Dante indeed succeeded in what no one had previously attempted, and his success has been the marvel of posterity. But Homer, like Shakespeare, used a well-worn form and made it miraculously his own. In the end the great poet does not care if the form he uses has been used before or not. What matters is what he makes of it, and what Homer made of the epic tradition of narrative has always been clear even to those who fail to understand how the thing happened.

This simple distinction between a poet's tradition and his own use of it has too often been neglected in Homeric criticism, and the result has been lamentable for the study of the poem. It has too often been assumed that different elements in the vocabulary or different sources of the story indicate difference of authorship. In one sense they do. The original users of the words or the inventors of the stories were many and various, and they were not the poet. But the poet made his choice of them and subordinated them to his artistic purpose. And it is with their use, and not with their origins, that literary criticism is primarily concerned. It is as if we were to assume that *The Merchant of Venice* and *King Lear* were written by different men because their action takes place in different places, or that the man who writes so well about wild flowers in *A Winter's Tale* cannot be he who knows so much about law in the *Sonnets*. The inquiries into Homer's origins have indeed been valuable, and their worth would have been greater if they had not been associated with a wrong view of how poetry can be written. To trace the style and the stories back to their farthest beginnings is an important and interesting task, but by itself it throws no light at all on the poet's achievement. The important thing is that out of these elements he made a poem.

Still less is it evidence for difference of authorship that one part of the poem may differ in tone from another. It is indeed remarkable that the poet of Hector and Andromache can also be the poet of the Διὸς ἀπάτη, but for such wonders gratitude, not doubt, is the right answer. Such a range of tone as Homer possesses can only be paralleled in Shakespeare. These two alone among great poets have fully explored both laughter and sorrow. Milton's majesty excludes laughter, and Dante's laughter is only occasional and sardonic. But Shakespeare and Homer make humour an absolute value which needs no other justification. When they are amused, it is enough for them. They, too, have the rare gift of laughing sometimes at what they love and loving none the less because of it. Homer may smile at the heroic simplicity of his most charming heroes, but he does not falter in his belief that they are all that men should be. Shakespeare in his most tragic moments can fling a joke at destiny and still keep the sublimity of his heroes fighting against fate. The combination of the tragic and the comic is so rare in great poetry that it may well give us pause, but it is foolishness to announce that the two can never be combined in a single man. Still less is it possible to distinguish various strata in the *Iliad* by tests drawn from other varieties of temper. The sentimentality, which Wilamowitz finds characteristic of the author of *ΣΤ*, may well be combined with the 'sly undertone' which he finds in the author of *A* and *Ε*.[1] After all, the same man composed Leporello's Song and the Statue Music. But these distinctions of temper are useful and indeed important, because they show the great range of Homer's poetical gifts. Some other great poets impose on their material the masterful impress of an intense personality, but Homer, like Shakespeare, is multiple and various. Most human emotions come naturally to him; he follows them and makes poetry out of them. Not being much concerned with preaching, he is not hampered, like Dante and Milton, by an exacting metaphysic, and he can safely follow his emotions as he pleases. What interests him is every phase of human, or rather of heroic, conduct. Outside the heroic world his

[1] *Die Ilias und Homer*, pp. 317–18.

subject hardly allows him to stray, and he gives us no low
comedy or vulgar farce. But his limits are wide, and he moves
freely inside them. The heroic standards with their great
emphasis on personal dignity allowed a wide curiosity about
human nature, and of this Homer availed himself. Provided
man was great and noble, he was a fit subject for poetry. He
was no use if he were base or dishonourable, and the *Iliad* is
free of cowards or cheats. The Renaissance, freeing itself
from Catholic tradition, found an emancipated pleasure in
delineating villains. But though Homer enjoyed a diplomat
like Odysseus, he was not interested in villains. His morality
condemned them, and they lay outside the heroic world.

The limits which Homer set himself give his poetry its
unity of character, though this unity is one compatible with
great diversity. Pervading the *Iliad* is the atmosphere and
character of the heroic age seen by a man who understood
it well and brought to his understanding of it an unrivalled
imagination and sympathy. His world is after all full of
variety and change, but it is also heroic, with the standards
and thought of a heroic time. The world of Shakespeare is
wider than this. He explores bypaths and depths which lay
outside Homer's scope, perhaps outside his understanding.
The Elizabethans trembled on the edge of great discoveries,
and asked with Spenser:

> What if within the Moones faire shining sphere,
> What if in every other starre unseene
> Of other worldes he happily should heare?

The itch for strange experiences widened their outlook and
turned them to examine everything that they could find which
promised novelty or adventure. But Homer's wonder fed on
the past, and was therefore limited in scope and character.
The miracle is that out of a perished world, out of old songs
and stories, he created something which is entirely true and
convincing. From the plain stuff of saga he made real men
and women, more real indeed than any of those about him,
simplified and sublimated by his creative imagination. Of
all the tasks of poetry this is perhaps the hardest, to persuade
us that the poet's vision is of something real. In this Milton

fails when he writes of Jehovah, in this great romantic poets like Spenser fail when they tread the dangerous path of allegory. Even Virgil, for all his knowledge of human nature, failed when he tried to create the ideal man. But Homer's touch was sure. He created not only individuals but a world for them to live in, he used a style not only of unsurpassed beauty in itself but admirably fitted to convey the high feelings and thoughts of his characters. So great was his mastery of his materials that the simplicity which results from it has often been mistaken for the work of untutored genius. He was a pioneer of poetry, and he keeps much of the simplicity of early verse, but he made this simplicity a triumphant element in his style and composition. Because of it he is always clear and candid, unrhetorical and unsentimental. These qualities, it is true, belong to early popular poetry like the ballads and are essentially the qualities we expect from unsophisticated men. But in Homer they are combined with a majestic style and a wide knowledge of human nature. The stuff of the saga is raised to a higher level by being subjected to consummate artistry, and the result is not so much popular as great poetry. To the study of the ballads, to the study even of *Beowulf* and the *Song of Roland*, we bring that indulgence which is allowed to the youth of poetry. With Homer no such indulgence is needed. Despite his mistakes, his exuberance, his carelessness of detail, he comes up for judgement in the highest of all poetic company, with Dante and Shakespeare. With the first he shares an unfaltering vision, with the second a boundless sympathy and understanding. Beside him the ballads are after all simple and perhaps childish, beside him much modern poetry is insincere and sentimental. Only the greatest of all poets can give this union of simplicity and majesty. Of all combinations it is the rarest and the most perilous. Homer, living in the aftermath of a great age and endowed with the unanalysable gift of writing great poetry, succeeded in being the perfect master of the intellect and the imagination, and, calling up from the past a world which he thought had perished, re-created it, this time for ever.

INDEX

Abstractions, use of, 231 ff.
Achaeans, 184 ff.
Achilleid, 9, 105.
Achilles, 2 ff., 15 ff., 17 ff., 32, 36, 193 ff.
Aeneas, 208 ff.
Aeolic dialect, 136 ff.
Aeschylus, 18 n., 26, 30, 229, 240, 249.
Agamemnon, 2 ff., 15, 17 ff., 202 ff.
Ahhiawa, 163 ff.
Aias, 3, 19, 32, 204 ff.
αἰδώς, 18, 240.
Akaiwasha, 167 ff.
Alaksandu, 179.
Alcaeus, 57, 62, 240, 256.
Alcman, 57, 256.
Allen, T. W., 71 n., 132 n., 135 n., 175 n., 181 ff., 251.
Andreus, 163, 169.
Andromache, 211 ff.
Antaravas, 163.
Anthropomorphism, 221 ff.
ἀοιδοί, 27 ff.
Aphrodite, 16, 22, 25, 223.
Apollo, 2, 37, 226.
Arcadian dialect, 143 ff.
Archilochus, 252, 265.
Argos, 40, 175 ff.
Ariosto, 98.
Aristarchus, 89, 97, 99.
Aristophanes, 89, 97.
Aristotle, 269.
Ariunna, 165.
Arnold, Matthew, 43, 45.
ἄτη, 19, 24, 26.
Athene, 18, 220, 221.
Atli, Song of, 47.
Atreus, 165.
Attarisiyas, 165 ff.
Atticisms, 129 ff.
Attila, 33.
Augment, treatment of, 148 ff.

Bacchylides, 33, 35, 61, 65.
Bards, 7, 27 ff., 47.
Battle of Frogs and Mice, 269.
Bechtel, F., 139, 149 n.
Bédier, J., 268 n.
Bentley, R., 146.
Beowulf, 32, 39, 47, 49, 64, 84 ff., 87, 114, 135, 157, 234, 238, 248.
Bergk, T., 59 n.
Bethe, E., 1 n., 31 n., 33 f., 53 n.,
58 n., 77, 99, 122 n., 179, 254, 262 ff.
Bolling, G. M., 51 n.
Briseis, 213.
Buschor, E., 260 n.
Busolt, 75 n.
Bury, J. B., 139 n.

Calchas, 3.
Callinus, 265, 270.
Catalogue of Ships, 70 ff., 110 ff.
Cauer, P., 77, 83 n., 119 n., 129 n., 145 n., 146 n., 175, 185 ff.
Chadwick, H., 87 n., 169 n., 235 n.
Chambers, R. W., 47 n.
Chaucer, 5, 68, 93 ff., 132 ff., 249.
Charondas, 48.
Chios, 42, 132.
Chryses, 2, 37.
Cleisthenes, 40.
Clytaemnestra, 3.
Combats, single, 31 ff.
Comedy, 237 ff.
Comparetti, 29 n., 32 n.
Corinna, 8, 33, 35, 57, 133.
Coriolanus, 23.
Cyclic poems, 8.
Cynaethus, 40, 42, 51, 251.
Cypria, 12, 269.
Cypriote dialect, 143 ff.
Cyprus, 30, 41, 143, 166.
Cypselus, chest of, 260.

Dalmatia, 34.
Δαναοί, 163 ff.
Dante, 5, 86, 94, 114, 117, 126, 131, 246 ff., 271.
Danuna, 163.
Dardenui, 165.
Death, heroic view of, 236 ff.
Delos, 42.
Delphic Oracle, 61.
Demodocus, 7, 27, 36, 39, 42, 47, 53.
Deschamps, 9.
Digamma, 146 ff.
Digenes Acritas, 51.
Diomedes, 15, 18, 19, 71, 205 ff.
Dolon, 213.
Dörpfeld, W., 159.
Drerup, E., 36 n., 53 n., 77 n., 94 n., 175 n., 179.
Dryden, J., 45.

DATE DUE